JAN 8-2c

Pony Tracks:
Renegades and Ranching on the Rez

To My honorable friend

Verne Sheppard

Written
By

Mel Anderson

Mel Arthur Ind
God Bless!

Library of Congress Cataloging-in-Publication Data

Pony Tracks: Renegades and Ranching on the Rez /
Mel Anderson

ISBN #0-9752839-5-2

The Cover:
Badlands Country in the Basin below the Stronghold.

73 Ranch Outfit making ready to trail cattle after a
long, chilly night of sleeping on the ground and night
herding---

75 miles to Chadron, Nebraska, 70 miles to Rapid City,
South Dakota. Nothing but blue sky and grass in
between---

Cover Design / Bob Anderson
Published by
Sue Breeding
Art in the Heartland
408 Washington Street
Columbus, IN 47201
812-376-3465
sbreeding@artintheheartland.com

About the Author

Melvin Arthur Anderson was the first son born to Arthur Burdett Anderson and Rose Magdalena (Fischer) Anderson.

He spent his early years growing up on Green Grass Creek with his two brothers and two sisters.

He traveled the vast prairies of the open range with a good horse between his legs, and was a stranger to none.

He spent much time with his American Indian friends and grew accustomed to their way of life. He was honored by the Looking Horse Family and given an Indian name by Stanley Looking Horse.

Attending school at Eagle Butte was a highlight. He traveled to and from school riding horseback, nine miles one way. Mel was favored by his teachers and was teased by being called "Teachers' Pet."

Mel quit school after his freshman year, planning to skip a year and go back to catch up and graduate with his class. This was not to be. He enjoyed so much the freedom of the outdoors that he could not make himself go back. This is something that he has regretted all his life.

The area representative for American Breeders' Service of Deforest, MN, Frank C. Bussel, from Armour, SD, taught a college course in genetic engineering from which Mel graduated second in his class of 80.

He became well known throughout much of the United States for his knowledge and ability in the cattle business. After experimenting with crossbreeding of seventeen different breeds, and establishing the Beefmaker breed, he spent most of his life raising Charolais cattle. The bulls produced by his 38-year seed stock purebred program became a much sought after product by ranchers throughout a multi-state area.

Mel lives on a ranch north of Wasta, SD with his wife of twenty-three years, Dorothy. They proudly display the "seven with the flat-top three" brand which once belonged to the early cattle baron and buffalo man, Scotty Phillip.

He has held ownership in cattle and horses continuously for 60 years, and still loves to ride a good horse. Mel is, indeed a "professional cattleman."

After many requests by friends and relatives, he finally accepted the challenge of writing <u>Pony Tracks: Renegades and Ranching on the Rez.</u> This is a book relying on memories and experiences of his childhood and early manhood. It is his hope that this writing will evoke gratitude and appreciation in many readers for the way their grandparents lived in days gone by.

Acknowledgements

I wish to thank my mother, Rose, for clarification of experiences recorded on these pages.

I also wish to express my gratitude to my parents, my two brothers, and my two sisters, who have had faith in me and helped me triumph through times of hardships and the difficult times in my life.

My sincere thanks goes to those whom I interviewed and were so encouraging and co-operative in giving me information to use for this book.

Thanks also to my loving companion and wife, Dorothy Lee, for editing and proofreading.

All thanks and praise go to my loving Savior for allowing me to complete the first one-half of this saga.

My English teacher, Mrs. Whitby, would be critical of my methods of writing, but in defense of poor English and writing style, my wish is to translate this book in to the language of the northern cowhands and the unique way of speaking of the reservation Indians I associated myself with in everyday life.

Dedication

This book is dedicated to all the older citizens of South Dakota who lived through the "Dirty Thirties," and learned to cope with the hardships of everyday living, as well as to the children of these early settlers, in generations to follow.

My hope in writing this historical fiction is that it will bring a twinkle to eye, and at times, laughter, to the reader.

Table of Contents

Chapter I
The Extra Dollar

We'd had a wet spring and the grass was lush and green on this June morning, when John Holloway came off the creek bottom, leading three broncs tied head to tail. I was fifteen, and for two years had been breaking colts to ride. At one of the Saturday night sessions, John asked my dad if I could handle a couple of colts. He said that he'd bring 'em down if I could. My dad agreed to this proposition.

My pay at the time, doled out by my parents, was 25 cents per week, but Dad had no objections to us goin' elsewhere to gather a little extra spendin' money. This horse breaking shore sweetened the pot, as it paid $10 per head.

As I sit here, and over 50 years have gone by, I still remember those three horses. (In those days a colt was a baby that was still nursing his mother, but after they were weaned, they were called horses: geldings-studs-fillies, or mares, and never again referred to as colts.)

Gypsy was a tall, chestnut sorrel with some refinement, a good disposition, a great mind, a long stride, and a set of lungs that would allow me to go down river to the Lee Robley place and on to Goose Creek, past Andrew Dupris', to gather a bunch of wild mares and colts. I could be back home on Green Grass Creek by 3:00 pm. There was just no "quit" in that horse and I loved to ride him.

And, then there was this chocolate palomino that was just a real knot head. He couldn't do much,

1

and didn't want to do nothing! I figured that after he bucked over the wood pile and into the buzz saw that his brain must not have been much bigger than a pea. He could have just as well stayed on flat ground and bucked around it!

My mother was sort of a worrier and spent a lot of time looking out the window. She saw this horse buck over the wood pile and flounder into the buzz saw. She like to have fainted! As for me, I was trying to figure out if I should jump off on that pile of wood! Anyhow, when the wreck was over, I was still aboard.

It could have been bad for the horse, because he hit that big 50" blade square on his chest, but he only had 5 teeth marks that required a little dab of pine tar, and away we go again.

Pumpkin—every young man that worked around the Hanging H (Holloways) remembers Pumpkin. He was the third member of the team that John brought me on that beautiful June morning.

Pumpkin was a shiny golden palomino with a pretty little head. He looked great with a saddle on— but ya better screw 'er down tight!! He was 14 hands high, and could jump about twice that if he took a notion to buck---and that was purt'neer every day!

There were a lot of WPA dams in our neck of the woods, and my job was to ride and open ice in the winter—every day. There were 8 dams that I had to tend, and also a ripple on the river that I had to keep open. Dad left an old ax at each dam. A hole 10 inches wide and 6 feet long was cut at each dam so that the range cattle and horses could drink.

At the ripple on the Moreau River (A ripple is shallow water, usually running over rocks) Vern Curtis taught me how to cut a trough and punch a hole through to water on each end, going with the flow. The water would some up through the hole upstream, and go down through the hole downstream. Sometimes it would stay open for days. I tried this same method on the Cheyenne River several times, and it was a mystery to me, but I never could get it to work that way on the Cheyenne.

The Moreau River looking west. This is an early photo—probably 1919 or 1920. Note the heavy timber. Years of drought and heavy use by domestic livestock, has taken its toll. Today the timber is sparse on this great little river.

Anyway, getting back to the pretty little palomino—I rode him to school a lot because it appeared like he needed that nine miles to school and back! He sure seemed to be forgetting about the bucking part of his routine—and then came Christmas vacation!

Well, he'd gotten a little thin standing in the old Eagle Butte Stockyards all day with nothin' to eat or drink all day, so I started giving him a gallon of oats morning and night. Boy, did that light a fire under this little pony!

I'd go out on my ice line of a morning, open a hole, cheek my horse and step aboard, and then the rodeo was on—at every dam, and at the river. To make matters worse, there was this little dip that we went through, and just for good measure, he'd buck there, too!

One time Russell and Vern Curtis were riding up the creek just as I went down into that little dip. I think that little palomino knew he had an audience 'cause he sure mopped up that day! I don't remember that horse ever bucking me off, but I sure took a beating. My legs were just black and blue. My feet would get so cold because I didn't wear overshoes for fear of hanging up in a stirrup.

January 1953 Photo
Holloway horse Pumpkin on left Mel and his horse
Skipper. Corduroy shirt with snap buttons made by
Mel's Mother Rose on her old Treadle Singer Sewing
Machine.

I learned not to feed a bronc a gallon of oats! Lots of miles and lots of wet saddle blankets later, he made a pretty fair little cow pony. Just to set the record straight, I was never a great bronc rider like Dean Reeves or Geno Hunt.

I was working for John and Shorty Holloway one fall and along came a bunch of Holloway relatives from Indiana or Illinois, or some such a place. The boys wanted to show the relation what a forked bunch of cowboys they had gathering cows for them.

They had this little round pen that they had just set up with ash posts and green cottonwood poles right near the house.

Shorty expressed his desire to gather the remuda, which was composed of about 80 horses, as I remember, including 10 broke cow ponies (kind of) and 70 as green as garden beans. We held outside this little corral and sorted off a couple.

John was as good with a half a lariat rope as anyone I'd ever seen before, or since. He used 15 ft., and, once over his head, (called a holihan) I never, with my own eyes, ever saw him miss.

Well he settles his loop over this little brown two year old with a white spot on his side that went by the birth name of Papigo. He says, "Mel, get your saddle!" This is the same horse he caught yesterday and called for Larry Walker. Larry says, "I ain't got no bridle for THAT horse!" — and Larry ain't with us any more!

Well, I kind of like my six dollars a day, so I'm sure not going to turn down no horse when John calls my name.

Well, I cinch my old E.C. Lee cak down and he's got such a hump in his back that the old steel horn is touching his mane. No leading him around now to get a little of that hump out 'cause today she's a spectator sport!

I jerk the horn a time 'er two to check for snugness, wrap the reins tight around his neck, run my hand thru the check on the bridle and step up. About jump no. 2 I felt things letting go, like somebody lit a fuse on a bottle rocket!

Needless to say, I landed in a heap, and nobody had to tell me to get back on, either, 'cause I had had training in that department from my dad! So, like a good little cowboy, I dust myself off a little and walk up to ole Papigo. I have a little visit with him, cheek him, step in the stirrup and spin him hard to the left, allowing enough time to sure enough get a good seat and – away we go, again!!! This time I ride him about four jumps, I think, and he throws me clean out of the corral.

There were about 8 poles left lying to the southeast of that little pole corral, and I landed smack dab on top of them poles on my right hip. I could still walk, but I was pretty much out of commission for about a week. Those were the days when doctors in West River, SD were scarce as rocking horse manure. You didn't venture to see one unless you couldn't stop the bleeding, or if the bones were sticking out without flesh on them.

By the way, Jr. Smith got on that horse after he dumped me twice, and he rode him, it looked to me like, plump easy!

I had special privileges during my recuperation. I got to tag along and holler, on a gentle horse called Dishface.

I never really spent all that much time on the Holloway ranch, but have vivid memories about cowboying there. I remember the first Saturday night. Everyone got paid. They put on their best shirt and got spiffed up the best they could, for a little frolicking uptown---maybe a movie and a dance.

There was no running water in those days, and with 12 to 15 young boys that smelled like goats, a tea kettle full of hot water and a sponge bath and shave (if you had whiskers) had to suffice. Then, you were good to go!

Town was Eagle Butte, Dewey County, South Dakota, in the heart of the Cheyenne River Sioux Reservation. It was located just 12 miles from the Holloway headquarters at Parade.

Getting back to this first Saturday night, everybody was getting paid and pulling out for the bright lights, but for Mel and Jr. We aren't getting our checks! We sure ain't saying anything, but we sure are a-wondering!

The boys were all cleared out except Tommy Maupin and Ray Braemer. Murphy called me aside and said that they hated to pay Jr. and me in front of the other guys because I was gonna get a dollar a day more, and so was Jr. We got $6 a day, and the rest only got $5! Boy, oh mister! That made me feel like the stud duck!

I really did earn the extra dollar because I was headed to catch the night horse by 3:00 am to go wrangle the cavy. Whoever was in charge of keeping up the night horse wasn't too particular what was left in for me to wrangle on. Most of them would pitch just a little, and those tree limbs slapping me in the face on a pitching horse in the wee hours of the morning made me feel like the devil, himself, was out to get me!

There was another little disadvantage to jingling horses—you were the last one to eat breakfast, and, if you didn't hurry, you were out of luck 'til noon! That meant 8 hours down the dusty trail.

I usually managed 3 cold eggs and 2 soggy pancakes with white syrup. I highly recommend this dietary regimen to any growing cowboy!

Before I get off on another subject, I'd like to give you a little history, as I remember it, about the Holloway holdings.

There were 3 brothers, as I remember: John, Glen (Shorty), and Jim, along with one girl, Velma. John and Shorty were partners, and Jim had a little holding along with his wife, Phyl and family. Jim always helped with brandings, dipping, and shipping. Jim's wife, Phyl (Eli) Holloway helped Murphy with the cooking, which was always hauled out to the crew where they were nooned up, ate and changed horses.

Jim later became chief brand inspector for the South Dakota Stockgrowers, as did one of his sons, Dan. Jim Jr., is and has been for many years, brand inspector at Faith, SD. Son Don is in law enforcement and has been the Pennington County, South Dakota sheriff for many years.

John and Shorty had a huge lease known as Armstrong County. This county was never populated enough to support a town, so it was eventually annexed into Dewey County.

The Holloway Brothers had somewhere in the neighborhood of 400 cows, which was a huge number for that era. One was considered to be a successful rancher if he had 100 head.

When I worked for them in the early 50's, they ran a lot of steers for I.C. Little. Nobody ever told you, and you knew better than to ask, but in one gather, it looked to me that there were about 4000 head! They were all colors of the rainbow, and of southern characteristic, with too much ear, and not enough hair for the North Country.

We held the herd and sorted the cut for shipping starting at 11:00 am with seven riders cutting. We didn't turn loose until about 7:00 pm. It looked like the steers were sorted about 50-50, and I assumed that they were going to keep the lighter end to scatter and over winter.

The Holloways also ran about 800 Matador cows, which they eventually bought. They sold approximately one-half to a big outfit up north, near Mobridge.

I never did get to gather those little Hereford cows, but the cowboys that did help gather them said that they were wild, and most times two ridges ahead of the cowboys, not stopping until they hit a drift fence.

Many times, if I went to gather horses, I'd ride one and lead one so's to have a fresh horse to make the first wild sashay. The first couple of miles on these range mares were pretty western, and one couldn't keep up on a tuckered horse. Well, on one of those occasions I left my winded horse at the Old Lee Robley Ranch. It had just recently been purchased by Russell Curtis, a bachelor. A finer man you never met.

The horse I left at Russell's was a Hangin' H horse that belonged to Holloways. The day before the big gather was to start at Holloways, I slipped down to Russell's and had supper with him. I stayed over night so that I could get an early start to the Holloway outfit on this horse of theirs. He was pretty well broke and ready to be turned back for my due reward.

I left out about daylight to travel the estimated 30–35 miles to Parade and the Holloway headquarters. A horse can travel a good 8 miles per hour on a brisk trot, so the sun was just up good in the east when I arrived. I'd say it was about 7:30 am. The only one at camp was Murphy, John's wife. She told me that the crew had pulled out at sunup with all the remuda, and that they were going to noon and change horses at the mouth of Fishgut Creek.

Murphy checked over my mount and asked if I thought he was good for another 12–15 miles. That was her way of telling me that he was sure enough ready for a little more riding, and make me feel important, and like it was my decision. Murphy told me to pull the saddle and come in for a cup of coffee and a sandwich while the horse's back was cooling.

I was still in my early teens and hadn't developed a taste for coffee, but I had a glass or two of water, and the best roast beef sandwich I ever ate in my life while she explained to me how to find the gather.

Murphy was one of the grandest ladies I ever met in my life. She treated every young cowboy like he was her own son. Murphy's maiden name was Tibbs, and I'm sure she had had a lot of practice with her little brother, Casey Tibbs, 'cause he sure enough never let any grass grow under his boots!

I headed south to Fishgut, and had no trouble finding the gather. There was the beginning of a small herd of about 80 Hereford cows and their calves, along with about 60 to 80 horses as well as, counting myself, 17 hands.

I checked in with John and he told me to turn my horse loose and he'd catch me a fresh one after dinner.

Young Johnny came riding in to check me out, and to inform me that I was late, and that most people never started their day at noon!

Johnny, John and Murphy's only child, was about 5 or 6 years old at that time, and probably was a little more of a seasoned cowboy than the three boys that had just come to South Dakota from Hearty, Iowa. Today Johnny is a very polite, mild-mannered man, with a great number of friends, including me.

We were served dinner, and no finer could be had. The remuda was brought up, and we were told to take our throw ropes in hand. We sort of eased around the saddlers and handed the end of our rope to the man on our right, progressing until we had a round rope corral. This was the norm for the entire roundup.

The first few times the horses experienced this, things were a little hectic. Most of the horses were not corral broke. I can still hear ole Bill Maupin holler, "Shake them ropes! Shake them ropes!" when a young horse would start crowding.

John was a seasoned hand and he would go in amongst the horses, swing that loop backwards over his head, and settle it over the head of his designated pick. After the horse was caught, he would announce, "Melvin! Jr.! Bruce! Larry! Ray!" or whomever he thought would fit this particular mount. Then the horse would be led outside the circle, bridled, and held along one's share of he corral until everyone had a mount. The ropes were coiled, and the extras, and spent horses were then turned loose.

These horses were all a little humpy, and had a little buck bred in 'em. Most would pitch a little when you first climbed aboard, but I don't think many guys got bucked off their fresh mounts. I really don't know 'cuz I was too busy taking care of business, myself!

Nothing delighted that ole John Holloway more than having 8 or 10 of them ole broncs break in two at the same time, with those young punchers hanging on for all their worth! I often think that this is why the Holloway Rodeo Company was formed. This was pure, true entertainment for John Holloway!

On one particular gather and drive of cow-calf pairs, it was slow going and everything was pretty well spent, including cows, horses, and cowboys (especially young cowboys). It was getting along about 10:30 or 11:00 pm on a partial moonlit night. I rode up to little Johnny to check him out, as it appeared that he was dozing.

I spoke up and said, "Johnny, are you OK?"

He said, "Yup—but I'm cold, I'm tired, and I'm hungry!!!"

I couldn't see, but I could tell that tears were about to come forth. I patted him on the back and said, "Cowboy up, little man. We're almost home," and rode back to my spot.

Johnny made it. And he still is! There weren't any sand boxes around his house. A Christmas present for him would have been a fine set of leather bridle reins and a new saddle blanket.

Johnny and his wife, Sharon, raised a fine family. It's still growing with several grandchildren carrying on the cowboy tradition.

Both their sons earned the right to appear at the NFR in Las Vegas, Nevada — Chuck as a pickup man, and T.C. in the saddle bronc riding.

Both Johnny's family and mine lost sons in tragic accidents. T.C. lost his life in a vehicle accident, and we lost our Jr. in a construction accident in Colorado.

The most famous cowboys, like Bill Linderman, Casey Tibbs, Deb Copenhaver, & Jack Bushbaum are more liken to John Wayne and Kirk Douglas or Randolph Scott. Some of the above-mentioned were sure enough good hands, but the real cowboys were the old boys who lived the life and were with their livestock day in and day out, through blizzard and drought, rainstorms and prairie fires. They risked their very lives for the welfare of their livestock, and were the good shepherds like God intended. And, above all, they treated their neighbors with honesty and respect. These old cowboys were role models and taught their

14

children to be God fearing, good, hard-working adults with a sense of accomplishment.

Some of these real cowboys that I was privileged to know as I was growing up were: Jack Hunt, Tarzan Anderson, Shorty Collins, Mike Shatz, Joe Zork, Sid Norvold, Bud Annis, Mark and Jim O'leary, Lee Robley, Albert Lopez, Andrew Dupris, Donovan Moran, Stanley Moran, Old Posey Moran, Glen French, Don Smith, Frances, John, Vern & Russ Curtis, Elmer (Slim) Berndt, Jim Keegan, Frank Macjeskie, Clarence and Robert Lawrence, Ervin Richardson, Leon Williams, George Webb, Ben Young, W. A. Hickman, Chauncy Johnson, and a host of Indian Cowboys who ran small outfits up and down the Moreau and Cheyenne Rivers, like Frank, Tuffy and Ed Ducheneaux, Kenneth West, Joe High Elk, Tom Looking Horse, George Madison, Thomas Hawk Eagle, Moses Bad Male, Sullivan Larabee, Baptise Red Dog, Leo Red Dog, Robert Blue Coat, Louis Thompson, Joe Yellow Head, Silas Elk Head (The Elk Head Family was known for their curley horses) Ed Lablanc, Charlie Red Dog, Blaine Traversie, Grover Cudmroe, The Linns south of Timber Lake, and the Lambs over in the White Horse country, and, of course, the T.O. Traversie outfit north of the Moreau in the Spring Draw country, and east of O'learys'.

Every one of these individuals has a story to tell, and not hardly one that you couldn't write a book about that wouldn't be more than a little interesting, and, sometimes, just down right astonishing. Most of it

15

would probably be about what these families had to do to just survive.

My family lived on Green Grass Creek on the old Starkey Ranch. Just downstream from us three miles where the Green Grass dumps into the Moreau, lies a little American Indian encampment called Green Grass Village. Most of the male Indians from there worked for my dad, Art Anderson, from time to time.

There was a wagon trail one mile to the west of our house that the Indians used to travel to Eagle Butte. They usually traveled by team and wagon, but sometimes by horseback, and often times a little of both. There were also visible wagon ruts where they would veer off and come to our house for a sandwich and a drink.

Mom would keep a watchful eye out, and if she saw "company coming," she would send us kids all over the place to gather eggs. She was of German descent, and a great bread maker. She always had a fine supply of freshly baked loaves. She would set herself up to make egg sandwiches and prepare a gallon jar of Watkins kool-aid. She stacked the sandwiches in the very same pan she kneaded the dough in. She met her guests at the gate where their lunch was consumed in rapid fashion, as the jar of hot kool-aid was passed along with a good drink for everybody.

There was no ice much after July those days because the ice in the icehouse was either used or melted by then. So kool-aid those days was usually cistern cool. (A cistern was a large bottle-like hole in the ground, grouted with plaster to hold water. The source of water for the cistern came from rain running off into eaves troughs, and then draining into the underground jug, or cistern. To retrieve the water one would tie a rope to a bucket and go for it. After you put the lid back on the cistern, you ran to the house with your bucket of water. You guessed – running water!)

There are very few of those old American Indians left, but they must have told the younger generations about my mother's hospitality, because a fair amount of the younger men and women still have a lot of respect for her. Mother Rose is 90, and she still speaks highly of her friends at Green Grass.

There was one particular family that started coming about every day, and Dad was getting pretty fed up with it. On one particular day, when the sun was straight-up noon, Mother had a big roast on, complete with gravy, potatoes, and all the fixin's, including canned vegetables from the root cellar, homemade chokecherry jelly and canned peaches.

Well, here came our dinner guests, the man, his lady and the two sons, driving in with their team and wagon.

Dad told Mother to set more plates because he was going to invite them in. Mom put up quite a fuss because they weren't exactly what you'd call tidy! The dog didn't even like the way they smelled. Mother finally broke down and allowed that they come on in and sit.

The old man and boys were eager, but the old lady was very reluctant to come in. She was finally convinced, and came in with her head buried deep in her shawl.

Everyone took a good bait of food on his plate. The roast beef was especially favored. All were anticipating a fine meal when Dad sort of glanced at Mother and said, "Rose, how old was this horse that we butchered? It seems kind of tough!"

Our guests politely and quietly set down their eating utensils and quickly departed. A Sioux Indian will not eat horsemeat.

This same family, and many more, still continued to get their egg sandwiches, and we are friends with them to this day.

Our Indian friends through the 40's and early 50's really had it tough, and they sure never all survived.

The Government sent boss farmers out to teach them how to irrigate and raise community gardens, but they never liked carrots and pumpkins. They liked meat! Hoeing weeds does not bring honor to a meat eater.

There were no commodities or food stamps, no welfare programs, and very few jobs. Their kids were forced to go to school at the Old Cheyenne Agency for months at a time, and the only consolation to the parents was that they probably had something to eat. But, what a price to pay. In those days there was no such thing as a fat Indian.

As a kid growing up on the ranch, one of my jobs was to ride bog. Our cattle, I guess 'most everybody's cattle, would get thin and weak over the winter, and after the spring thaw, they would go into a drainage area for a drink. Sometimes they would mire down in the mud, and one would have to throw a rope around their neck and pull them out. Those days a good share of our saddle horses were at least ¼ Percheron, and they were hell for stout—so stout that it was foolish to use a little grass 7/16 throw rope. Most people of the day carried a fairly new 40-foot piece of ½ in. sisal. In this case, with the stouter rope, the cinch would break, or the saddletree would end up in your lap before the rope would break!

These little creeks would usually twist and meander here and there, and as a kid will do, I got lazy and cut across a bend in the creek without taking a good look-see.

Well, 3 days later I was going over this same ground, searching for stuck cows, when I saw ole Moses Bad Male backed up to the creek bank, pretty as you please. He had a log chain dangling off into the creek. Sure enough! I had missed a 3-year-old in the bend of the creek, and she was dead. Read dead! Down by the dead cow was a whole lot of live maggots surrounding the carcass, along with ole Moses.

I says, "Moses, what you gonna do? She's dead!"

"Oh, ha! Pull it out and eat it, you know---good, tender meat—boil it you know. Kills all the germs!"

I sat there a horseback and watched the whole procedure. He sure never left much for the coyotes. Like I said, they are meat eaters!

Moses later became a good Christian minister and lived a long life. He was a wise old man.

It was about the first week in August, and my dad decided it was time to start turning steers back to have them a little handier for shipping to Sioux City. Because it was pretty hot, we started about 3:00 a.m. for the mouth of Red Earth Creek. That was our designated ride for the day.

We got just about 1 ½ miles northwest of Curtis's branding pens, and we heard voices in the Native Lakota tongue. It was just about breaking daylight, and we rode over a bench near the river. There was this sort-of-dugout in the bank that had two big wooden doors on it.

Dad wasn't scared of nothin', but I was! He stepped off his horse and swung open one of them big doors. There stood ole Thomas Hawk Eagle, Claude and Sylvester! They all had butcher knives in their hands. Hanging from the ceiling of that dugout was the biggest, fattest Hereford cow I ever saw in my life. I should say, half hanging. She was so big that about half of her was still on the floor!

Dad said, "Butchering one of my cows, huh, Tom?"

Tom says, "Nah, Art. Course I know you wouldn't tell, but it's Curtis's."

Dad flopped the hide over to reveal the brand. It was a C+. That brand belonged to the Curtis sister, Marge.

We ride off with me a little spooked of those three huge Indians holding butcher knives, and with a 22 rifle propped in the corner to boot. I'd heard stories!

As we rode away my dad said, "Today Curtis's, tomorrow ours—somebody has got to feed them. Then he rode in close to me and made contact with his foot. He looked me in the eye and said, "You didn't see anything, did you?"

I answered, "No!"

There was not a deer to be found, and buffalo were gone. Our neighbors were all meat eaters!

Chapter II
Curtis Brothers

As a kid growing up on the ranch, I was always making pony tracks on a green horse, with no particular destination in mind. I'd most often find myself 12 to 15 miles from home, usually thirsty and hungry. So, I would find a high hill to climb and scout the area for a sheep wagon.

Nearly every outfit in the 40's and early 50's had a band of sheep along with their cowherd. The sheep were called mortgage lifters.

Vern and John Curtis standing on truck loaded with woolsacks.

Once I spotted the shiny white canvas-covered wagon, I would head in that direction, knowing that the sheep herder would be just a little hard put to find someone to visit with, and he'd be plumb willing to give you a hot drink of water from his canvas water bag, and would probably ask, "Are you hungry?"

Let me tell you, a growing kid that's been wrestling a "broomtail" for 6 or 8 hours, and can get a sheep tender to cook you up a skillet of side pork and fried potatoes—oh! This is the epitome of fine dining—depending, of course, on who's doing the cooking!

These little prairie homes were built on a wagon running gear with the main body fitting between the bolsters of the wagon, which were some 44" wide and 12' long, with 24" sides flared out to 7 ft.

The flare between the wheels was enclosed, allowing for storage of canned good and chuck, such as beans, canned milk and side pork, which was the staple meat. Side pork was a big, smoked slab of bacon that would keep for days, wrapped in an oilskin tarp.

The wagon's tongue was the step into the door, which was a Dutch door, allowing you to open the top half for a look-see at your bedded band of sheep, or for cooling.

Just as you stepped in the door, and always to the right, was a bolted-down, very efficient little wood-burning stove, complete with oven. Most wagons had no table, so the plate and cup were set on the flare along with other trappings. But, weather permitting, your host would allow that you should eat outdoors, and out of the skillet so's not to mess up his living quarters. Also, water conservation was usually a consideration. The camp tender usually came with camp chuck and supplies. He would hook on to the wagon with a team and move the wagon to a new location for fresh grazing and a clean bed ground for the sheep.   Never in a low spot because the sheep preferred higher ground.

At the far end of the wagon was the bed, the length of the flare and 40" wide, with a screened 2x2 window above the bed, which allowed for breeze and circulation, making things surprisingly comfortable.

Curtis Lambing Camp
Sheep Tepee by stream

Sheep Wagon – Cooty Wagon and Wood pile on left. Main tent or "house" on right with range tent in back.

The storage under the bed was usually accessible from the outside where the herder kept his clothes, oats for the horse, and various and sundry other items necessary to do the job at hand.

There were three to four wagons in the vicinity, but the one I visited the most was the Curtis Brothers' wagon. Francis was the sheep man of the three, but not necessarily the one that stayed with the wagon.

Curtises liked to have boys from the Webb Family or the Jochim Family because they were seasoned, and of good character.

My mother would often send an invite with me to give to those young men to come in and have a meal. This invitation was gladly accepted. It would always be a noon meal, as the sheep would settle around a water hole during the hot part of the day.

I remember once when I was very young, Francis rode old Sweetheart in for a little home cooking and homemade ice cream. He made a deal with Mother—if she would put together the fixin's he would crush the ice and do the cranking. My part of the job was to jump on old Speed, and, with sack in hand, go to the icehouse and bring ice home for the freezing machine.

Mom scolded Francis for taking the lid off and peeking to see if it was done. You could always tell, if it was done by how hard the crank turned. The harder it turned, the harder the ice cream.

I must have been pretty young, because I was playing with this little toy called a "top." If you took this top and put it on the door of the root cellar, and pushed the plunger down, the thing would spin and make pretty noises. Old Francis took the thing apart to see what made it sing, and couldn't put it back together! For a long time after that, I wasn't that happy to see him riding in, for fear he'd take something apart!

The Curtis Brothers were involved in a big part of my growing up, and I have vivid memories of them. It seemed as though' we would run across one or all of them every day or night.

My dad had two old model "A" Fords, and, one night, upon his arriving home after a big Saturday night on the town, he found John and Vern sitting on top of the spare car in our yard. Our old 3-legged dog, Jack, was a herding them close, with his shackles up, and exposing a lot of tooth!

My folks had gone to the dance that night, and stayed until the piano player, Agnes Rousseau, went home! Therefore, it was about 2:00 a.m. Dad calls off old Jack, and John and Vern dismount from the top of the old car—MAD! Dad mentions something about "grub," and Vern mumbles something about it's almost breakfast time, and if Dad would allow them to sleep in the fresh hay in the barn, maybe they'd have breakfast in a couple of hours.

Sunday morning Dad took pail in hand to head for the barn just below the house, to milk the cow and pitch a little hay to the saddlers in the stalls.

Dad brings up the pail of milk along with about eight eggs in his hat, followed by John and Vern, who had had a short night in the barn. They were sure enough hungry and thirsty — and still mad!

Breakfast was a big meal at our table. Anyone who dined there can attest to that! Always buttermilk pancakes, fried potatoes, eggs and some kind of meat such as bacon or liver or even sometimes, steak. Dad usually made breakfast, but this time Mom and Sister Betty Jane made it, as Dad was busy discussing range conditions and cattle prices with the "boys."

Our visitors had taken on a good fill, rolled a couple of smokes and were about to leave when John asked Dad if he would be allowed to "teach that dog a lesson." Dad asks what he had in mind. John says, "Gol, Art, after I saddle up, I'd like to ride up here and take my catch rope down and double her up and dunk 'er in the rain barrel, and make a stand. You hold the dog 'til I'm ready, and you turn old Three Legs loose, and we'll let 'er rip!

He did, Dad did, and the dog did! About the time John had the rope behind his back on the second revolution, Old Jack jumped at his chest and had him by the bibs. Dad had to wade in there and pull Old Jack off! The training session wasn't very successful, but no blood drawn!

(Note: About 80% of the cowboys in that era wore bib overalls, bought too long in the leg so they could roll the bottom up on the outside, using the roll for an ash try for their roll-your-own smokes while indoors.)

Old Jack mysteriously died about 10 days later. Jack was not a pet. He lost one of this hind legs in a coyote trap. He was also snake bit by a rattler once. He hated snakes with a passion, and Dad and Grant (Grandpa) would take their two dogs, Jack and Slobbers, up to the big snake den on the ridge, and flip the rattlers to the dogs. They would literally tear and shake those reptiles to bits!

The Curtis Brothers branded V/C on the left rib of their cattle, and in that big, open country, they roamed far and wide. My dad would scold and warn me when we approached a bunch of cattle "to be quiet—don't talk!" If you would set your horse up for a little while so those old, wild range cows could have a look-see, and you circled in slow, you could ride amongst them and make a sort. But, if they heard a little kid's squeaky voice, they were long gone and over yonder!

The Curtises weren't very flashy dressers, nor did they ride fancy horses, but they sure knew how to make do with what they had.

Those big old horned Hereford cows were very impressive with their dewlaps flopping between their front legs, and them giving you a stare like they meant business! I don't think there was a coyote born that could snitch a bite out of one of their calves. They would have gotten the business end of those antlers!

One thing that always impressed me about their operation was the bulls. They took great pride in them, and dug deep in their pockets to buy the best. The Evan Mischief bloodlines is what they favored, leaning

29

more toward the yellow color than red. Vern pointed out to me that this bloodline had black hairs at the tip of their tails, and that characteristic was certainly carried on to their offspring.

John and Vern would spend a little time talking about their bulls — not really bragging, but pointing out that theirs were the best on the range — maybe even better than Lee Robleys! Lee raised registered Herefords fro a long time.

The country has since all been ruined with barbed wire and steel posts, but at the time while they were upgrading their cow herd, they were also upgrading the cattle in the entire county, because cattle were run in common, no questions asked.

Cattle have a tendency to migrate with the drainage, given a chance, and that means downhill. And, that also means it's down hill 'till you get to the river.

This was a time you could ride from our house to Mobridge, SD, some 80 miles, with no gates to open. It was the same way going west downstream of the Moreau. I've rode west past the Diamond X Diamond on highway 65 without an obstacle.

The cattle had the capability to roam some 110 miles up and down the river, if they weren't turned back once in a while. This meant that the Curtises shared those good bulls with just about everybody that ran on the river, and that was every outfit that had a cow!

My Dad was one of the guilty parties, along with O'leary Brothers, Slim, Bud and Johnny Berndt,

Harold Brewer, Robleys, Chick Anderson—that's just to mention a few, not counting all the Indian families that lived the whole length of the river, clear to the mouth of the Missouri.

So, yes, the Curtises were grand old stockmen that shared their range, their bulls, and their branding pens.

Branding pens on the Moreau River. These pens were the only good corrals on the river for many miles. Hundreds of calves were branded here each year in a two-week period. Note wood branding fire in center.

For years, all interested parties would throw the whole shebang together, from up river and down river, and points in between. The herd would be held at the branding pens on the east side of the river, usually at the end of June, and before the 4th of July.

The smaller outfits would cut the herd to sort out their own, in an orderly fashion and trail home to brand before they turned loose. The bigger outfits were appointed a designated day to sort and brand at

31

the pens where the help was all gathered at one spot. The next day, it was a new set of irons in the fire. Sort of a community branding.

Dad was sort of clumsy with a rope, but always rode a horse that would sure lock on to a cow. So, he was always in the midst of cutting the herd. It took quite a handful of cowboys to hold the herd and hold the cut, me being amongst them.

The big day was when Curtises took their turn, which was usually the last, as the branding pens were on their home range. They could just turn loose and ride away when the branding chores were done.

Most all ranchers had an "ear mark" for their cattle. My dad's was a notch out of the top, and one out of the bottom of the right ear, with the Bar Lazy S brand being on the left shoulder and ribs.

In this way you could recognize ownership from either side. Also, in the wintertime, when long winter hair covered the brand, the ear would tell the tale. Those old cowboys knew earmarks as well as brands.

The Curtis Brothers didn't bother with a little notch on the ear. They had the mark of a dewlap, just like the Matador Outfit that was long gone from this range.

Most dewlaps were made by grabbing a handful of loose hide under the brisket, and slicing in an upward motion from the bottom up. Old John Curtis made an art of this. He would cut from the top down. The farther you go, the narrower she gets. When those cows reached the age of 7 or 8, those dewlaps hung down about 10 inches. For all practical purposes they looked like a bell with out a clapper. They stuck out like a sore thumb!

Those huge Hereford cows with their horns pointed towards the stars, and with dewlaps dangling were a sight to behold!

I'm sure that those four brothers are still a-riding on those old Herefords and rolling smokes up in Cowboy Heaven.

Francis was a good cook, and could make as good a roast beef or leg of lamb that ever came out of an oven. Sometimes a fellow sort of wondered about his sanitary measures, and, I'm sure Betty Crocker wouldn't approve of some of his recipes!

Come branding time one summer, we were needed to lend a hand with gather for the branding. My dad allowed that he needed time to put new ledger plates in the 5 ft. sickle mower, and replace the pittman stick. So, he sent me down river to the branding pens with two horses. I had two army blankets over a jacket tied to the strings behind my cantle for an overnight stay.

During branding time, the brothers pulled the sheep wagon down near the pens to use for a base camp, and for cooking. I arrived about 3:00 p.m. No riding was going on for the rest of the day, so I went with Vern up in the short draws off the river to gather ash wood for the branding fire, cooking, and such. The cottonwood along the river was in abundance, but not desirable for hot coals and long burning like the hard wood ash.

Vern was the slighter built of the brothers, but he took pride in his sharp blade. He was proud of his axe, and he sure knew how to use it! I was the loader and he was the cutter. When we got back to the wagon, I was treated to what was their version of "sheepherders dessert," which consisted of a slice of bread on a plate, topped with a generous helping of apple sauce with a little canned milk poured over the whole works. You'd chase flies and eat fast 'cause it's good!

The staple of the day was what didn't spoil in the heat, and it wasn't much! Lots of fried potatoes in bacon grease, side pork, beans, campfire coffee, store-bought vegetables to balance the meal, and canned tomatoes with a good helping of sugar sprinkled over the top for dessert.

The evening was spent visiting and planning a strategy for the next day's ride. As a young boy, I loved to listen to those guys spin yarns and amuse themselves, as well as listen to Jerry O'leary sing those old Irish songs. With a shot of grog in his snoot and one in his pocket, you'd swear he'd just docked at Ellis Island!

There's something about sleeping outside that allows for total rest. You can breathe that fresh air under the stars, take a three-or-four-hour sleep and be totally rested. That is, if the mosquitoes don't decide to go to bed with you! Also, you would want to be sure to check for anthills. Ants make for miserable bed partners!

I woke up early and rolled my blankets, caught my horse, rode him to the river to water, and hobbled him by the wagon to get my breakfast and take my riding orders for the day.

I was to go up Red Earth to the ONO outfit where Glen and Nora French lived, to pick up 3 cows, 3 calves and one dry, and to look for more, both going and coming. I'd be expected back about noon.

On the way to French's, I rode thru the Hawk Eagle cows, which numbered about 80. The calves were peeling fresh brands, mostly belonging to Benny, and with the telltale ID branded on the hip, meaning "Indian Department." In order to legally purchase one of these cows, it had to be accompanied by a permit signed by the boss farmer in charge who was paid by the government to oversee the cows issued to the individual Indian families. This was known as "The Replacement Program."

I ran into Claude down in the timber and had a little visit with him. He said there were no strays. Claude never did much good in school, as he was a little slow in the "think tank." But he was pretty honest. He rode a lot and kept the Hawk Eagle herd pretty near the family dwelling at the time.

I could tell old Claude had something tied to the saddle strings on the offside, and as I would try to ease around to have a look-see, he would lead his horse in a circle so I couldn't look! So, I says "So long," and rode off about 100 feet, and spun a cookie. It sort of surprised ole Claude when I came thundering back, but I wanted a peek at what he had hung up on his saddle that was so important!

He had a big old skunk hung by the neck, pretty as you please! Thinking he's probably going to skin the critter and send the pelt to Sears and Roebuck, or some such thing, I asked, "Claude, what you gonna do with the skunk?"

He says something in his native tongue, then says, "Bury it in the sand for 3 days, you know---tastes like chicken." The biggest mystery to me was that skunk had absolutely no smell!

On up to Glen and Nora's, where I was welcomed with open arms. In the house we go for fresh oatmeal cookies and a glass of milk, with conversation as to why I was there in the first place which was to take the dewlaps to the branding pens.

Glen allows that he will go along and help me thru the gate. I went down to the horse pen with him and he catches this black horse with a stripe and a snip.

Now this deal is fancy! This old gelding is a shiny and top-notch No. 1 good-looking cow pony, shiny as can be with his mane combed, and his coat brushed. It was first class all the way with both horse and rider. A nearly-new saddle with a pelican horn and a Navajo blanket of Indian design sticking out of all four corners. Glen, himself, was a sight to behold with his wool Pendletons stuck inside the tops of his Blucher boots, and a respectable Stetson perched atop his head. Well, I thought I was cowboying with Gene Autry, himself!

The whole French Ranch was like that--- everything in its place, everything painted, and nothing broke. I thought for sure that they were millionaires, although I didn't know for sure what that word even meant!

You know, after all that fine entertainment, I am a little late getting back to the gather with my 4 cows— about 2 ½ hours late---and I am HUNGRY! I ride up to the wagon where Francis is taking a little siesta in the shade, so I go in the wagon to grab a handful of cowboy grapes (raisins), making just the proper amount of noise so as not to get hollered at, but enough to wake up the main cook of the day.

Francis wakes up and scratches a little and says, "Are you hungry?"

In a low tone I replies, "Kinda."

So he stokes the fire and puts in a couple of sticks of ash in the firebox, and hands me three big spuds to peel. He goes to the storage compartment in the back of the wagon and comes out with a fair-sized onion and the side pork wrapped in the oilskin tarp.

By then the ash is doing its job in the little stove, and it's just jumpin'. He deposits two slices of side pork in the pan and proceeds to slice the onion on to the meat and it's a talk'n to me with a lot of sizzling and popping. I'm drooling! Out comes the pig and in goes the spuds into the well-lubricated pan. The onions and taters are cooking now with the cast iron lid holding 'er all in place.

Two turns with the spatula and the grub is on the home stretch, with Francis reaching in for a taste to test for tenderness. Almost done to his liking, he pops open a can of cream-style corn and tops off the whole kit'n'kaboodle with corn.

He very gently grasps the handle on the cast iron skillet and sets 'er out on the ground to warm the corn and blend the aroma! Then he proceeds over to the corner of the wagon to scratch his back. I notice that the wagon is rocking just a little bit, and he slides his hands under his bibs, what sort of looked like to me, towards "forbidden territory," and he started scratching there, too! With a fair amount of satisfaction, he pulls his hands out and check his fingernails — they are full!!!

All of a sudden I was longing for my mother's cooking! Yes, I did eat. I was hungry, and you never wanted to make the cook mad!

Francis Curtis was unique, and I could write an entire book about him, but, I know more than I need to know about a lot of people, and I have to be careful not to point fingers, as fingers can be pointed back at me, and I do live in a glass house!

Mrs. Curtis and son Francis.
All the conveniences of home.

Francis purchased a fine, made-to-order saddle-probably a Hamley—with a huge horn the size of a skillet. He was very proud of it, as there were very few new saddles floating around in Dewey County. With intentions of showing off his fine, hand-tooled saddle, he came riding in on his little saddle mare, Sweetheart, patting her on the back side with a little lath stick. Cowboys of the day liked horses with a fast-running walk. This was his method of crowding her in to that gait, which would cover five miles per hour and not tax horse nor rider.

There was cow work that day, and ole Francis got in the thick of things to lend a hand.

Old Sweetheart was more used to herding sheep than sorting cows, and was slacking on the job. Francis knew she could do better, and told her so. Just to get her attention, he tapped her ever so lightly on the forehead with that little lath stick. She dropped like rock---DEAD!

Francis didn't have any use for a dog, but he got very attached to his horses. He walked away, not even able to bear the pain of pulling his new saddle off. One of his brothers went back to pack his gear home.

The Curtis Brothers always thought I bordered on the edge of being as wild as a peach orchard boar. They were a little suspicious of me, I think, as I made a lot of pony tracks. They also quizzed me about goings-on in the neighborhood, like, "What's old Pat Miller up to?" or "Did you see any dewlaps in Don Smith's outfit?" or "Have you been down river as far as Joe Guinvilles?" or "Has Andrew Dupris cut any hay yet?"

I saw a few things that I wasn't supposed to see, and my dad told me to keep my mouth shut. But, I sure would tell the brothers when I would spot their V/C cows.

I was riding out on the big flat gathering horses on a little white mare that belonged to Father Golden. Coming down a long ridge into an ash-laden draw, the little white mare tripped up in fallen timber and went down, throwing me free. I've got a hole in my britches, and a little skin off my knee, but none the worse for wear. No way would that little mare let me walk up to her, and away she goes with the wild bunch! There is, as I recollect, only two times that I had to walk home.

It was about 5:00 pm., and I'm tired! Dad is gone with Blackie, the only other horse we had in, and by the time he came in, it was late. I reported the events of the day to him, and he said he'd gather the bunch with the saddle mare in the morning, and not to worry about it. These were pretty kind words from him!

I'm down by the little white bunk house next morning, about 6:00 a.m., and I see this big cloud of dust coming from the west, caused by a huge herd of horses. I'm wondering, "What the heck!"

Old John and Vern were out riding early and spotted this white mare with the saddle still intact. They knew it was my tack, and they sure enough were Worried that I was lying in a heap some place! This is some 57 years later, and I still remember and appreciate their concern and act of kindness!

By the way, there was another young boy that made pony tracks on that same open range. I was about as wild as Grandma's house cat compared to him. His name is Anthony Lamont Johnson, affectionately known as "Curley."

Chapter III
History & Family

Fate allowed me to spend my early childhood in this great Moreau River Country. Dad bought the Starky ranch in 1934 or '35 for $500, which was about all the money he had, and a lot more than most had.

Times were tough and money was in short supply. It was called The Great Depression. No money -no grass -no water - and grasshoppers so thick that when they flew overhead they blotted out the sun.

The $500 allowed for possession, but there was no deed with the name Arthur Burdett Anderson on it! The taxes hadn't been paid, and the land was reverted back to the county for "back taxes."

My dad was a conservative man, to say the least. He could make a dollar stretch ¾ of a mile! By 1939 he had enough money saved to buy a tax title and deed from the County for $700.

The counties in West River, South Dakota never had enough money to govern, and were willing to take any reasonable offer for the land to get it back onto the tax role. Most of the land in the area, over 1 million acres, belonged to the Cheyenne River Sioux Tribe, but a large tract within the reservation boundaries was declared open to homesteaders in 1910.

Many ranchers squatted long before 1910 and had large, established herds of cattle and horses. Many were of French descent and several other nationalities that were riverboat men and fur trappers that worked for the American Fur Company to trap, buy furs, and establish trading posts in the area. These trappers, traders and riverboat men took a liking to the American Indian girls, who were more than willing to get acquainted!

These men, new to the land of the Dakota, broke away from the tradition of the buffalo hunt.

Most had big families and big herds to feed them. When one of the sons or daughters got married, they would have a weeklong feast, celebration and "give away" (where the host would give elaborate gifts to the guests), along with lots of horse races.

Fred Dupris from the Ridgeview country, was one of these old ranchers that my uncle, Rusty Anderson, broke horses for. Rusty said that Fred had horses numbering in the thousands. And although Scotty Philip was credited for saving the buffalo, it was actually the Dupris family that managed to salvage a small herd. Scotty bought that little herd, and the buffalo multiplied in numbers from there.

Some of the names I remember from that era are: Narcell Brothers, Lebeaus, LeCompte, Ducheneaux, Garreau, Arpan, Claymore, Dubray, Gunville, LaPlant, Rousseau, Traversie, and others.

The Indians that were the true buffalo hunters all took names from animals or birds as they were earned, or, from warring with their enemy or counting coup. Names such as Fast Horse, Looking Horse, High Elk, Bald Eagle, Chasing Hawk, Hawk Eagle, Black Bull, Black Crow, and Blue Coat were just some of them. Each family knows how their ancestors earned that name. But this is not for me to tell, as I would make errors.

Of all the people living during the drought and depression of the thirties, I think the American Indian suffered the most. They were taught to live off the land, and the land yielded little.

Alex Garreau worked for the C.B.C. Horse Company. He said horses would stagger into the Missouri from as far out as thirty miles for a drink, as the stock ponds were few. All the creeks and smaller tributaries, such as the Cheyenne and the Little Moreau, as well as the Big Moreau were as dry as a bone.

Instead of branding colts and cutting studs, cowboys were sent into Montana, North Dakota and Canada looking for water and grass for these C.B.C. horses. Most were finally shipped to South Saint Paul, Minnesota to a packing plant, and slaughtered.

I can only imagine what kind of cowboy it would take to rope and throw 70 or 80 studs a day to brand and castrate. They must have had stout ponies and strong cinches. I wish I could have been there. Too young.

The drought and depression went on and on. Then the USA went to war in 1941, just as the grass was coming back and things were getting better.

The Second World War drained us of our most valuable asset, young men. The men that weren't called into service moved to larger cities that offered jobs in factories and hope for a future.

Back at the ranch my dad was struggling to put a few cows together and hold his horse herd intact, as he and Barney Downing had a government contract to sell horses to the army. Also, there was a large demand for draft teams in Iowa farm country.

My mother is my favorite subject, and although I don't think she got much credit for it, she held the family together, providing clothes, food and love. I went hungry lots of days in my younger years, but that's because I was too far from my mother's kitchen, not because there wasn't food on the table. There were three meals a day, every day, and dessert twice a day. And, if two or three cowboys came riding in hungry, day or night, she fed them with a willing smile.

Dad would be home most nights, but would usually be gone building dams for the W.P.A., a program the government came up with to employ the people. He would get paid moving dirt with a team and a Fresno or dump wagon. (A Fresno is a large scoop-like device that was pulled behind two horses. If held at the proper angle, it would scoop ½ sq. yard of dirt that the team would drag to a designated area where the driver would lift a long handle, approximately 6 ft. long with a rope attached, allowing the dirt to be scattered 6 to 8 feet. The handle was left up until you went for another load. The handle was then pulled down by the rope to be positioned for reloading.)

This allowed Dad to get horses broke to drive and pull while making money moving dirt. He also rented teams for $1.00 a day to people who couldn't afford to buy them. There were plenty of takers.

One of the projects he worked on for a long time was Bruske Lake, north and east of Eagle Butte. He would come during the weekend and prepare a load of hay to take back Monday morning for his teams. Anyone that knew my dad would tell you that he wasn't lazy. He worked every minute of every day.

Mother had an old Singer sewing machine that she sewed all of us kids' clothes on. She got quite good at it. Some of the Indian ladies would give her material as a gift. I allow the government might have had an issue program that allowed them to receive material, as most of them wore better "home-made" clothes than we did. Mother took great pride in handing me or my brother a new shirt, or my sister a new dress. (There were five kids in the family, but the youngest two were not yet born.)

Mother Rose was a generous giver! Rose's parents, my grandparents, Joseph and Hannah Fischer, migrated from Germany to Russia, and then to Strasberg, North Dakota. They finally settled south of Eagle Butte near Rudy Creek where the Ganjes, the Heils, Bushes and several other German families lived. They were tough and sort of took hardships for granted.

Both my parents' folks had large families. The Fischers practiced the Catholic faith in regular attendance, and had a brood of 12 children. That's my mother Rose's family.

My dad's parents, Ulysses S. Grant Anderson and Nellie Walker Anderson had a total of 15 children. They were Methodist. They lived apart for 20 years. Hard to tell how many kids they would have had if they had gotten along a little better!!!

Anderson Grandparents Wedding Picture
Grant Anderson & Nellie Walker
Married April 27, 1898

My mother is short in stature and always was small. She was just not stout enough to pitch wheat into a header box. So, in her growing-up years, she was left with the yard and house chores—mainly cooking and washing dishes, washing and ironing clothes, baking bread, butchering chickens, tending the garden, milking the cows, separating the cream, and making butter. In her spare time she baby-sat her younger siblings, while all the rest of the family did field work. They were tried and true farmers—good ones, and proud of it.

The first house they had was of the old country "Germany" style with the barn attached, allowing one to open a door and step from the house into the barn without going outside. The barn housed the milk cows and the chickens, and also served as a nursery for the old sow, if the weather did not permit for outside birthing. Every nationality has its traditions. This was a tradition from the Old Country.

It was the brothers' (Pius, Pete, Andy and Wendelin) job to keep the barn clean—very clean, which they did. They hated it so much because they always smelled like cow manure when they went to school. The girls teased them to their wit's end and they would ask the teacher if they could study on the other side of the room.

Another German tradition was the way they picked their soul mate. They didn't. Their parents did. When a girl was old enough to be wed, her father would start searching for a boy with good standing in the church, of good nature, with ambition and prospects for wealth. The father of the bride would approach the father of the prospect, and if they could reach an agreement, a wedding date was set.

Hannah never met Joe until the day they got married. Did she love him? She said she learned to love him. And love him she did with all her heart and soul.

Personally, I was scared to death of my Grandma Fischer. She was tough and loud, and ruled her household with an iron hand. She would go out early in the morning to the hen house, ringing the neck of a couple fryers—one in the right and one in the left!!!

We'd have cream-style chicken and homemade bread for breakfast, pickled watermelon for lunch, sausage for dinner, and blood sausage for supper. There is talk about Indians eating the innards of their animals. You haven't seen nothing 'till you watched a German butcher a pig! They even can the squeal and the oink!

Once I was privileged to stay at my grandma's house to study the Bible. One morning I'd just got up, and she instructed me to go feed the duck, which was "setting," hatching eggs, which were about due for ducklings to pop out and see the daylight.

Nothing doing but on the way back, I hear this blood-curdling scream come from the direction of the chicken house. A big, old sow had entered into chicken territory, and old Grandma was going to have war with her. The sow decided that was about all the verbal abuse it could stand and ran right between Grandma's legs, hauling her out of the chicken house backwards, with a chicken in each hand. I figured we'd probably have headcheese for supper!

Once a year Grandma Fischer would take a horse-drawn wagon load of wheat up over High Elk Hill and over across the Missouri on a barge to Forestburg, and on eastward to the gristmill. Here she got her year's supply of flour. The trip was about 80 miles, and it would take 5 to 7 days. She always wrapped a white shawl or turban around her head, but never could seem to figure out why the flying ants always wanted to taunt her!

Flour was the staple food of the day. Her oldest son would often say, "All Ma needs to feed a bunch of people was flour and water!" That seemed to be true, as she was always kneading dough for bread, noodles, coogan, piecrusts and the like.

It was hinted by one family member that maybe the trip to the gristmill was to get away from Grandpa for a week!

Grandma was a fair-sized woman of German descent and she had a lot of grit! One spring day she came walking in behind the team that she had been using to harrow in the field of wheat. She put the team in the barn, walked in the house, went to the privacy of her bedroom and gave birth to a baby! She sent son, Andy, on the run to get Mrs. Heil, the neighborhood midwife. By the time Mrs. H. arrived, business was taken care of, with the new baby fed and in his mama's arms!

Now, Grandpa Fischer was, indeed, a "piece of work!" He was always jolly and full of fun when the grandkids came to visit. He would use me for an excuse to "go fishing," but never let me touch his bamboo pole! You've never seen excitement until you've seen Joe Fischer pull a bass or crappie out of a dam on a bamboo pole! He would whoop and holler and dance around like he was doing the rain dance!

**Wedding Picture Joe & Hannah Fischer
German Immigrants
Mel's Maternal Grandparents – following German
Custom –Theirs was an arranged marriage.**

Playing cards was the same way. He was boisterous. He would slap the cards on the table and stomp his feet and let out a holler when he took a trick. He loved to win, and if he had to cheat a little, he thought that was okay, too!

I played Casino with him for 5 years and never won a game. Nobody is that lucky! It was worth it just to watch his every move, but I never could figure out his underhandedness.

Joe had many friends, and that is what he worked at the hardest! He was the "king of his castle" and every family member jumped to his tune. To his credit I will say, he worked extra hard tilling and planting the ground for spring seeding, and it was "all hands on deck" for harvest, he being in the lead.

His pride and joy was his header box, which was pulled by 6 stout horses. It had a sickle twelve feet in length, which cut below the heads of ripe grain by about 5 or 6 inches. The cut grain was then conveyed into a large box in tow, with about four kids pitching like the dickens until it formed a stack of about 4,000 pounds. It was then deposited in a row in orderly manner for arrival of the threshing crew.

Joe also took pride in plastering cisterns, which were underground storage tanks that held water for household use. Plaster was a cement-like substance used to form a seal between earth and water.

There was always company after church on Sunday, as Hannah would put out an invite for all in the community. She and her girls were, by then, well known for their good German cooking. No recipes were allowed, as Grandpa and Grandma Fischer did not learn to read or write.

Another thing that would allure bachelor cowboys and family men alike was Grandpa's "fermented squeezing" as they were called. These were the days of prohibition—no hard liquor was allowed.

On one of our little fishing trips on Bruske Lake grandpa told me he would, maybe, sell a jar or two of his homemade booze at the schoolhouse dance and box social. One of these dances was held somewhere every Saturday night.

He would go to the designated site on Friday night and bore 5 or 6 holes that would hold a quart fruit jar. He was careful to leave the soddy grass intact to be saved for the "lid." He'd place the jars in the holes for safekeeping and for sale at the Saturday night shindig!

He'd been told that this was a Federal offense and to be careful. But as with all things done illegally, one is bound to get caught! In this case it was by a competitor squealing to the Feds. Old Joe was caught with booze in hand, as the revenue men lay in waiting! Two Federal marshals took Joe away, and Joe is look'n at "time!"

The next day two suited gentlemen came pulling into the homestead, big as you please, scaring the whole family into thinking that those fellas were gonna take Ma, too!

Out jumps Pa, and the revenuers go on their merry way! Joe is pretty relaxed about the whole thing, and tells the lawmen that he's tired and needs a rest and THEY can feed his brood for a while! They turned him loose! It was called a "hardship" case.

There were certainly hardships and trying times at the Fischer homestead, too. Leo, my mother's baby brother, died at three days of age. Hannah had a very difficult birth and the baby would just keep moaning and sounding these little grunts. He refused milk and finally succumbed. Mother was 14 years old at the time of Leo's departure. Her father handed her a pan of warm water and instructed her to clean the baby and ready him for burial. This was very hard for Mother, and it haunts her 'till this day.

Mother Rose also had another younger brother that went by the name of Baby Joe. Baby Joe had had an affliction since infancy, and Mother was the primary caregiver to this precious little brother whom she loved very much. He was very sweet and kind. Baby Joe passed away at the early age of five, and Mother was so heartbroken that she couldn't go back into the house. She was allowed to live at the home of the closest neighbors, Jack Heil and his wife, who was the midwife of the neighborhood. She reluctantly returned home to her family after two months had passed.

Jack Heil donated a little corner of his homestead quarter for a graveyard, and those two little brothers, and others, were buried there, including a member of the Ganje family. The grave is marked by a homemade cement cross of great dimensions.

Still another incident that had a lasting affect on my mother was when a summer storm passed over the Fischer homestead. Dogs are more frightened of lightening than probably any other thing. The family dog was howling and clawing the screen to be let into the sanctuary of the house. Note was taken of his fearsome behavior and he was allowed to enter the home.

The dog found Mother, who was asleep in bed, and he took refuge under her bed. Lightening struck the house, knocking Mother unconscious but the dog was struck dead beneath her, probably saving her life.

I remember, as a young boy growing up on Green Grass Creek, how fearful Mother was of lightening storms and how she warned us to stay away from windows, because the screens were made of wire mesh and they may draw lightening. Although she became very attached to our ranch dogs, they were never allowed in the house.

My father, Arthur, was Mother's second husband. Her first was Elroy Pommorin. She met Elroy at a dance in Faith, SD on the Fourth of July. It was "love at first sight." Rose was 18 years old when they were married. They moved to Wisconsin to seek their fortune and start a family. My sister, Betty Jane, was born to that union.

Elroy had a wooden foot that Rose never discovered until their wedding night! The bottom of his foot had been cut off by the sickle bar of a horse-drawn mower, most likely in a runaway. (A team of horses out of control was known as a "runaway.")

Times were very hard and jobs were nonexistent. People were begging to work for food, and young men were hopping freight trains, going from city to city looking for work, with very little success. Rose and Elroy lived in a little house where they raised a garden, doing day work wherever they could find it. No task was too hard for $1.00 per day.

They were a very popular couple and had much company as their popularity grew.

One evening company arrived, and it was decided to throw a little party. Rose and one of her friends cut across the alley into town to get crackers, baloney and cheese to snack on.

Mother was always courteous to their bachelor neighbor, John Combs. She would sometimes take him pie or cake to be neighborly.

While Rose was gone to the store, John knocks on the door. When Elroy answers with, "Hello, John, come on in," John pulled a gun out and shot Elroy in the head. He died the next day. John was mad because he hadn't been invited to the party!

Rose was a widow at the age of 19 years, and Betty Jane was without a father. They had no means of support. Telegraph was the technology of the day, and a message was sent to Rose's parents, Joe and Hannah, informing them of the tragedy and time of funeral. They were asked to please come. Rose says that she barely had enough money to send that telegram.

Very few people had a dollar to spare, and Joe and Hannah, with a large family to feed, were no exception. The train tickets to Wisconsin were $9.00 each, and where were they to get the money?

Conrad Held had told them of a horse trader, Arthur Anderson, that was living with his brother,

David, over in the Parade Country. They thought that Art might buy a team from them, as he was breaking horses and hauling them by rail to Iowa to sell to the Amish farmers.

The connection was somehow made, but Joe hated to part with a team because a good work team was the lifeblood of a farmer, and acres would lie idle with no power to pull.

Joe tried to borrow money from Arthur, but to no avail. Dickering was the order of the day! Arthur spotted a new, nicely constructed building that was about 12' x 14' that Joe had recently built to store grain. Art offered $25 for the granary. Sold! With cash in hand, Joe and Hannah headed for the Milwaukee Railroad depot in Eagle Butte, leaving for the sad reunion with their daughter and granddaughter. (That little granary was moved to the ranch on Green Grass Creek and was used to store horses' oats for over 50 years.)

Rose remembers how shabby her mother looked at the funeral with her torn and tattered, and not too clean, wardrobe, as well as her unpolished shoes. She had come with what she had, and made the best of it.

Rose was left in Wisconsin, almost in abandonment, as there was no money to bring her and her baby back to South Dakota with her parents. Two of Rose's brothers, Pete and Andy, scraped together enough money to buy train tickets which were sent to her so that she could come home.

Now this "horse trader" (not a very good title to have in those days, and which was often associated with gypsies) starts to show up at the Joe Fischer place for visits, bearing sacks of oranges and bags of prunes and such as that. Rose's sister, Cecelia, is teasing on her quite a bit saying things like, "I think he's sweet on you!" Rose would reply, "Oh, you mean that old bowlegged Art Anderson? He's the homeliest man I ever saw in my life!!" It was also suggested by her brother, Wendy, that Art might have fleas!

Chapter IV
Trying Times

The Saturday night dances and frequent visits by Art to the Fischer place finally evolved into a romance between Art and Rose. They were married and moved to the Starky place, just 9 miles straight north of the little town on the Milwaukee Railroad Line, called Eagle Butte. That town was named for a little butte where the natives would lie in wait to trap eagles for their plumage and feathers for making their magnificent headdresses and other regalia.

Times were tough, but everybody was in the same "boat," and we sure didn't know we were poor. Those lean years were character builders, and provided us with an education that no college could ever provide! People learned responsibility and work ethics, and to be God fearing, have good attitudes and, most of all, to get along with what God provided from day to day, as he did then, and as he does today. He provides us with all that we need.

Thanks to Mother Rose, our family never went one day without an abundance of food on the table. I can remember, so vividly, the huge garden, to which half was planted to potatoes and in which we all worked so hard to keep clean of weeds and insects.

Dad would take his team and walking plow into the plot, tie the lines of the harness together in a knot, and slip them over his head and under one arm, so that both hands were free to steady the plow. The plow had long, wooden handles connected to the center of the plow lay (the knife used under the sod) that protruded to the back, where both hands were needed to steady it.

Two furrows were thus plowed and us kids and Mom would punch the seed potatoes into the side of the furrow. Two more furrows would cover up the newly planted potatoes and make ready for the next row to be planted, thus spacing the rows 28 inches apart.

Betty, Larry and I each were assigned certain rows to be kept clean of weeds and to keep the constant invasion of potato bugs off the growing plants by plucking those creepy, multi-legged insects off the vine and dropping them into a tomato can full of kerosene. (Turpentine and kerosene were used for everything from fueling lamps, starting the fire in the stove, for disinfectant and cold medicine, as well as being mixed with other concoctions for home remedies to cure everything from colic to diarrhea.) How I did hate "garden duty!" It sure did interfere with my circles around the ranch on my horse!

Besides potatoes, many other vegetables of all descriptions were grown in that garden. My favorite was watermelon! The production was dependent entirely on the rainfall of the season, as there was no way to water it except to take the team and stoneboat (a sled-type contraption about 4′ wide and 6′ long) to the dam. Upon the stoneboat would be placed two wooden 50-gallon barrels. This would be pulled into the water a ways, and the barrels would be dipped full with a bucket and taken back to the garden to unload. The round trip amounted to about ¾ mile.

(Dams are called different things in different parts of the country. Down South they are called tanks. In several parts of the country they are called ponds. Dams are not natural reservoirs, but are constructed by moving vast amounts of dirt into a drainage area to stop the flow of water. A spillway was usually cut near the top of the dam fill for the overflow, unless there was a natural spillway.)

Rose would harvest vegetables from the garden for everyday use and can the surplus in a steel chamber called a pressure cooker. Electricity had not yet become part of the scene, so this was all done in the kitchen on a cook stove or range fueled by wood. It would be 100 degrees outside and 150 degrees inside, next to the wood range!

As different varieties would be ready at different times of the season, it seems as though she was always washing quart jars and canning as high as 600 quarts per year. We were always trying to grow a little patch of field corn for our livestock. We would also pick field corn for Mom. She would scrape the kernels off the cob and can many quarts when the maturity of the corn was in the milk stage. I usually inherited the job of gathering, as I could commute back and forth from the field with a sack of husked corn dangling from either side of my pony.

The second week in September we would harvest the potatoes — a family affair! Dad would plow them out with his one-bottom walking plow, just as he had plowed them in. The second pass would spill the potatoes to the top. As each row was uncovered, the pickers would hurry as fast as possible to pick up the potatoes, being careful not to retrieve any bruised or cut ones, as they would rot. The spuds would then be dumped in the wagon to be hauled and stored in the root cellar.

A root cellar, or cave, as some were called, was an underground dwelling that was constructed by hand by digging out a large square hole, tapered on one end to allow for entry. On the hole was set a large ridgepole, usually of the hardwood ash variety, and about 10" in diameter, going the full length. Then smaller poles were laid over the ridgepole as closely as possible. Over the top of the log roof then, was spread coarse native grass, usually taken from the swampy ground known as slough. This would not deteriorate like the finer stemmed grasses or straw.

The framing lumber and hinges for the entryway door and steps were all that one needed to purchase. This cost around $12.00. After the entry was framed and the door was hung, all the excavated dirt was thrown over the poles and grass in a mound-shape fashion in order to shed water. There was also a little vent that protruded out the top that reminded me of a chimney with a little pitched roof on it for ventilation.

This efficient little earth dwelling served as a storage facility for the potatoes in the right-hand, rear corner where the potato bin was located. On the entire left-hand side there were sturdy shelves from top to bottom where 600 to 800 quarts of homemade chokecherry, currant, plum, and buffalo berry, and grape jelly were stored, all of which were grown and picked on our little ranch. Also on the shelves were the canned vegetables from the garden and the 150 to 200 quarts of canned beef. That canned beef was the "fast food" of the era.

When peaches were in season, Art would go to town and buy bushels of them, as well as pears, plums and apricots along with an endless amount of sugar that Mother and Sister Betty slaved over on that hot kitchen stove, preparing for canning.

Dessert was always served at Mother's table after dinner and supper.

This little cellar was also a sanctuary from storms. Rose would gather her little brood and head for the cellar when mean storm clouds rumbled overhead. A kerosene lantern was always in preparation for a storm, as it would have been very spooky in that little dark hole in the pitch dark! It was cool and damp down in this little sanctuary, and it usually housed 5 or 6 creepy little creatures called lizards. The way they would slowly crawl around on the dirt floor, waving that slimy green-striped tail back and forth, for all practical purposes, reminded me of baby crocodiles!

In addition to this little creation being the only means at the time to keep things cool, it was also a detention center, and quite often used as a discipline tool! If we did something either of our parents didn't like, we would have to churn a batch of butter. There was this substantial glass container with a mechanism that had wooden handles that revolved near the bottom when you turned a little crank. With a little luck, and a whole lot of cranking, and if the temperature was right, the liquid would separate from the fat and one would have butter. I might add that on a fresh slice of home baked bread, one never tasted anything finer than fresh-churned butter! Plus, the buttermilk was used for the morning pancakes.

The temperature was just about right in the cellar, and brother, Larry, and I were "on notice" just about all the time. We did hate that job of churning butter!

Our spread on Green Grass Creek, in years gone by, was heavily laden with ash timber, although it was mostly dead in my day. The old timers that worked for my dad, like George Madison and Moses Bad Male would talk about the timber being so thick on the creek bottom that you couldn't ride through it.

When Art and Rose took possession of the Starky place, the timber was nearly all dead due to many years of drought and grasshoppers stripping the bark off the limbs.

Farmers and townspeople, alike, would come down off the hill with their team pulling a running gear (what is left of a high-wheeled wagon after the box is lifted off) destined to cut and haul a load of ash logs. Art would charge all comers $1.00 a load for all that they could pile on between the bolsters.

We hauled many loads each year for ourselves. Straight logs being thrown aside for posts, and the rest bucked up in the buzz saw for firewood used for heating and cooking. The man who took the wood away from the saw after it was cut into approximately 15″ lengths would make two piles. The wood with the large diameter was put in one pile for the heating stove, and the smaller diameter, up to 3 inches, saved for the range or cook stove.

I know for a fact that we were still burning wood in 1952, as I took it upon myself to haul the year's supply of wood in for sawing. I took the box off the wagon, and with a good team, Dick and Captain, I hauled nine big loads of logs for sawing. Some were sticking out the back so far they would drag when going across the creek.

The champion wood hauler was old Bill Berndt. He could stack it up between the bolsters to the height of about 6 feet, throw a chain around the load and over the reach, and put a twist in it with a long stick. He'd climb aboard his pyramid and head for home. He sure got his dollar's worth!

I never will forget that old man. He always wore bib overalls and, it seems, he only locked one suspender up and let the other one flop! He had big ears, and you couldn't help but notice that the wind would set them in motion! Bill was a soft-spoken man, and he raised a fine family: Elmer (Slim) with the B brand, Gerald and Johnny with the arrowhead brand, and Bud. As I remember, there was one girl, Phyllis. Finer people you will never meet.

In the days of the open range, the Berndt cattle would run to the river and we would often gather them. At one time they had an albino stud. Johnny had a string of curleys that originated from the Elk Head Family herd. I broke a little brown horse of this strain for Johnny. He was fun to ride because he had a lot of bottom.

Those curley horses were sure different. When you would get one hot and sweaty those little curls would look like pin curls with little beads of sweat dripping off them.

Not all neighbors are fine, upstanding people like one would like, and not all abide by the "Golden Rule." Taking matters into one's own hands sometimes carried out frontier justice!

There was this cocky neighbor kid — the only son of a prominent rancher — who was favored to be the heir of the family holdings. This guy, about 19 or 20, had smart tack, dressed the part of Tom Mix with a brown hat short on brim with a wide hat band decorated with conchos adorned with silver. His outfit was complete with pants tucked in boots, which were holding up his Crockett spurs. He wore chaps and an ever-present pistol strapped around his middle.

He came riding in one day for lunch, knowing Dad would most likely be gone. Mom was always afraid of him because of the pistol. (Mother was deathly afraid of guns after Elroy was murdered.) But, she invited him in for coffee and a sandwich, nevertheless, as it was her custom to never let a person leave her home hungry. All of the time she was feeling uncomfortable about the whole situation.

After accepting the hospitality, he arose as if to leave, but grabbed Mom with the intent to take her to the bedroom. Mom fought like a demon, and his intentions were not completed. Mother was bruised and very shaken, and her clothes were torn from the incident.

Dad came home to a wife in tears who had to give him an assessment as to the events of the day. Although it was late at night, and Dad had no food, he went out after that young cowboy in hot pursuit, not knowing whether he would be at his home which was a good 14 miles from our place. It was well into the wee hours of night, and breaking day, when Dad reached his destination. Not wanting to awaken the parents, he snuck into the house like a thief in the night. He found his prey sleeping in his sanctuary as though nothing had happened. He opened his eyes with a 25-20 rifle resting between them. Dad issued the ultimatum: "If I ever see you anywhere in Dewey County again, I'll kill you!"

The lad shook his head in agreement, and left the county. This boy's father ranched in Dewey County for many years, and upon passing it was said that if he did pay his last respects, it wasn't at the funeral.

Another sad state of affairs, along these same lines, happened to one of our neighbor girls, only this time the law was involved. These people, new to the community, rented the old Abair Ranch on Bear Creek. They moved in with a fair number of cattle and horses. They spoke with the accent of the South, and looked to be Spanish. These folks seemed to be respectable and probably were, but they mostly kept to themselves.

They had two boys somewhere near my age. I would run into them occasionally up on the big flats where large herds of horses had located.

The younger of the two boys acquainted himself with a young lady from Portland, Oregon, Lynette McBride. She had traveled by train to Eagle Butte to visit her cousins. This boy performed an unthinkable act upon Lynette, causing much grief and unrest in the neighborhood.

He was arrested and a trial ensued. Pat Morrison, a well-known attorney from Mobridge, was retained to defend the boy. The case resulted in a not-guilty verdict.

This same attorney got an acquittal for the man who shot Murdo Mackenzie's son at the little cow town of Evarts. Pat was 21 years of age at the time. He was slick!

This would never do! A meeting was held at the old Butte View School, and a committee of 5 was appointed to go visit the family, my dad being amongst them. They were issued an ultimatum. They were given 30 days. In that time period, they moved, "lock, stock and barrel," never to be heard from again. Not a handful of people even remembered their last name. Maybe that was somewhat satisfying, but small consolation to the young girl.

CHAPTER V
My Hero, Uncle Chick

One of my heroes in these early days was my Uncle Leslie "Chick." He was easygoing, soft spoken, and happy-go-lucky. His mother said he was born fearless, as was proven in his short life.

My first memory of him was when Dad and I rode down on the river to his place. My dad had business to discuss with Chick, who was his younger brother, as well as the youngest in the family of 15.

Chick had this waspy black horse in the corral, scotch hobbled and blindfolded in the process of putting blanket and saddle on his back, in an attempt to ride him. I don't know how old this horse was, but he was mature, and appeared to be 6 or 7 years old. He was not taking kindly to the bonds of civilization! After the saddle was put in place and cinch attached to the latigo, Chick gave a mighty pull, with about all his strength, in order to get his outfit good and tight before the horse sucked in too much air.

This old black just threw a stuttering fit, bawling and squealing, and trying to buck with the one hind leg tied up under his belly. He landed on his side, getting rid of any extra air he had in him with a loud rush of air coming from just directly under his tail!

The old pony finally figured out it would be much easier on himself, and he wouldn't be quite so beat up, if he just stood still. After softening Old Black up a little, Chick let his back foot down, took the sack off his eyes and handed the reins of the hackamore of the exasperated horse to my dad, and explained to him that he wanted him to lead the horse away from the river and up on the bench so he wouldn't run off over the river bank. Dad's job was to haze him up over the hill to the west.

We took off up on a little plateau, not far from his house, with Dad leading the soon-to-be transportation, with Chick riding double behind me on Old Speed.

Chick says, "This is good," and Dad snubs the horse up close and reattaches the sack with some degree of difficulty. That done, Chick instructs me to ride in close, and he just leaps off my old grey, lands right in the middle of the bronc and gathers the reins, one on each side, and jerks the sack off his eyes. He let out a holler, buried his spurs and fans the horse with the sack! Barnum & Bailey never displayed such an act, and with an audience of only two!!

Chick loved to ride a horse that bucked, and he could do it with the greatest of gusto. He had a bucking chute attached to his corral and would often perform for his American Indian neighbors to their great delight. He'd try out the bad ones for the O'Leary Brothers' bucking string.

I was 11 years old, and he thought it was high time I got aboard something a little more exciting. He had this Hereford bull eating out of a hayrack that he pulled into the corral and in a very soft voice, questioned me about if maybe I'd like to ride that bull!

Say, I wasn't about to tell this guy I was a scared of nothing! He was my hero! I says, "I'll give it a try," glancing at Dad, hoping he'd say, "No, you better not!" Instead he says, "I'll help you run him in!"

I can still remember the snugness around my fingers as Chick pulled the loose rope "two hands down," doubled it back, and showed me how to grip it. He grabbed my skinny behind and slammed me up against the rope, jumped down, and swung the gate! I guess the bull was bucking pretty good, and I was a little uncomfortable up there for the new experience. The old bull was bucking right toward the hayrack, and my big concern was him running into it. I hear Dad yell, "Jump off!" so I turn loose and make a flying leap. Chick was so proud of me! He ran up and whopped me on the back, knocking the wind clean out of me!

Dad bought a bay horse from Jerold Berndt. He had great expectations for making a good saddle horse out of him because of his good conformation and kind disposition.

Dad took this good-looking bay that was of mature size, and weighing about 1400 pounds, down to the little Indian camp at the mouth of Green Grass Creek, to the Janis boys, Andrew and Wilbur. They were the established bronc stumpers of that community, and had ridden several horses for us in the past, which were sent to Missouri for Army training. The price was $5 a head for the Janis boys' efforts.

These boys could conquer for breaking about any horse, even if they had to resort to the Janis method, which was to tie them to a large fallen cottonwood tree for a period of time without food or drink.

The next time we see this horse, he is headed towards town with a man aboard, but he was snubbed close and between two other horses. This was probably a well-thought out plan, and it probably would have worked, had they not run into a bootlegger (someone who would buy whiskey for Indians, because at that time, they were not allowed to buy it)! They bought a bottle to generate a little courage!

They run into Kenny West, who is the meanest, baddest bronc stumper of them all, and maybe they brag a little about how they got this salty old pony down at the stockyards. This tall, long-legged Kenneth is up to the challenge! This is only hearsay, but it was told to me that the big gelding piled Kenny in the corner in quick order, along with all comers.

Well, this horse comes home a little gaunt, but nothing that won't be fixed with pasture time. The Janis boys say this just ain't worth the $5! Dad knows just the guy who can put the "salt on his tail"! And down we go to the river and Uncle Chick's place, leading this horse.

When we got there, Chick is waiting, and has invited quite a crowd of the natives, along with Peewee Johnson, Chick's hired hand, and Mark O'Leary.

He walked up and took the lead rope, stoked him a few times on the neck, and in his soft and friendly tone, talked to the horse. He said, "You can't be so tough." I don't think that he should have said that. They lead him to the bucking chute, and he didn't put up a fuss of any sort. Chick pulled his old Hamley down and climbed aboard. He says, "Open the gate!" I never saw a horse buck so hard before or since!

Along about the 5th jump, Chick's cinch broke and down he came! I thought he would say, "Run him back in, I'll get another cinch!" No such words were spoken!

The market for a good, gentle saddle horse was about $35, and Mark O'Leary offered Dad $225 for that horse to put in his string of bucking horses. Dad sort of hung his head and said, "No, Mark, I have to offer this horse to Bud because he did me a huge favor, and I owe him one back."

Chick was married to one of the O'Leary girls at 18, and at this time was rodeoing and building a fine herd of Herefords. He was one of the first in that country to own a tractor with a mowing machine attached. He worked long hours to cut hay for himself and others, making friends with everyone who crossed his path.

He would load his family in the cab of his old pickup on Saturday night and load all the neighbors he could haul in the box, and head for town. The first thing he would do upon arrival is go in to Austin's store and buy a pack of tailor-mades (cigarettes that came in packages, as today, and not roll-your-own), open them and offer each a cigarette, which was gladly accepted.

Chick owned a racehorse for the purpose that he took to all celebrations. There were horse races at nearly all the celebrations, like the Days of 1910 at

Timber Lake, and the Faith Stock Show. He won his share!

This big runner was well over 16 hands at the withers, and his name was Gype. I have no idea where he came from.

Things were going good for Chick as he was building his cowherd and was gaining ground, having just built a new house for his family, which included 3 young daughters.

He came riding his classy grey horse, Snuffy, into the yard one morning, to make a deal with Dad to trade his steer calves for heifer calves. In this way he could increase his numbers quicker. They made the trade.

The next day, he changed horses and headed north toward Timber Lake to visit his brother, Russell "Rusty" to make the same proposition. It had been raining a lot that year, and there must have been a huge downpour up river, because when he got back to the crossing, just adjacent to his house, the riverbank was full and raging. The Moreau carries a lot of mud in flood stage. There was a good, sturdy bridge just 2 miles to the west, over highway 63, but he decided against it, and jumped his horse in.

He was 30 years old —

My uncle Vernon came at night and there was whispering, "Art, you'd better come." I knew there was something wrong. They went immediately to the river, but soon lost hope. Charlie Red Dog, from across the river said he heard Chick yell, "Hey! Hey!"

Chick was an efficient swimmer, but the horse evidently got the upper hand and pawed him under. The horse scrambled out of the river, rider less.

A massive attempt was made to retrieve his body, with airplanes flying, and men in the current, hanging on to a long rope strung from one side of the river to the other.

All attempts failed to yield the body. Nine days after he entered the water, the river went down and his body was found on a ripple at On The Tree Crossing, by my friend, Bobby LeBlanc and his grandfather while they were watering horses.

My grandfather, Chick's dad, was summoned to identify his body. It was badly decomposed and the catfish had discovered him. My Grandfather recognized him only by his Blucher boots. A wife had lost a husband, three little girls lost their daddy, and I lost my hero.

This was the second son that Grant and Nellie Anderson lost in the river. The first was Melvin Boyd, being my namesake as well as my cousin, Boyd. As a young child he was referred to as "Boydy."

Grandmother Nellie was running the boarding house in Fort Thompson, South Dakota, and water had to be hauled from the Missouri River for domestic use. Young men usually did this job in the confinement of the jail. However, the water was not forthcoming, so grandma asked John Heartly if he would haul her some water, because he had a truck.

John agreed to do this and was accompanied by Paul, Art, and little Boydy. Upon backing into the river, the brakes failed, and the truck slid sideways on the ice and broke thru. Paul and Boydy were thrown from the truck into the icy water. Paul managed to crawl out of the water over the truck to safety. Art, my dad, and the driver, John, jumped out the driver's side and were in no danger of drowning. John went around to rescue little Boydy, and actually had a hand on him, but the strong current of the Missouri pulled Boydy under the ice. My grandfather looked for his little son for one entire year. Even with the help from many others, the search was of no avail. Boydy drowned on February 12, 1923, at 8 years, 4 months of age.

My grandfather, Ulysses Simpson Grant Anderson, was a very ambitious and enterprising man. Although small in stature, he was very strong. He was known to lift 55-gallon barrels of produce off a drey wagon and carry them into his general store with ease. One of his two general stores was located at Alpena, SD. On one occasion two men entered with intent to rob Grant of his cash box. Grant grabbed them both and slammed the would-be bandits' heads together, and bodily tossed them out the door. Word soon got around not to mess with Grant Anderson! His young sons already knew this, as he was a very strict disciplinarian.

Grant owned two general stores, a shop that manufactured buggies and sleighs, two large ranches, and a lumberyard. He also purchased an orchard in Texas.

Grant Anderson was considered at that time to be the wealthiest man in the area because he had a large enterprising system in place.

And then came the Depression, and his empire came tumbling down along with just about every business in this great new state.

Grant went from wealthy to flat broke in two years, leaving his older children to fend for themselves. There was no choice! Grandmother, Nellie, ran the boarding house in Fort Thompson, and later was post mistress in the little town of Oacoma, just across the Missouri River, and to the west of Chamberlain, for 31 years.

Grant somehow got word of the vast prairies west of the Missouri, and thought there may be an opportunity to get a new start farther west.

He packed two loads of meager belongings and gathered up what livestock he had, and headed west with his sons.

He never went back to live with his wife, Nellie, for 20 years. He only went back when his youngest child, Chick, drowned in the Moreau.

His goal was to get all his sons started, and to help them along whenever he could. He spent most of his time at Uncle Chick's, and Uncle Rusty's, but also herded sheep up in the Parade country for the boys. He would drop down on the Green Grass Creek to spend as long as two weeks at a time.

Grant would not allow us to call him "Grandpa." He said his name was GRANT!

Our grandpa never did quite get over losing his holdings, and he was really a saver (kind words for being a tightwad!). He would come riding in to check on the progress of his cheese and for a little visit, always wearing old wool, olive-colored Army pants and old, worn-out oxford shoes. Sometimes they were not a match! He pretty much looked the part of a bum.

He made the best cheese I ever ate out of goat's milk. He would line a steel cylinder with cheesecloth and pour his ingredients inside. He'd wait about a month for it to age. I was always so anxious to taste his new batch! When I was an infant, my mother said that neither her milk, nor cow's milk agreed with me, and I was doing poorly, not able to hold down my fill. Grant came to my rescue by leading a goat all the way from up the river so that I could have goat's milk. It totally agreed with me, thus revealing the secret of why I have been mischievous all my life!

Grant never owned a car, and to the best of my knowledge, unless he bummed a ride in a car, his mode of transportation was on horseback. His horses didn't look like much, but they had to have a fast walk, or be gaited, known as pacers or single-footers. His old horse was just awful lazy and it was a real effort for him to cover any ground on that steed. So, he bargained to come get a snappy little white mare that belonged to Father Golden, the Catholic priest at Eagle Butte in order to upgrade his means of transportation a little!

Grant dropped in to our house one day, for the noon meal. Dad, Mother and we kids sat around for a couple of hours visiting with him. About 3:00 p.m. Grant pulled out for home with the new mare in tow. He wasn't gone but about 15 minutes, and he came back to the house with a bloody handkerchief wrapped around his fist! He dismounted and went to the house. Mother, sensing something was wrong, met him at the door. He reached in his shirt pocket and pulled out his thumb! He asked, "Rose, can you sew this back on?"

Dad drove him into town to Dr. Green, who did sew it on, but it never "took." He spent the rest of his life short his thumb.

What had happened was that when Grant crossed the creek, which had a little stream of water flowing through it, his horse decided to jump it, but the white mare sat back on the lead rope. He evidently had it wrapped around his thumb unceremoniously, and the jerk of the rope plumb tore it off!

Grant could not stand idle hands, and he would often drag out a pail of bent nails or staples, along with 5 or 6 hammers that had self-inserted ash sticks for handles. He'd line up his grandsons and give us a little demonstration on how to straighten them, production-line style.

Cousin, Gordon, and I used to hide from Grant so he wouldn't get the opportunity to put us to work!

Grant was a good Christian man, and believed in the teachings of the Bible. He was always very careful not to use God's name in vain. If he got very excited about something, he would spout his favorite expression: "Judas Cousins!" or "Judas Priest!" being very careful, even then, that there were no ladies around.

CHAPTER VI

The big wheat farmers from the South discovered South Dakota with its vast open prairies, and came to invade my little kingdom with John Deere tractors and wheatland plows, gaining control of all the rich farmland up on the big flats in the Fox Ride Country. This forced ranchers to start fencing in their units.

Also, the government was involved in declaring a vast stretch of the Missouri River as Eminent Domain, offering a large settlement to the Tribe under the able leadership of then tribal chairman, Frank Ducheneaux, the reason for this being plans to build a large earthen dam known as Lake Oahe, across the Missouri near the SD capital of Pierre. This dam would back water way up into the Missouri River and its tributaries, such as the Moreau and Cheyenne Rivers, flooding the most productive and beautiful ranch lands in the state. This forced out most of the old established ranchers, Indian families, and the old Cheyenne Agency where most Indian children got their education. I don't know what the settlement was, but, however great it was, it was not near enough, because that area was taken away forever from our American Indian people, and all mankind. We can no longer see God's creation there as he meant it to be.

Along with the settlement of cash, a program known as the Rehab Program was set in motion to rehabilitate the Indians. The program allowed for an

Indian family to take out a lease of approximately 4,000 acres. They were issued a number of cattle, usually from 100 to 200, along with a pickup truck, a little Oliver tractor complete with mower, rake, loader, hay rack, and sometimes, a two-bottom plow, as well as a small amount of money which was put into the bank in each participant's name, all of which was to be paid back in time.

This program took very nearly all the tribal lands for the participants of the rehab program. This looked promising to all concerned, and was also allowed for enrolled tribal females married to white men, of which there was a significant amount.

When you lose a million acres of open range, and all the flat ground is being fenced for farming, where do you go? (Most Indian grazing lands were leased to white ranchers. These lands were known as Range Units, and given numbers. My dad's range unit was #34 and located in the rolling hills east of SD Highway 63 and north, starting on the north side of the Moreau River.)

My dad was in a particularly bad predicament because, although he had not a large herd of cows, he had horses numbering in the 100's. The army quit buying, and tractors were taking the place of workhorses, except with the Amish. They were for the most part raising their own horses that were far larger and much gentler than the West River South Dakota horses.

Horses were worth very little. When you've got a lot of horses running on the neighbors' range, it has a festering effect, and causes a huge strain on relationships.

One evening the Dewey County sheriff drove in and told Dad he had a bunch of about 65 horses carrying his brand, Bar on the jaw and lazy S on the shoulder, left side, locked up in the stockyards at Eagle Butte.

A Kansas wheat farmer had hired Gene Brugier and the Janis Boys to gather them and lock them up for damages done to wheat fields. This all came with the proper papers, signed legal. These horses were going to be loaded in boxcars and shipped to Yankton the next day to pay for damages.

Dad did some thinking on it, and figured he had a boy that knew the route to the Eagle Butte railroad yards pretty good, day or night, as this kid rode there 5 days a week going and coming from school, and if he had a mind to, he could get there in about 45 minutes!

He mounted me on a big ½ thoroughbred, ½ Morgan stud turned gelding, and sent me on a mission with a hacksaw and an extra blade wrapped in my jacket, which was tied on the strings behind my cantle. My mission was to go cut the lock and turn 'em loose, and not get caught with the saw! I was about 15 or 16 years old, and scared to death, but I got 'er done. Those horses boiled out of those pens and headed north, probably right back on the wheatfield!

Dad drove his old '36 Ford coupe to town the next day to confront the wheat farmer, and hinted strongly to the wheat farmer that he'd probably stolen the horses and sold them, and Dad wanted to get paid $50 a head right then and there!

To make a long story short, Dad started shipping his horses out of that very same yard onto railroad cars receiving 2-1/2 cents a pound. No colts were accepted. He gave every kid in town that would take one, a colt, and turned the rest loose, unbranded.

Those horses brought an average of $31.00 each, and he put the money in the bank in Chamberlain, SD. He left it there, along with a check he had received from Jack Hunt for a band of sheep. He left it there for over 20 years, without making a withdraw, and with no interest because in those days banks never paid interest to depositors.

When Dad went to get his money, they refused to give it to him because no one there knew who he was! Dad's mother lived in the little town of Oacoma, just across the bridge from Chamberlain. She was known to all for she lived there and was the postmistress for over 20 years. She had to identify my dad as her son, Arthur, and the bank reluctantly surrendered the money! They had had free use of it for all those years!

One of these trips to town with a bunch of wild mares ended in near disaster. We had gathered a small bunch of about 35 or 40 horses for shipment. My friend, Dean Reeves, was staying at the ranch for a time, breaking out some old Diamond A broncs that were running loose down at Mossman Camp. He consented to help drive our horses to the stockyards on his mount of the day.

86

Amongst the bunch we were trailing was an old sorrel mare that was a sure-enough bunch quitter. Dad had tied a wagon burr in her foretop for the purpose of distraction so she'd stay with the main herd. This old mare carried on something awful with that ½ pound wagon burr bouncing off her head! She squealed, pawed and kicked until she got tired of beating herself up. This old mare forgot all about leaving the main herd, and with her head held low, she loped all the way into town like a good little girl!

We were just turned lose and headed south when all hell broke loose for old Art. He was mounted on an old buttermilk buckskin stud with the OK brand burned into his jaw. That old stud blew his cork! I can attest to the fact that when this old boy bucks, he lands like a load of rocks, and he don't quit bucking until he's good and ready. He never did buck me off, but there were times when I wish he would have. Hitting the ground was small consolation compared to the beating the old stud gave you on the hurricane deck!

Don't you know—Old Art got bucked off not 100 yards from the house and Dean and I proceeded to turn the bunch loose and check for damages. I loped up and asked, "Are you hurt?" Art was laying there, holding his leg and I'm thinking that for sure it's broke! He said, "No, I lost my pliers!"

Art was very uncomfortable in boots as he was just a little bow-legged, making the heels of his boots turn over so bad that he just gave up on that kind of footwear, resorting to lace-up shoes. From the very beginning, 'til the cows came home, he wore bib overalls.

This outerwear was handy, with protection up front to keep your shirt clean, and with a host of pockets to pack your "possibles" (something you might possibly need!). On the lower right-hand side there was this little pocket that was just right for a pair of pliers, and designed for that purpose. Art made good use of that little pocket.

Thinking back on it, I'm sure he wasn't near as concerned about those pliers as he let on. He was more concerned about getting bucked off in front of two young punchers with grins on their faces like coons eating cactus!

Dean offered to take the buck out of Art's saddler, as I had him caught up and brought back. Art declined the offer, and I'm remembering the same situation in reverse, when I'd hear, "Get back on!"

I guess the old stud was satisfied with his results because he moved out just as fine as frog's hair, and never offered to take to the airways any more that day. It took less than two hours to regather the ponies and gain access to the stockyards 10 miles to the south.

This is where the near-disaster part comes in. Those big, old stockyard gates were made of heavy plank, and were about 7 foot high by 12 ft long. And although they had good hinges on them, there was no way to open and shut them big heavy gates horseback.

Dad had to make a sort of some kind, and Dean, being the good hand that he was, grabbed the gate without hesitation, to allow for separating the horses.

About that time the train locomotive started coupling railroad cars, which began a series of very loud crashes as one car was connected to the other!

Those old broomtails spooked and hit the gate, piling one on top of the other in a mad scramble to escape. Dean was smashed behind that big gate with tons of horse flesh in motion! We almost didn't have any more Dean. To this day, I still don't know how he came out from behind that gate, shaken, but without a broken bone! (Not that he'd have admitted it, if he did!) He was tough, and he must have a king-sized guardian angel!

Dean Reeves
Heading To School on a Diamond A Bronc
January 1954

Going back to the buckskin stud that Art was bucked off from that day—that stud was a colt killer. I can only guess that it was to get the mares to come in heat. Before Art discovered that he was killing colts, he had killed somewhere around 60. He was gelded at the age of five, and we rode him on the ranch for many years.

Right about that same time period, Dean Reeves and I were riding broncs to school, taking the long way around. It was three miles further, but there were no gates, and three more miles made no difference to the horse or rider.

On one particular morning, Dean was mounted on a big bay 8-year-old that had just a few rides on him. I was riding a nice little sorrel 4-year-old that I was breaking for Jerome O'Leary who lived over south of Highway 212 in the Lantry Country.

It was sort of a foggy morning and we were just west of Slim Berndt's and Dean said, "Webb's house is gone!!!" I answered with, "Oh, it's there, we just don't see it for the fog." We rode on in to school and put our horses in the stockyards on the south end of town. We walked back to the north end of town to the schoolhouse. I was detained outdoors by some boys with idle chitchat, and Dean went on into the schoolhouse. He soon returned with a look of shock and sadness on his face carrying the distressing news that George Webb's house had burned down, and that two of the brothers had perished in the flames. The other members of the family had bad burns.

George Webb was an early riser and his first chore in the morning was to kindle the wood-burning stove so that the old house would be nice and cozy for the morning breakfast. Every old timer, including George, had a little kerosene can full of fuel to recharge the reading lamps and to light the fire. George, in an effort to give the fire a little quicker start, doused the fire with a little shot of kerosene. The stove blew up, engulfing the entire house in seconds. Some of the boys, who had been sleeping upstairs, jumped out the upstairs window to escape the flames. Most of the rest made it out safely, but Ray and Lee were lost.

(If you live in Boston or Pittsburgh, you have never heard of Dean Reeves, but you have name recognition in Dean and Emma Lou's son, Tommy Reeves, the World Champion Saddle Bronc Rider.)

The old Eagle Butte School carries some memories such as Freshman Initiation. The seniors would put the freshmen thru all sorts of misery on initiation day. On our eventful day, the seniors mixed flour and water to make a glue-like substance, which they plastered on our heads, thus gluing our hair to our scalps. They took our pants away from us and forced us to wear a bed sheet in the stead.

You know, Dean and I made enough pony tracks to know that this was not fun for us, and it bordered on abuse. Ole Dean is thinking on how to get even. He remembered that there was an old setting hen in the manger of the horse barn. Thinking that the eggs were probably good and rotten, maybe we could pull our own initiation! So, we allowed we needed to go home and do chores before the evening festivities in the big schoolhouse gymnasium. Things were going along just hardy-har-har for the senior class, until Dean unloaded his batch of eggs on the primary suspect! Dean could have easily been voted class president the next day!

Oh yes! We got called to the superintendent, Dewitt Butler's, office. He couldn't keep a straight face. He told us we'd better behave and that we had to pay the cleaning bill of 60 cents each. The best money we ever spent!!!

Not counting being shot at a time or two, I've had several brushes with death, myself! I've risked my life many times to save a newborn calf or colt, and even lambs, but three things stick out in my mind as being very close calls!

Art Moran was a good friend. His father, Stanley, was the son of Old Posey. Posey was the stepson of Scotty Philip, an old cowman of some notoriety, who had a frontier town named after him — Philip, SD. He branded seven with a flat-top three anywhere on the left side.

July in South Dakota is long on day and short on night. We were haying up on the big flat, so it was about 9:00 before we got home for supper and chores. Supper, as the evening meal was called, came first and chores after in the pitch dark. The milk cows were usually waiting at the barn door to nurse their calves. Horses would be in the corral waiting to be watered. On our outfit, there was no water in the corral, so everything left confined in the corral, like work teams or saddle horses, had to be trailed ¼ mile to the west to be watered, if the creek went dry. We had in a pure white ½ albino and a chestnut sorrel that we had just rode a few times. We thought that they handled good enough to trail the little bunch to water and back. Included in the bunch was a wild mare. She crowded the gate, which had a crotch, or forked log, propped up against it, to serve as a brace to hold the wire tight. She got a little too close to this fork that protruded beyond the post, and ripped a huge chunk of hide loose from her ribs in a "V" shape. This rip was about 20 x 20 inches, and the race was on! With that skin flopping on her side, and with all that pain, she was quitting the flats with me in hot pursuit on the 3-year-old chestnut. I was trying not to bend her back, NOT having a whole lot of luck, and not really concerned about where my horse was putting his feet! I'm still young and dumb as a pile of rocks!

We're just sailing thru this hard pan spot with all the cactus, sagebrush and holes, when my horse just falls out from under me and rolls plumb over the top of me. Now, things get interesting! With my right foot all the way thru the stirrup, hanging over the left side, and old Sorrely trying to kick me in the head with all intentions of getting rid of the whole unfamiliar package! The Lord said, "I'm not ready for you, yet!" And my boot came off my foot and down I come with most parts intact, and nothing lost that wouldn't grow back!

Now, it's a little tough walking in the dark at night thru the cactus, with only one boot on, and me worrying about Art Moran all this time.

I walked back home to a concerned father, and a sympathetic mother, but no Art Moran!

I suppose I was home about ½ hour when Art came riding his little white albino in along with every other horse we left the corral with. He was triumphant!

My dad fore footed that wild mare early the next morning and filled the wound full of yellow powder called Sulpha. He sewed her up and loaded the wounded area with pine tar, but she kept biting at the wound and pulling the stitches out. She went to horse heaven. No penicillin in those days!

As for my boot, I never did find it. I looked and looked, but to no avail, and I'll bet my Sunday socks a coyote liked the aroma of my dirty feet and took it away to chew on for a little nutrition! Boots for me were about as hard to come by as hen's teeth, and I sold a good horse for $25 so that I could order some from The Miller Stockman catalog.

Our corrals and holding pens were void of water in the early days, and when calves were weaned from their mothers, they had to be held in the corrals for about a week to allow their mothers time to get used to getting along without them. During this time we would haul water from the dam with the team and the stoneboat, adorned with two barrels, in order to water those thirsty little critters. It was quite a job requiring several trips, depending upon the number to be watered. The big advantage of this labor was that the wild little buggers got used to seeing a two-legged, talking human in their midst, and soon figured out the delivery of essential drink was soon to come after the arrival of this foreign monster!

After about a week, we would catch our saddlers and move all cows from the area and turn the calves out of the pens. We then drove them to the dam for their daily fill of water. Now you know, when you turn those little fresh-weaned calves out into the freedom of the wide-open spaces, the calves would exhibit a great deal of frolic, such as bucking and running, usually in about six different directions! Our job was to try to keep them bunched so they wouldn't disappear over yonder ridge and back to where they came from in the first place.

The first couple of trips over to the dam were interesting, and probably would have been a whoop-te-doo good time, if your dad wouldn't be hollering at the top of his lungs, shouting instructions that you could no way understand in the first place!

No broncs allowed, and the best horses caught for this task, and all goes well moving our herd of weaners in a tight bunch, until a lonely white jackrabbit darts over the fill of the dam!

The race is on!! The calves split in two bunches, one bunch going straight west with my dad in hot pursuit, and me going hell bent for leather on my little horse, Skipper. We just got to the lead of my little bunch when Skipper stuck both front feet in a little washout about 18 inches wide, throwing me over the deck and he lands upside down, all four feet in the air, and using me for a cushion to break the fall!

On that particular morning it was snowing and blowing, causing a ground blizzard, therefore the washout that my horse stuck his feet in was full of snow level with the ground. Had it been void of snow, my horse would have avoided it by jumping over it.

I remember being in this unfamiliar bed with this strange lady, donned in a white dress, talking to me. I was in the hospital at Gettysburg! I had seven herniated discs in my back. This resulted in the longest stay, up to this point, in a hospital! No operation was ever done. I still have seven V-shaped discs in my back.

The one other time I thought I "bought the farm" was at a different location, many years later, and far south of where I grew to adulthood. This also involved a horse!

Mel saddling Bronc tied to snubbing post in pole corral on Green Grass Creek.

Chapter VII
The Green Grass Picnic

People in our neck of the woods enjoyed gatherings and get-togethers, which were few and far between! Some examples were the Days of 1910 Rodeo at Timber Lake, which served as the county seat of Dewey County. Then there was the Sitting Bull Stampede at Mobridge, just up river from LeBeau, the infamous little town in which Dode McKenzie was shot by the town saloonkeeper. It is now an underwater ghost town, flooded by the vast Oahe Reservoir. It was burned and abandoned by the long-gone Murdo McKenzie and the Matador Cattle Company. Another event drawing large crowds of ranchers was the Faith Stock Show and Rodeo.

In our county, the event that excited me the most was the Green Grass Picnic. People would load all residents of their household and head for the gala event. This, by all accounts, was the "Dewey County Olympics" with foot races for all ages, fat men's races, sack race, scoop shovel race, father and son race, pop race, and wild cow riding. Cattle, sheep and sometimes, swine judging took place, as this was dubbed a 4-H event complete with county agent! And there was the annual saddle horse race that all comers took very seriously, especially delighting the many American Indians that lived in the area. There would be as many as 30 in number, racing in a straight line to the designated finish, skimming over badger holes and drift wood, for the honor of having the fastest saddle horse in the county. And, believe me, there were some "imports" in the mix and all for bragging rights and a first place cash prize of 50 cents!

This annual affair assembled a crowd of nearly 300 country and town folk alike, coming from home with homemade ice cream and fried chicken in tow, to watch and participate in the festivities, and especially to watch the big men in the tug-o-war.

This involved a rope 100 feet long and 1-1/2 inches in diameter, made from the material of the day called sisal. A stake with a ribbon was driven in the ground with three ribbons being tied to this long rope, one centered over the stake, and another one on each side of the center ribbon. The object was to pull the opposing team's ribbon past the center stake, thus declaring victory and acquiring bragging rights. This tug-o-war was always the North against the South, with the river being the dividing line. If you lived on the south side of the river, you pulled for the South, and thusly.

These giants of men would take position with leather gloves for protection against rope burn. The largest, biggest, baddest was on the very end, taking up the position as anchorman. After the signal was given all were grunting and pulling for all their might, seesawing back and forth until one side became victorious, all hands being totally exhausted for their efforts! Francis Curtis was the anchorman for the South, and Lee Robley for the North. There was a total of thirty men in the contest. Not once, but often, they would break this brand-new, just-came-from-the-hardware-store-rope, and everybody would land in a heap, rear end over teakettle, being rewarded by loud roars of laughter and applause from the spectators!

In the case of a blowed out rope, there was a time out. The rope was neatly spliced, navy style, and they'd have another "go."

This was also a day for the 4-H kids to judge cattle. Usually a herd of about 25 cows and calves, whatever was nearby and were of mixed ownership, along with two bulls, were penned in the little corral for judging. Some of these cattle were roan or brocklefaced of Durham origin, but most were Hereford. Then the 4-H club members, with pencil and pad in hand, would select from the pen, which, in their opinion, were the best, and document the findings on their pads. These were to be graded by the county agent who was educated along these lines, and who was in charge of such matters.

But, don't turn 'em loose yet, 'cause there is wild cow riding coming up and the rodeo stock is already in!

This wild cow riding was right up my alley! After all had ridden in the contest for one of the three places paying cash prizes of 50 cents, 25 cents, and 10 cents, there would usually be a few cows left for exhibition. So, some of the older punchers could show their stuff, me being right in the mix with the "old guys" riding one right after the other.

One of these "old guys" was Ervin Thompson, who lived on my Uncle Chick's old place. He could sure enough ride a saddle bronc as pretty as you please, and he had sure enough earned his badge as one of the all-time greats! Being "old" meant that Old Ervin was in his 30's!

Ervin came as a spectator, but he allowed that he might just get on one of them old bulls if I'd loan him my spurs, because he never brought his along. Now, this chute that we rode out of wasn't a modern day outfit! You climbed down on the cow and held your feet up so's not to get rubbed off on the discharge. The gate was just lifted away from the front delivery chute, and you were out in the wide, open spaces! When, and if, you got the cow rode far enough, you got to thinking about how far it was to trot back, and you'd step off!

The equipment was simple. A half-inch circingle, or loose rope, was doubled and wrapped around the middle of the cow, strung thru the loop and pulled snug. Most rides made those days were "two hands down," meaning both hands were securely gripped in the rope.

Old Ervin came out on the Hereford bull, just a spurring and jerking his knees. This was quite a crowd pleaser! He came back and handed me the spurs, and with a look of disgust on his face, issued a statement to the effect that those spurs were no good, and that I should throw them away, as they were "bent!"

I had just received that new-fangled pair of spurs as a gift from Jim Scott. The spurs were made by Crockett, and designed by an old twister by the name of Jerry Ambler. The shanks were purposely turned in to make it easier for you to get a hold, and old Ervin, not knowing about this new equipment, had put them on backwards!

For a short-legged kid, I was pretty swift in a foot race, winning several 50 cent pieces in a good sprint, as well as in the sack race where you would climb into a burlap sack that was acquired by purchasing cow feed by the 100-lbs, and hop to the finish line, trying for all you were worth not to trip yourself up.

The scoop shovel race, in which one was required to bring their own scoop, was another of my favorites. This race required a team of two and one horse. The rider would ride to the scoop tender fast as one could go, and throw this 30 footer over the scoop handle. You would be towed back over the line, helter-skelter. If you were smart, a little practice was in order at home! Nowadays, I suppose it would require a crash helmet! My method was to tuck my pants in my boot tops and slide my heels right on the ground for stability and keep my pant legs from filling full of grass. It didn't take long to dismount the shovel when you went over the finish line, on account of the friction warmed up that scoop pretty good! This event was hilarious, as ropes got tangled and cowboys went flying. My brother, Larry, and I had this thing down pat, and were always in the hunt.

The pop race was another good one. The boy had to buy a nickel soda and find a girl who was willing to take a chance and be a good guzzler. The object of the game was to race from the designated starting point, with the soda, being careful not to spill any, because you would be disqualified, and hand it to the girl to drink. (I always bought a bottle of orange because it didn't have as much fizz, and was easier to pour down the gullet. I thought that this gave me the "edge.") After the pop disappeared, you had to hold hands with the girl and pack the empty bottle back to the finish line. The only time I ever won this, I asked Jeannie Miller to be my partner, and we won by a fair margin.

Then there was the father and son race — fathers on one side of the track, and sons on the other. This is where I had my work cut out for me! My dad was so bow-legged that he couldn't even run a straight line, let alone run fast! I remember once going out to meet him to take the baton from him, and therefore won the sprint. The judges said, "Thumbs down! You cheated!"

Two of the horses that us kids raced at the annual event were Speed and Frog Legs. Frog Legs belonged to my sister, Linda. He was an iron-grey gelding with big black spots running down his front legs that reminded you of frog legs. So, he was thusly named. We ran him in the saddle horse race for four years, and he won three out of four, only to be beat by Myron Mayor and his big, tall sorrel, with his son, Buddy, as jockey.

Speed wasn't named Speed for nothing! This horse was actually ½ Percheron and ½ Thoroughbred. Gentle as a kitten and ridden by all comers. He loved to run, and if you got behind a bunch of horses, you could hardly hold him when he got hot. Myself, taking many a wild ride on him bringing in the wild bunch.

So, this racing was right down his alley, and he was always amongst the front-runners.

One morning Betty decided she had a chore to do on old Speed and made him ready with saddle and bridle. She backed him out of his stall and proceeded to lead him out the barn door. The old horse had different ideas, and planted his feet, thinking it would be a much better idea to stay in the barn and munch fresh-mowed hay from his manger!

After three attempts by Betty to introduce the old boy to the great outdoors, I decided I'd better lend a hand. I grabbed onto the well-used hayfork to give him a little tickle on the backside with the tines. Just as I made contact with the old boy's rear end, he pulled back on the reins. The tines of that fork penetrated a good two or three inches, but he left the barn, nearly leaping over my sister, with her shouts of "Don't do that!"

The horse got dreadfully sick, and my dad said he had "blood poison." Mom heated water with Epsom salts in it, and we put hot packs on his swollen rear quarters, trying to draw the poison out, but to no avail. Dad said that there was a new vaccine called penicillin, made from mold that could have saved him, but the soldiers needed it, being the time of World War Two.

All in our family loved that horse, and although we were by then used to our animals dying, there was a time of mourning for old Speed.

My Dad never once scolded me, or ever brought it up. I remember him saying that a good child punishes himself, and that is, by all standards, the very truth!

When I get to heaven, I expect to see a very heads-up white horse with wings, soaring the heavens in readiness to forgive me.

All comes with a price, and at one of these annual events, an Indian boy, about 14 or 15 years of age, was laughing and running with his friends. He ran smack into the back of a horse, which jumped forward and kicked back with both feet, striking the boy in the chest. Blood started oozing out of his mouth and ears, and he was probably dead before he hit the ground. I witnessed this with my own eyes, and it is vivid in my mind today.

Chapter VIII
Big Wagon

How these two mares made it all the way to South Dakota, I'll never know, but Dad bargained for them. One was a sorrel and the other a black, branded OE on the left shoulder. They were registered with the Jockey Club, and of English origin. These two mares were acquired from Eyolf Orbeck over west of Dupree on Red Owl Creek. Eyolf was married to Dad's sister, Esther. They had had about all the fun they needed to have in this God-forsaken country, and were pulling out for greener pastures.

They were both dandy horses, and far outclassed our old range mares, but then, there comes the problem of trying to keep the sorrel mare on her home range. Home to us just wasn't the same for her, and she was the cause for many miles horseback.

Dad would ask around about this mare's location. At one time she was gone from her home range for three years. Dad was visiting with old Pat Miller at the annual Green Grass picnic, and he told him that Don Smith over on Goose Creek had a sorrel mare in his little band with the EO brand on her, and that he should probably check it out.

I was commissioned to go see, and bring her home if she fit the mold, and to be sure to bring the colt along if she had one.

It was about 35 miles to Dan Smith's spread, and then after one got there, the horse herd had to be found. So, I knew I had to leave early and be pretty well mounted to boot. I picked a big, stout blue roan four year old that I had a lot of rides on the year before. He had a lot of snort, sort of what I needed to take on such an endeavor. I catch Blue and pull his tail to rid him of burrs and long hair. I stabled him so there is no fooling around. The next morning I got a good, early start, with a pint of milk wrapped in newspaper, along with 2 sandwiches all wrapped tight in my jacket, which was tied tight to my cantle, compliments of my mother.

I'm headed east on a long trot and making good time and at the mouth of Goose Creek about 9 o'clock. Then came along this sort of little distraction.

I ran into this pretty little Indian girl at the river, watering her horse, and I ride in to say, "Howdy." A prettier little gal you never have seen. And with big brown freckles on her nose to boot. If she would have had a ribbon tied around her neck, she would have looked like a china doll. I kept trying to make conversation with her, and all she would do was hang her head and say ahh. I finally persuaded her that I had the makings for a pretty good picnic tied to my cantle, and maybe we could sit in the shade of one of those big cottonwood trees and I would share with her, and that my horse needed to be unsaddled any how so's to cool his back.

That little meeting went pretty good and she promised me she would meet me right here in this very same spot next Friday about noon. Then I set myself to thinking that if I sorted off that old mare and took her home, I wouldn't have any excuse to come back up this way. So, I just sort of amble back up the river and back home, getting back with a whole lot of sun left before it went down in the west. Dad says, "Did you see her?" I was sort of startled by the question. I went on to tell him I never saw Don Smith's horses, anywhere I rode, failing to tell him about the part where I never looked. But, I believe that I'll give it another try about next Friday, which was six days in the future. I'm sure glad he didn't look me up close in the eye, because he would have figured something just wasn't quite up to "snuff."

Dad had bought this big quarter horse stud from T. J. and Elliot Rickles. He was sure to my liking with a neat little head and smaller feet than I was used to. He was void of all the feathery hair on the hide around the cannon bone. Because he was new to the outfit, I sure wanted to give him a try, and maybe take him up river to show to my new-found friend with the curves in all the right places.

Come Friday, away I go again, thinking at this rate, and due to current events, it may be a long time before I get this old mare home, and I'm wondering if maybe next time Dad's going to tag along to lend a hand! That would shed a whole different light on the situation.

I leave early on the old stud that goes by the name of Big Wagon, and sure have time to kill, as I don't want to get to our big shade tree too early, so I swing off the river for a visit with old Russell Curtis. He's working on one of those old red water-cooled engines with a big flywheel that fires and then goes around about three revolutions and fires again. He was using this engine to power his pump jack to draw water out of the well. He said that he was cleaning the magneto and the plug.

The Big Wagon Stud

Russell sure is admiring this old stud, and asking all kinds of questions. He's all set for a good visit, and invites me to stick around for dinner. Shucks, I'm too nervous for that 'cause I got other things on my mind, and tell him I have to tend to business and head off for the rendezvous. I get to the tree, and no pretty freckle face. Wait till the sun is shining on one o'clock, and still no show! Darn, I guess I just as well go check on the old sorrel mare. But my heart ain't in it.

Smiths' horses were confined to a pasture, which involved opening, sorting thru, and shutting a gate, which is no easy task for a lone rider. I might add, it borders on the impossible! I spotted the little band of mares from a high hill just very shortly after I rode into the pasture, but now, this is a different deal than I'm used to. This is a well-bred bunch of horses and wild as coyotes, probably because old Don done his horse gathering with an airplane!

Now this bay stud of Don Smith's isn't hankering for company! Especially company that could be competition like the old boy I was riding! The stud makes a couple of passes to check things out, and I'm sure enough swinging my rope, 'cause this deal is scary.

The old mare is in the bunch with not only one colt, but a yearling following close behind. Everybody in this family looks alike — the old mare, the colt, and the yearling, so I know I've got to cut three horses out that gate! Well, don't you know---that bay stud helped me more than 5 riders could have! He kept his little band in a tight bunch, and wouldn't let them run. I broke into the circle just at the right time to separate the mare and her two colts out the gate. The stud allowed that he'd better protect the rest of his little band and drove them straight away!

The old mare and her brood just sold out on a dead run, and was quite a ways ahead of me by the time I got the gate shut. It was a hard gate to shut because the wire loop over the gate post was a little skimpy.

Old Big Wagon is up to the challenge, and he's running so fast, he's bringing water to my eyes. About where Andrew Dupris lives, the mare turns up this little draw and heads south and out of sight into a big, long draw that has drainage to the river. I turn my old stud loose, and allow for room to get ahead of the old girl to turn her back west. When I got to about where she should be, NO HORSES!!! I look behind me and the old skank had turned back on me just as quick as she was out of my sight, and by the time I spotted her, she was a good ½ mile ahead of me---running not over, or around, but along a shale bank that NO horse should have been able to even stand up on 'cause it was steep and tapering right off into the river.

The old mare and her colts were gone! The only chance I had to catch up to them was to jump my horse into the riverbed onto the sand bar, and that was 9 or 10 feet straight down. No horse is going to do it! With nothing to lose, I take my throw rope down and ease the loop around my horse's neck and jump down, holding the rope with a little tension so it would break my fall.

I'm down there coaxing and giving light tugs on the rope and the horse is on the edge, bending his knees, doing his best to please me. Another little tug, and a "Come on Boy," and he sails off that bank pretty as you please. And we're back in the race. That old mare is getting pretty winded, going thru all that rough country on a dead run, and her colt is plumb tuckered out, as we've run hard for about 10 miles. But, old Big Wagon is taking it in stride!

110

When we got to Green Grass Creek, that old mare ran right up the bottom of the creek bed the rest of the way home. Thinking she was hid she trotted into the corral like a gentle little puppy dog. This is the very same mare that Dad tied the wagon burr on when we trailed her to town!

That Big Wagon stud took us a huge step forward in our horse-breeding program. He bred some brains in his offspring, and being bred to those old cold-blooded mares, he put a lot of refinement in them.

Chapter IX
Leaving Home

One time, when I was about 15 or 16, I was leading a bronc through a gate just opposite the barn over by the old granary. I was also carrying a gallon of oats. The oats was bait so I could give the ole pony a little treat when I turned him loose, to make him easier to catch next time. Just as I was going through, but still hanging on to the gate stick, my brother lit a firecracker!!! When that firecracker went off, the horse spooked and tried to jump over me. He popped me on the head pretty good, and spilled the oats as well.

Boy! That made me mad! And there stands Old Brother with a big grin, thinking this is great fun! I turned loose of the horse and was about to let him know what I thought of his little prank! Mother hears the ruckus and yells, "Don't you touch him!!!"

I made a decision that if I couldn't defend myself against firecrackers and flying hoofs, I'd better find a place to stay that was little more void of assailants! I packed a few "possibles" and rolled them in my jacket. I saddled a black and white paint 3 year-old that I had just recently acquired in a trade from Fat Bringman, the Diamond A foreman, for horse breaking. I headed south with one dollar, forty cents in my pocket and not an idea in the world where I would lay my head that night.

It was well into the afternoon when I hit town and ran into my friend, Dell Louis Yellowhead. One thing led to another, and we got the local bootlegger to buy us a can of malt liquor to share for a dollar. In this way, "Scope," Dell Louis' nickname, could help me drown my sorrows. Scope's mother and father, Joe and Mamie, were in charge of the Government Barn, just a couple of miles south and east of Eagle Butte. I overnighted with them. The conversation was composed of two dialects, one of which I didn't understand.

Young Riders Standing Left to Right Mel Anderson-Dell Louis Yellow Head-Jr. Smith-Dean Reeves. Kneeling Toby Stally-Buzz Reeves-Larry Anderson-Chuck Smith

After a fair night's rest, I saddled up old paint, thinking that home might not be the worst deal after all, but being Art Anderson's son, with stubbornness "bred in," I decided to explore other options, I headed west, thinking the little cow town of Faith was only forty miles away, and I could surely get a job with Milt Sturgis or Billy Richardson at the sale barn.

I'd rode about 10 miles to the west, and nearly to the little Lantry Community, when my horse decided that he wanted to cross the railroad tracks and go south. So I decide to just ride at a walk and follow his nose for a spell. I got south of the track about two miles and ran into a little cowboy named Jimmy Keegan, headed towards town in his pickup. This was the first time I ever laid eyes on the man. Jimmy slowed to a stop and asked, "Where you headed?" and "Where did you come up with the paint?"

Gail Whitney riding The Paint Horse I left on to go to work for Jerome O'Leary.

I told him that I was looking for a job, and that the horse was a Diamond A that had been shipped up from Wagon Mound, New Mexico.

Jimmy told me that ole Jerome O'Leary, just down the road, was going to build a new fence, and that he was looking for help. He advised me to stop and inquire if I thought that I was man enough to handle a 16-pound maul.

I was pretty young, and didn't have much hope of getting a job fencing, even though I'd had experience driving sharpened posts at home. My stomach is rumbling, and I'm hoping that someone will take pity on me and offer me some grub. So, I mosey on in to Jerome's yard.

Jerome was out under the lean-to with an old big-titted Hereford, which was tied to a post, a calf shoved underneath her. Jerome was trying to get some milk in to the calf because Mama Cow had such big tits that the calf couldn't get his little mouth around them to nurse, and had pretty much given up. I dismounted my steed and proceeded to help milk the old girl out, in order to reduce the diameter of her tits so the baby could get a handle on 'em without assistance.

While helping out, I was making conversation about that I would probably fit the bill on the fencing job if he was willing to give me a go. The wage was $5 a day plus "keep." I got that job, and a place to hang my hat with two fine folks!

My boss man had already made the stretch points in the fence, and had one strand of barbed wire strung tight on the ground for a guide. My job was to sharpen a wagon load of 80 white cedars, and take along two rolls of wire, then head for the breaks with team and wagon. At the designated site, I was to put the two spools of wire on the wire unroller, which was attached to the back of the wagon, and unroll as I went. I was to drive posts the wagon length apart for spacing, along the guide wire on the ground. The posts were to be driven to a depth of 20" or more, if possible. This was all done while never leaving the wagon box, as I needed the extra height to slam the maul on top of those 7-ft posts. The spools of wire were 80 rods long with just a little extra, so when you got to the H brace, it was just right to tie on and stretch. The only thing left to do was staple the three wires left to complete the job.

This procedure was repeated for six days a week, with Sunday off to rest. Labor on the new fence was costing $20 a mile, and there were no complaints from either party.

On one of the Sundays, there was a rodeo at the Old Cheyenne Agency. Mr. And Mrs. O'Leary decided it would be a worthwhile event. They asked if I would like to join them. Of course I was very excited to go and thought I might enter the bull riding. But, Jerome said, "No," that he wouldn't give me permission 'cause them brahmas were really mean, and I might get hurt bad. I was very disappointed to hear that because I thought I'd mastered this cow-riding thing pretty good!

Upon arrival, Mrs. O'Leary set out her picnic lunch, and we ate our fill before we took our spots on the fence for good position to view the rodeo. We saw many a wild ride by the Indian cowboys.

The announcer informed the crowd of a special event that was free to all. A hundred dollar bill was being tied to the tail of a particularly mean Brahma bull, and all comers were welcome to try to remove it — finders, keepers!

I look at ole Jerome, and he says, "Go ahead!" Well, that poor beast never had a chance with about 100 men competing for the big money. I came out of there more than a little bruised and scratched, but with a very smelly one hundred dollar bill and a smile on my face like a wave on a slop bucket! I'd just earned a month's wages!!

My dad caught up with me at one of the Saturday night dances at Eagle Butte, and in no uncertain terms told me to get home and help him hay! There was no agreeing to that on my part, but it was "obey your parents or suffer the consequences!" I told him that I'd be home within the week, as I had to pick up my "possibles" and my long-time-turned-out-paint horse.

Jerome's horse trap was small and flat, allowing him to pen the horses with his old Dodge pickup. There were only 5 horses in it, with my horse making 6. His horses consisted of the work team I used to build fence, and one saddle horse with two big geldings along for company. One was a black-seven-year-old, and the other a nice little sorrel four-year-old. I was curious about these two. Jerome said he was looking for someone to ride them, and that he would pay $15 a piece to get them broke. I took the job on the spot. I'm thinking that ole shiny black would sure enough make a quick trip out of going back to Green Grass Creek.

Mel in his play pen.

The black wasn't even halter broke, so, the night before I left for home we put a hackamore on him and tied him up so, maybe, he'd get a little sore under the jaw for easier handling. Maybe he'd even lead a step or two! The next morning, Jerome saddles up ole Brownie, for hazing purposes, and I climb aboard Midnight to have a go at it. I let the Scotch hobble down so all four feet were on the ground, and the horse crow hopped around the corral just a little. He seems to be responding to pressure, turning in both directions, and I'm thinking, "This is sure going to be an easy $15! Jerome opens the gate and rides out ahead of me with ole Midnight just following along, pretty as you please, down the road toward Lantry and

Highway 212. Jerome follows along about two miles and tells me that I'm getting along just fine, so he turns ole Brownie south and don't look back.

Well, the old bronc is getting sullen and sour, not liking to see this strange country without company. I'm having quite a time keeping him lined out, even to the point of sticking my thumb in his eye to get him to navigate in the proper direction. All this time the horse is getting madder, and me getting the worse for wear!

Then I see this cloud of dust and hear a rattling noise. As this commotion closes the gap, I see it's old Matt Tiernan and his relic of a yellow International pickup, belching smoke and with fenders waving! Ole Horse takes one long look and gives out a loud snort, and heads north on an emergency basis. That yellow monster looks big enough to eat him, and he ain't stopping, no matter how much whoa I put on him! There just ain't any brakes!

The State had decided they had better improve Highway 212, and were doing considerable work right in my flight path. Old Black goes across at about full throttle---right between two big dirt-moving rigs, which were also yellow! He finds another gear and leaps over Don Farlee's fence, heading north, and I hear wire creak, but I'm sure not stopping to fix it.

I still have very little control, and we're going north like I'm carrying the mail!!! I slide that ole black to a stop up against the cottonwood corral at the Diamond A 24 Ranch on Bear Creek and got off. What a trip!!!

But, I got friends here, because my sister, Betty and her husband, Dick Schrempp, have settled here, and call this "home." I have had all the excitement I need for one day, and accepted the offer to stay over night. I had traveled about 25 miles in a very short time! Tomorrow was another day!

The next morning, on a much more co-operative horse, I rode the rest of the way home which was about 10 miles "as the crow flies."

The black horse was about all I rode all summer. He had a bad attitude, and was just overall rank! One of his bad habits was when I dismounted, he would sure put a lot of effort in to trying to jerk the reins from my hands and make a mad dash for attempted freedom. He'd usually break both reins in the process, by stepping on them.

His habits presented quite a problem, because, after six hours or so of riding, I'd need to relieve myself! If there were any trees around, I would just drop my throw rope over the horse's neck, dally up short to the tree, and step down to do my business. Even then he would test the rope a time or two with the noose around his neck.

Well, don'tcha know, up on the Big Fox Ridge Country, trees are few and far between — but you still have to "go." Well, there is this little round hole in your saddle, under the center of the swells, called the "gullet!" Well — my saddle blanket needed to be thrown over the top rail on the pole corral more than once for aeration purposes!

One day when the sun was just past center, this rider came in, leading a very shiny well-proportioned horse. He had come up from the Cheyenne River, 44 miles to the south. This was the first time I ever laid eyes on Bud Annis. Now, in my eyes, this fellow was all cowboy! Very neat with crease in his Stetson, showing no sign of dirt, bat-wing chaps with outside pockets, Crockett spurs with oversized rowels on a pair of made-to-order boots. He was sitting on his mount with the posture of a drill sergeant! He had a copper complexion, showing his American Indian heritage.

After exchanging greetings, Bud was asking for Art because the purpose of this visit was to deliver this stud that he had in tow. Dad was always out doing something during the day, and he wasn't available. No one seemed to know his whereabouts. My mother and I did considerable coaxing to get our visitor to stay put! I surely didn't want him to be leading this fancy young stud off, and I'm already thinking about who I can impress aboard such a fancy steed!

Dad finally showed up, to our relief, and he agreed with Bud that the horse was probably worth the asking price of $125. Dad took the stub pencil and the Dewey County Bank check blank out of his center bib pocket, and ownership changed!

This stud turned out to be a dandy. He was ½ thoroughbred and ½ Morgan, looking similar to today's Quarter Horse. We kept him stalled in the winter to ride and turned him with a large band of mares in summer.

I, myself, broke many young geldings sired by this stud, and after a couple of weeks of riding one of these geldings, you could pretty much go do what you had to do on them. They were fast to catch on to the job at hand.

Bud Annis and O'Leary Brothers threw together and put on several rodeos each year. They'd trail their bucking horses to the days of 1910 at Timber Lake, and Sitting Bull Stampede at Mobridge. Volumes could be written about many of their individual broncs, as they were gosh darn awfully hard to cover. The buck-off rate was usually more than 50%.

On one occasion Bud and his helper, Johnny Iron Lightening, were trailing around 40 head north to meet up with the O'Leary string. They turned loose around the dam west of our house to water and rest.

Dad had got word to Bud about this big bay horse that had bucked off Kenny West, the Janis boys, Chick Anderson, and just about everybody else that ever tried to ride him. Bud wanted Johnny to give him a try so he could have a look.

Everybody knew John Iron Lightening. He was a hair lip, and didn't have much of a place to store his snoose, which he always chewed. He was very difficult to understand because he couldn't pronounce his b's but it was an undisputed fact that Johnny would stick the steel in a bucking horse! The result was that the horses would buck like scalded dogs, with him to finish what he started on a good share of them.

This big bay horse was easy to catch and stood, very patiently, when Johnny snugged his old

Committee down on him. Old Mr. Bronc Rider was thinking, "The longer I wait, and the more scared I got!" so, he just steps right up and lights the fuse!

About the third or fourth jump, Old Johnny is dangling off the side of the straw-roofed shed. Then he makes a comment---"That's enough!" in plain English and for all to hear!

Dad had already turned down a very good offer for this horse, but he owed Bud a favor. Bud had a look-alike pair of draft horses, not yet broke to drive, but very much favored by my dad, and the only thing that stopped change of ownership was $250, which Dad didn't have. Bud let Dad have the horses on "time." Dad, thinking that he could break them on a farm Fresno building dams, and ship them by rail to Iowa for a hefty profit. Some things just don't work out. Came a thunderstorm one late afternoon, with considerable lightening, and one of the two horses was struck dead right along-side the chicken house. My dad and mom stared at that dead horse for a long, long time.

Bud was the best flank man in the business, knowing just how much torque to put on the pull strap for any individual bucking horse. He piled many a big-name cowboy in the dirt with his skill. One of those horses was the big bay he bought from my dad. That horse's name was Broken Bones, and to the best of my knowledge there were only three qualified rides on him in his career.

In later years, when I moved to the Eli Place in Ziebach County, Bud and I were neighbors. I would go down river to his arena and play cowboy. I was also involved in hauling roping calves to different rodeos for him. Bud's son, Keith, is a master with a rope, and his four beautiful daughters all rodeoed. But, that subject is short, as they are all married to very jealous husbands!

Bud Annis had the backing of a good wife, who is to this day, still among the living. That family had a lot of class!

Picking up wool off dead sheep and skinning dead cows and horses probably don't appeal much to me today. However, when I was a young man with empty pockets, it was sure a good way to make a dollar, or, quite a few dollars, as far as that goes!

My parents were able to get along with little or no money during The Depression, and were definitely self-taught conservatives. This meaning if us kids needed money, we had to just figure out how to get it.

Most of the banks went broke and closed their doors in the late 20's and early 30's, and all the accounts were lost. My father's was among these. Dad had scraped up a small fortune for the time being-- $217.00, but had no way for safe keeping but to hide it. The logical place to hide it was the root cellar, which came to mind, as it wouldn't blow away, and it was safe from fire. Dad went to the potato bin in the cellar and made room for his stash, which had been placed in a fruit jar. He dug a hole for concealment, planted the jar, being careful to brush dirt over it so no disturbance could be easily detected. He then covered it all with potatoes. He thought this was all done in the greatest of secrecy, even though there were people around. He probably forgot that there was the air vent protruding skyward that could serve as a peephole. My dad thought the cellar was a safe haven, and he never checked it for a long, long time.

Dad made a deal with Sullivan Larabee for a rather large number of Indian ponies, whereupon he went for his stash, only to find that it had been stolen! No finger pointing, because someone might be falsely accused, and no law was called because you dealt with your own problems according to unwritten law. This incident wore on my dad, and never went away, because all who had been present at the time he buried his treasure were thought to be friends.

So, after the spring thaw, the winter kill became prey to my skinning knife and wool sack. (Winter kill pertains to livestock that perished in the harsh winter months.) I would scour the countryside, looking for dead cows to skin, having been warned repeatedly to only prey on cattle with our holding brand, which was the Bar Lazy S. This was, of course, to avoid being accused of butchering the neighbors' beef.

Hides were a very good price in those days, with 8 cents a pound being the average with a grown cow yielding 100 pounds. Salt was 2 cents a pound, so be sure you put lots of salt on for preservation and added weight before rolling!

I would ride a bronc up to one of those dead critters, and he would usually display a great deal of resistance to the look and smell! I'd dismount and introduce my horse to confinement by both hobbling and jacking up a hind foot. This skinning is going to take a while, and I sure enough don't like to walk!

After freeing the hide from the carcass, the next job is to take down the Scotch hobble, which would be used as a tow rope to drag the hide home. Now, the first mile or two of this could get a bit western! There were a couple of rules to follow: drag your prize on the grass so the hair wouldn't rub off, and never, never turn your old bronc around to show him what you are dragging! Taught from experience!

Nothing stinks like an old dead sheep!!! But, there is money in the wool. After a short period after death, an old ewe slips, or releases, her wool from her body. This is where the term "easy picking" came from. Two fleeces to the gunny sack is about seven dollars worth of wool.

The old range horses were survivors, and very seldom would you find a dead horse. If you did, the coyotes usually had the hide mutilated, as horse meat was their preferred diet. If you did run across a fresh carcass, it was much easier to skin than cows. Horse hides were usually bigger. I remember Cliff Ralston giving me $10 for a horse hide.

You remember hearing stories about how the buffalo skinners smelled. I must have made an impression on my mother, because upon my return from one of my skinning trips, she had a wash pan, soap and towel in waiting "outside, " and trousers and shirt in hand. No words were needed!

I need to tell about one especially good haul of wool, which consisted of four gunny sacks, chucked plumb full, and bouncy. I was breaking a little red and white paint horse for Gumbo O'Leary, and he was my mount for the day. I tied up a foot on him and secured a sack of wool on all four corners to allow for him to get a little used to the idea of being a pack horse for dead sheep droppings.

This little horse is pretty gentle and for all practical purposes, ready to turn back to his owner. I surely didn't expect any problems. The trouble began right after I let his foot down and tried to mount. The wool sacks stuck up so high that I had a heck of a time getting my foot over the top to straddle the saddle. In other words, getting on kind of reminded me of an elephant climbing a tree! By the time I got somewheres near where I was supposed to be for departure, ole Paint had had all he needed of this madness! He goes to pitching making an all-out effort to unload me and the whole works in the creek! Wool sacks were smacking me in all directions! I often wish I could have been a spectator to that sport!

Delivering the Aberdeen American News another of my enterprises. I truly believe that paper carriers have a special place in heaven, with them being at the front of the line!

My idea was to "pony express" those papers, with the big canvas container secured around my saddle horn, because by now I'm told it's almost a sin for a cowboy to walk! My route consisted of seventy-five subscribers and 150 dogs in defense of their owners' front doors!!! This pony express idea went out the window for good and was melted down on the very first attempt! I never realized that there could be so many dogs in a little frontier town such as Eagle Butte until they volunteered for home guard duty! I had 50 dogs yapping and growling at the heels of a terrified horse, and me afraid he would buck me off and I would surely be dog food, and headlines in the very paper I was attempting to deliver! Those dogs didn't allow for delivery of even one of those papers!

I delivered papers afoot, piggy-back style, for two years during the months that school was in session. But I never walked—I ran! Once a week, money had to be collected from the subscribers. This was always a very enjoyable day for me, as I met many a lasting friend in always a very enjoyable day for me, as I met many a lasting friend in my little community. The rewards were great in the form of cookies, candy bars and sometimes money, given me for a job well done.

I was also the town messenger, delivering notes here and there. I'd also take time to shovel the elderly widow ladies' walks, and maybe, hauling a bucket or two of coal for them. I especially loved one poor lady who had hands gnarled with arthritis. I never did know her first name, and her mail was always addressed "Mrs. Lawrence." She'd have hot pudding in the ready for me, the taste of which compared to no other. My route varied from 35 minutes up to two hours, depending upon distractions.

I could stand back a ways and pitch the paper up on Charley Ralston's step with old Shep snarling and growling, but making no attempt to attack. I eventually got to knock on this man's door to collect for the week. I retained the counsel of my wise old mother as to the strategies needed to surmount such obstacles as defensive dogs! As always, mothers have the know how. She fixed me 3 little round hamburger balls to be delivered each day along with Charley's paper. On the third delivery, the dog came out from under the step with his tail wagging. Come time to greet Mr. Ralston with the bill by knocking on the door, and Old Shep is sidled up next to the paper boy, looking up at his master with much approval. Old Charley said that he never thought he'd ever see the day! He informed me that his dog had never allowed any human other than himself to lay a hand on him. I am, to this day, gratified by the compliment and the $5 tip old Charley gave me.

The main source of water for the town was the well at the Spiel Farm, which was located on the west edge of town. There was also a dairy on that farm that provided about half the milk for the town. This required the washing of many quart milk bottles by hand before being filled and delivered.

The dairy was operated by a man by the name of Danny Rice, and his family. I took employment during the milking operation. Milking was done with a stool, bucket and two strong hands. My job was to clean the gutters, and watch to be sure that a cow did her job ahead, or in, but not behind the gutter. My pay each day was 2 quarts of milk, which I happily carried home to my mother, who gladly paid me 25 cents a quart for the milk. By any standards not bad pay for 1 hour's work.

Danny also ran a livery stable of sorts. We would house our horses in his barn for overnight stays in the winter. He offered feed and shelter for a fee. Danny had a big iron grey gelding that I broke for him. I used this big, strong horse to travel back and forth from town to our ranch north of town.

Another dairy of long standing was operated by the George Matz Family on the northeast edge of town. He furnished milk for the residents of Eagle Butte for many years. Us kids stayed clear of his house with never even a prank on Halloween, because we were plumb leary of this old fellow. If things didn't go right in the milk pen, you could hear him curse and beller all over town!

There was a rumor going around that, while positioned on his stool, his head buried in the flank of one of his milkers, another milker, this one with horns, walks up and gives the one he's milking a little nudge with one of them sharpies. Of course, this, caused the cow being milked to jolt, knocking old George butt over teakettle. George responded by releasing his resentment with an ash post, dehorning the intruding old sister with determined force and no sanitation or sanity required!

I'm saying that nobody in my crowd ever had nerve enough to tip George's toilet!! That yard was off limits to all trick or treaters!

George was a hard worker. He put up a lot of hay with his old grey team. He would load huge loads of hay from the low ground and lake beds onto his rack. His loads were always picture perfect with access to the top of the pile by a ladder permanently affixed to the center front. He would climb atop his well-rounded load and holler, "Joe! Jack! Heet Ahh!" his big grey team which had turned white with age, were named after the boxers of world renown, Joe Lewis and Jack Dempsey.

George's brother, Gus ("Fatty"), Matz, made his living by repairing harness and saddles, as well as putting half soles on shoes. Fatty was confined to a wheel chair. He had had to have his legs amputated. The story goes that he had ingrown toe nails and got blood poisoning.

Hunting jackrabbits was a lot of fun, and also very profitable for me. In my rounds as paper boy, I ran into this man, Frank Ganje. He had been drafted into the Army and had a Remington single shot 22 rifle for sale. The price was $5, and I just happened to have that in my pocket! That gun with the open sights was a good shooter. Or, maybe, I was careful because I knew I only had one shot! Anyhow, I shot many a nice jackrabbit with my $5 investment.

On my rounds opening ice in the winters, I would see this nice, white furry head sticking out of a hole, and it wasn't much trouble riding a horse up within range to get a good clean head shot. I soon figured out which horses would allow you to approach them and tie a bloody rabbit to the saddle! On a good day, there might be four or even five rabbits. Horses really can smell fresh blood, and are fearful of it. The only way to get the horse to accept the smell is to put blood on your glove and rub it on their nose in order to neutralize the smell. In the toughest of times I remember rabbits selling for 20 cents each, and, if the pure white ones with good pelt were sorted out, there was often a premium.

My dad had bought a brand new 1950 Ford V8 pickup of which he was very proud. I asked him if I could use the pickup to hunt. Night hunting was legal in those days, and everybody did it.

There was a certain time of the night that the rabbits would just come out in droves to feed. There seemed to be no rhyme or reason as to when! Some times it would be nine at night, and the next night it would be midnight. On this particular night I had very good luck, shooting about 40 rabbits. I only had one box of fifty 22-shells, and was totally out. But, I had borrowed Dad's JC Higgins 12-guage shotgun and a full box of shells for it. Dad warned me to always get out of the pickup before I loaded the chamber to shoot, which I did. On this particular moonlit night I could see Mr. Rabbit, and I started my stalk. I would shoulder the gun to fire, and Mr. Rabbit would hop away just out of range. Finally, I was able to get a good shot and let fly!

I sure did kill that rabbit, but what I never realized was that my game had run in a circle as I was stalking it, and when I pulled the trigger, I was directly in line with the passenger door side of the pickup!

Dad never scolded me about it. He just never fixed the door, and for the next 15 years I had to look at that perfect 14-inch round buckshot pattern in the door. Of course, all comers would ask about this unusual decoration. Dad would point at me and say, "Ask Melvin!"

Chapter X
The Joenses

There were a large number of children in the Joens' Family, our closest neighbors across the creek and 1 ½ miles to the southeast. The girls outnumbered the boys, and in most instances, outweighed them! They were all of joyful nature.

When my parents got married and moved to the Starkey Ranch; they were greeted by the Joenses with open arms, gifts of food, and livestock. The "livestock," being an old "cluck" and a bunch of not yet-hatched eggs. (A cluck was a hen bent in the direction of maternal instinct by the rooster, to lay eight or ten eggs and set there until her little chicks popped through the eggshell into their new surroundings.) This gave Ma and Pa Anderson the advantage of more layers to put eggs on the kitchen table, and young roosters for the frying pan. Mother Rose said this old setting hen was the best wedding gift, ever!

There was a big rift about Dad's cows getting into old Hans's cane field. The casualty count was 8 head. Cane was very poisonous, especially during the drought years. The nitrates were sky high. Most ranchers never took the chance of planting it for fear of livestock getting into it and dying. There was, by mutual agreement, a 10 wire fence built between Dad's range and the old Hans' field. No more cows in the trespass, but bitter words, which can never be taken back, were spoken in haste. This caused "hard feelings," and the visits stopped and the communication ended for a very long time, probably for about four or five years.

During one season of above-average rainfall, everyone who farmed had a "bumper" crop, including old Hans and my dad, with his 36 acres. When the crop was ready, Dad had us kids all out shocking grain. In the distance we could see old Hans (There were two Hans Joens—Old Hans and his son, Young Hans.) shocking grain. He always used a fork to avoid being rattlesnake bit while picking the bundles off the ground. Shocking with a fork was much harder to do than bare handed, but Old Hans had mastered the art quite well.

Pretty soon we see Old Hans walking in our direction, and my dad is wondering out loud, "What the devil do you suppose he wants?" We keep right on shocking our oats and Hans walks right up within hearing distance to announce to Dad, "Art, I shouldn't wonder I got bit by a rattlesnake!" He pulled up his trouser leg for my dad's observation. His leg was already very badly swollen. The order of the day was to lance and draw the poison. Dad sets him down on the ground and pulls out his pocketknife for the lancing. This old Hans, has the look of a man about to get his leg amputated without any 'shine for deadening the senses.

Dad is sucking blood out of this man's leg, and I'm thinking, "They haven't talked to each other for years, and now Dad's sucking blood out of his leg and spitting like an old coyote.

Luckily we had driven up to the field in Dad's '36 Fort two seater, or that bite could have been fatal. Dad never took time to put gas in his old car, and never had enough to make it to his destination of Dupree, which was a very long distance of 30 miles. That is where Dr. Creamer, the nearest doctor resided. Dad stopped at the filling station at Lantry to put gas in, not taking time to top it off, telling the attendant he would pay on the return trip because, "This is an emergency!" The patient made it to Dr. Creamer's office none too soon. The swelling had gone all the way up his leg and side. Even his arm was starting to swell. The doctor pulled Old Hans through, and after a time of recuperation, he resumed a normal routine. Relations between him and my dad got considerably better after that.

Old Hans finally moved to town and Young Hans moved into the old homestead with his wife, Otha, and their little brood of kids. Now this outfit knew how to make do with what they had. My mother told me that they could make silk out of a sow's ear!

My brother, sister and I had many jovial times traveling back and forth across Green Grass Creek playing games with the Joens kids that we made up as we went along. Freddy, the oldest boy, and I would ride Dad's work horses just to see if we could!

The Joens Homestead was really too small to make a decent living on, so Young Hans sold it to my dad and moved up closer to town to be neighbors with Carl Pedersons, Faye Lavender and his sister, Eva, and her husband, Erik Bruske.

My dad and a hired man by the name of Bonny Brannon from Arkansas, who was strong as a bull, six feet tall and dumb as a dead tree, were over in the old holdings at the Joens place after his acquisition. They were making a shed ready to skid home with a four-horse team. While taking a break and being a little snoopy as to his new purchase, Dad walked over the hill a short distance to the west where there was a little earthen dam with a small amount of water in it. He wanted to make an assessment of it to see if he could, maybe, enlarge it if the drain-off warranted the extra work. Below the fill of this dam lay four stout planks about 8 ft. in length. Thinking maybe he could use them for his moving project, he lifted one to check for soundness and discovered a hand-dug well, complete with wooden curbing under the planks. After removing all the planks, the sunshine allowed for a good look-see into the old, abandoned well. There was what looked to be a fair amount of water and something hairy, like an animal had, maybe, fell in and drowned. I was instructed to go get an old sheep hook out of the shed that Dad and Bonny were making ready to move. This was a contrivance with a large hook on the end, enabling you to fit it over the back leg of a sheep to subdue it. This hook was attached to a nice, smooth wooden handle about 12 ft. long.

Dad wrapped some barbed wire around the hook end and lowered 'er down the well to see what he could bring to the surface. All the time he was giving me the "spook" by saying, "I hope this ain't no dead body!"

The snaring process was successful, with the results producing a cowhide with a good-sized square chunk missing. Bonny and Dad retrieved seven cow hides from this old abandoned well, all with the square chunk missing. I'm sure Dad was looking for something that would have missing hide from the location he branded his Bar on the Shoulder and Lazy S on the Ribs, but gave up after laboriously pulling hide no. 7 from the well. All 7 hides had the missing piece cut out in the same place, right where the Curtis brothers branded their V/C.

It was common knowledge in those days that there were people that would butcher neighbors' beef. If, by chance, you rode by a place with smoke coming out of their chimney and you detected the odor of burnt hair, you could bet your Bull Durham sack that somebody was burning a brand. In the case of finding the hides in the old well at the Joens Homestead, one might suspect the former occupants, but the fact is, they were not the culprits! The truth is they were hauled in from the southerly direction. This was admitted by a family man that was beyond suspicion. This gentlemen lubricated his tongue at the old horseshoe-shaped bar in the liquor store at Eagle Butte on a Saturday night. He admitted the theft and cover up to one of our neighbors. My father told me there was nothing more dangerous than a kid with big ears and 20-20 vision, and to keep my mouth shut!

I'm sure that the news of the hides in the well was spread on the "hush-hush," but not by me! That is, until now. I kept the secret for 56 years, and the hired man, Bonny, never had a clue because he thought we were looking for a dead body.

Bonny Brannon came to South Dakota with a dream of being a gun-toting cowboy, and although he was born about 50 years too late for his dream, he did make a mark of great importance to our family. My Dad and Slim Berndt were real good hands at cutting studs together. Ole six-foot-six Bonny, although a brute for strength, just couldn't get the hang of throwing those studs! That required perfect timing. After about the third horse, Dad is worried. This big old boy is just going to get trampled, so he tells ole six-foot-six to go dig a well some place!!! This was quite a statement! We had dug test holes up the creek, down the creek and over the hill with very poor results. But, off goes Bonny with auger and four foot extensions over his shoulder, out of the danger of flying hoofs!

This stud cutting business was down to a science for Dad and Slim. I don't think you could call either one of these guys handy with a rope. The idea was to flip your loop just ahead of a running horse to catch both front feet. This was called "fore footing." When the horse felt the loop tightening on his front feet, he would jump, thus allowing you to tip him over with very little effort because all four feet were off the ground.

Dad and Slim used the snare method. There was a piece of baling wire placed three feet high on the wall of the old straw shed. That was also the west part of the corral. A large loop was then made and hung on the wire, with both men hanging on to the loose end of

142

the rope. Then I would run the horse around where he would try to jump the loop, and nearly always catch both front feet. Down came the stud!!

My dad told me many times that there was no one better than Slim Berndt on the head of a horse. After the horse hit the ground, he would immediately try to get up, but for a big man, Slim could move like a cat and grab the head and tip up the horse's nose. Once Slim had his big paws on a horse, there was no chance of it getting up. Without my going in to more detail, those two guys cut hundreds of studs that way.

Now back to Bonny — Dad and Slim were only about two-thirds done with the bunch, and Six-foot-six comes and sits down in the shade, and rolls a Bull Durham smoke. He's been gone about two hours. Dad mentions to him, "you weren't gone very long. Did you get thirsty?' The old kid says, "Why would I be thirsty? There's all the water I needed to drink in that hole I just dug." That stopped Art Anderson dead in his tracks! This is hard to believe, and Dad starts quizzing him about how deep did he go, and how far down to water, and so forth.

The business in the corral was finished before Dad went down below the barn to have a look-see for himself. Sure enough, the hole was full of water!! Dad had tested for years with his test auger to no avail, and Six-foot-six, by chance and by gosh, dug a well in two hours that is sill in use today!

Bonny Brannon was from a different part of the country and was rather unpredictable and somewhat amusing. He spent every spare penny on western attire, and he stuck out like a sore thumb with his high-crowned, 5-inch brim Stetson and his buckskin shirt with long fringes. He wouldn't ride with a saddle, always bareback, Indian style. He frequently asked for cornstarch to relieve his sore behind.

My dad usually started his day around 3:30 or 4:00 a.m., and the first order of the day was to pitch a little hay in the mangers for the horses, and milk the cows. He also often times made breakfast which always included buttermilk or sour cream pancakes, fried potatoes, some kind of meat, usually bacon or sausage, or sometimes steak. There would be lots of eggs and of course, coffee and milk to drink. This big giant of a guy that we called Six-foot-six could do one thing better than anybody else---EAT! One morning my dad decides he's going to see just how many pancakes he can get Bonny to eat. Bonny stalled a little after about 5, and Dad said, "You'd better eat a couple more just in case we don't get back for dinner." Bonny eats a couple more, along with another helping of eggs and bacon. He sets down his fork for the second time. Dad is really getting a kick out of this and says, "If we get in late, Rose will be in bed, and if you eat a little more now, you probably wouldn't have to bother her for supper." Bonny smothers a couple more cakes with chokecherry jelly and eats away. When he finished, he was obviously full to the point that he was miserable. He slid his chair back and started to climb the ladder up to the attic where he slept. Dad asked, "Where you going?" The big old boy replies, "I usually go to bed after supper!"

Chapter XI
Scotty Gill

There were events that happened before my time, or, maybe I just wasn't old enough to be involved, but I learned about them by listening at sheep camps, brandings, or when the threshing crew would over night at our place.

I overheard men talking about Scotty Gill. The old Scotsman had a fairly large band of sheep and lived in a sheep wagon year 'round. Although he had a team of horses that he could either ride or drive, he preferred to walk with his sheep dog like they did in the Old Country. This being the case, his team was just usually turned loose to fend for themselves, and he would just pay someone a few dollars to gather his team when he needed to move camp. My dad was one he depended on to keep an eye out and fetch them on demand. On one occasion, upon arriving at Scotty's sheep wagon, dad found it empty and cold. The oven door was open, so he closed it for lack of room in the wagon, and stoked up the fire. He set on a pot of coffee. It wasn't long and the sheep tender showed up, expressing his gratitude in a big way for having his team at camp, because he had to move. His flock was out of grass.

The two men were sitting in this cramped little quarters and Scotty started sniffing the air, thinking there was something wrong with the smell of things. In his Scottish brogue he asked, "Art, have you seen me cot?" Dad said, "No, I haven't seen your cat."

No sooner said and the old Scotsman opened the little oven door, resulting in much smoke spilling forth. Scotty, with a disdainful look said, "Art, you son-of-a-butch, you cooked me cot!"

Scotty met his Maker by having his throat cut with his own sheep shears. Many an old timer had the answer, but not for sure. Some say he committed suicide, some say he was murdered. Scotty made 'shine whiskey both to sell and to drink, and my dad said, possibly to lure visitors to his camp, as a sheep herder's camp is a lonely one. George Webb and Old Mike Keller were the last ones to admit they saw him alive, leaving him in a jovial mood as they had spent a good deal of time playing poker and drinking his home brew before departing.

The Indians avoided that deep draw where he had set his last fateful camp. They said they heard Scotty ringing his sheep bell when the wind blew. They were very superstitious of his spirit. This camp was located in a deep, timbered ravine just east of Elder Ferguson's holdings.

The wind was blowing, but not much. I listened for the bell, and sure enough, I hear ting-a-ling-a-ling. Oh boy, I'm ready to go see Mama, but I have to test my courage and ride on in.

The old Scotsman had erected a sturdy stand from ash, made complete with tail fin and propeller. When the wind blew, the propeller would turn and hit a little paddle that would hit and evaporated milk can which had a couple of pebbles in it. This caused a spooky dinging noise. This device was invented to

146

deter the coyotes from entering the sheep bed ground to steal a lamb. I have no idea how, but our family claimed title to Scotty's team of horses. One was a bay we forever more called Scotty, and a brown we called Tony.

Scotty had a little galvanized tank that he dipped his sheep in to kill ticks and mange. That tank still is in good shape and remains in our family's possessions today. The sheep shears were taken as a trophy and shown to me by a sheep man who used to live twenty-five miles south of Eagle Butte in Ziebach County. He also had the "recipe" and used it.

Chapter XII
Quarantine

Medical doctors were at a premium in Western South Dakota, and sometimes, nonexistent or were so far away that it was considered a waste of time to travel great distances to be attended by a licensed physician. Many home remedies were put to use. I sometimes think that this is where the saying "kill or cure" came from! Turpentine was the number-one remedy at our house. This clear, not too odorless liquid, was diluted with honey for strep throat and sore throat, and mixed with pine tar for open wounds on both man and beast. If the quart container of turpentine was not replaced when used up, the kerosene was brought out! This was purchased in 50-gallon drums because great demands were put upon it to start fires, to fuel the wick-burning lamps and for use as disinfectant and on insect bites. The kerosene was used in place of turpentine. You haven't had cough syrup if you haven't swallowed a tablespoon full of turpentine and hot honey. It stopped the coughing immediately, mostly because it took a bit of time to catch your breath and begin the process of breathing again!

Mother and Father Anderson had rented a house in town from Elmer and Lucille Berndt. It was located just across the road to the west of the school playgrounds. It was at this location that Mother and the kids lived during the school year. Transportation was poor and at that time, no one would even think of

149

driving 12 miles twice a day in a cold and very unreliable automobile on bad roads, to haul children to school.

While living in the town house, all of us kids, Betty, myself, Larry & infant, Linda, who were still nursing, contacted scarlet fever. This disease was very contagious and life threatening. The county officials came to our yard and placed yellow quarantine signs on our driveway, and also posted one on our front door. This meant that no one in the community could come in contact with our family, and no possessions of any kind could be taken from the premises. I also remember the children playing in the school playground, scolding, and making unkind remarks to us if we happened to be outside during recess. My mother forbid us to go outside during recess, which was hard for me because my sister, Betty and I were never very sick. Mother, in an attempt to entertain us, made rag balls about 4 inches around, and Betty and I would go outside and play ante-I-over the roof of the house for hours.

Brother Larry was very sick with a high fever for what seemed an eternity. Mother was very fearful that she was going to lose him. She put cold towels on his body day and night. Since I believe in the Almighty power of God, I think Mother's prayers were what pulled Larry through this very dark time in his life.

Linda, who was about 8 months at the time, had such a sore throat that she refused her mother's attempts to nurse her. This was an added burden to this poor, isolated lady's responsibilities.

The town constable was a very nice man who all respected. He could be forceful enough to keep law and order in our town, and yet kind enough to help those in need. We were isolated from the world except for this very caring human being. He was an American Indian named Boldt Lafferty. Every day he would come to our driveway and stand by the quarantine sign to take Mother's order for groceries, which were allowed to be charged at Austin's store. Boldt would, everyday but Sunday, deliver groceries and mail as far as the quarantine sign for ready access for Mom. This went on for the full 21-day quarantine. This was our salvation. This town cop was truly a genuinely caring and kind-hearted man.

After 2 weeks, by God's grace, and with Mother's loving hands, we were all pretty much back to normal, but crisis number 2 arrived at the door, namely, Art Anderson. Dad was very ill when he rode in to the yard. He was so weak that he could barely stay on his horse, and could not speak. It was a wonder that he was even able to mount, let alone stay on his horse for the journey to town. He needed help to get off his horse, and much more help to get in to the house.

There was another man in this little frontier town that could be counted on in a crisis. He was called on many, many times to haul sick people to the Pierre hospital, which was located 100 miles to the southeast. That's not all he did. He could just be counted on for help if someone was in a bind. He was not of sound limb. He walked with a stifling limp. His name was Adolph Hohertz.

Time was definitely running out for my dad when Adolph and his friend, Conrad Held, arrived to help load the patient into Adolph's Ford for the emergency trip to Pierre. The route was difficult because of poor roads and snow, but they were successful in getting Dad to St. Mary's Hospital where he was diagnosed with spinal meningitis. For a time, Dad saw two of everything, and had to have corrective glasses. It was a very long time before he had a full recovery, if he ever really did!

Dad's brothers, Rusty and Jim, took charge of the ranch chores and hired J.D. Kessling to fly Red Sloesher and my cousin, Boyd Anderson, to take care of the cattle feeding and the various other chores. The feeding was still done with a team and hayrack, with the hay being pitched both on and off with a pitch fork. Much labor was required to load and unload, I believe, 3 loads each day.

All heals with time, and eventually got back to normal. All of this had really been a setback for our family. I don't think that my dad ever fully recovered from it.

Chapter XIII
Snake Den

We were always running in to rattlesnakes on our rides around the country and were rather accustomed to seeing them with the "you leave me alone, and I'll leave you alone" attitude. There is a long, narrow ridge that meanders to the north and a little west of the present site of my brother, Larry's ranch that stretches a far piece, pointing towards the Moreau River. In the process of some disturbance, this ridge shifted, allowing the earth to settle about five feet. This allowed for a narrow crack about ½ to ¾ mile long. One could only guess how deep it was. Rattlers and other snakes of all descriptions, such as bull snakes, blue racers, water snakes and puff adders would instinctively migrate to this ideal habitat in the default to den up for the winter. In the spring of the year this location and the surrounding area got pretty interesting. Horses would trot along with their head in a position for a better look a where they were stepping, and they'd have one ear cocked for better listening. Myself, I never had nerve enough to dismount and whop the snakes' heads with a throw rope like my dad used to do! I was too afraid that those slithering creatures might gang up on me!

Now, to my dad and my Grandad Anderson, this was great sport! They would take their two dogs, Jack and Slobbers, up to where the snakes were departing from the den. They'd flip the snakes to their dogs with sticks. The dogs made short work of Mr. or

Mrs. Snake by shaking them into several pieces! Dad and Grandad would be dodging flying snake parts in the process!

In a given day, Dad claims that the two of them eliminated more than 70 rattlesnakes while a fellow horse back rider watched from across the divide. This big, tall fellow is still alive and well. He's probably about ninety. I don't really want to embarrass him by revealing his name here, but he sure was afraid of flying snake fangs!

There was a fellow who hunted rattlers for a living, probably for the purpose of milking the venom from their fangs for anti-venom serum, but I'm not sure. His name was A.M. Jackley. He would visit our residence twice or more a year. He invented a large trap device that attracted the snakes into it. In them there was a shiny object that would flip open with the pressure of the snake crawling in, but there was no way for them to get back out. This trap was constructed with two 4 x 8 pieces of plywood and screen. The trapping was done in the spring when the snakes came out of the den, and also in the fall when they came back to hole up for the winter. Jackley would come periodically to empty his traps, using his near six-foot snare-like device. He'd pick out the rattlers and drop them into a cardboard box, ridding himself of the unwanted reptiles. All that he kept were the rattlesnakes.

One fall Jackley never showed up to check his traps. Out of curiosity I rode by the trap just about every day, as I was sort of fascinated by this huge entanglement of 300 or more snakes! This went on for, I think, about three weeks, and no Jackley. The snakes started to disappear! First the garter snakes. Then the blue racers, then the feisty little puff adders, and so on until everything was gone but the biggest rattlers and fat bull snakes. The last trip I made to the den that fall, I made a startling discovery—the bull snakes were constricting the rattlesnakes and swallowing them! I opened up the little trap door and allowed the survivors to escape. I have, after that sunny fall day, never killed another bull snake.

Another sunny day, about 10:00 o'clock in the morning, Mother was on her way to the clothesline to hang out her wash when she discovered a very fat rattlesnake in her path. She dropped her basket of laundry and headed for her trusty garden hoe. It wasn't long and her foe was in two or three pieces! Her job was not quite yet done, however, because Ole Mama Snake was packed full of babies—eight, to be exact. Mom hoed down the whole herd, as those little reptiles are just as poisonous as the big ones. My mom told me that was how the mama shakes transported their young. They just opened their mouth and told the little ones to get in!

Now, I just have to tell my story about the blue racer! They never called them suckers "racers" for nothin'! One night our wrangling horse got away, leaving us plumb afoot. I could see ole Peewee about ¾ of a mile away, southeast of the house, and on the south side of the creek. I took a quart of oats and my bridle and headed out across the creek wading in knee-deep water, in hopes of catching Peewee. All the time I was pretty happy with myself in general, whistling a little tune. I just knew I would have good fortune catching this little bay with my quart jar of oats.

I heard this little ruckus and spitting sound behind me, and lo' and behold! There is this slimy 3 and ½ foot blue racer snake trying to make love to my bridle reins, which I was dragging along behind me! That son of a slime ball put the spook on me, but good!!!

I won many a 100-yard dash in my day, going to school at old Eagle Butte. My old friend, Francis Zacher, who owns an interest in the bank, can attest to that. I attribute my racing ability one blue racer! Oh, by the way, if I step on a rattler, I can jump five feet straight up, and that can be verified, too!!

Chapter XIV
The Diamond A

Jobs were scarce in the rural community, and very few of the younger generation could afford college. They just mainly stayed in their respective area an worked with their parents, or if they were lucky, they could land a job with the State Highway Department, the railroad, or the diamond A Cattle Company.

The Diamond A was founded by Captain Mossman of the Texas Rangers, and later came under the ownership of Leon Williams. The Diamond A had holdings in Miles City, Montana, Wagon Mound, New Mexico, and, in my time, large holdings in Dewey, Ziebach, and old Armstrong County. (Armstrong County never had a town or a county seat!)

The Diamond A had a general foreman overlooking all operations, and a camp foreman at all the separate locations. In order to be foreman of the Diamond A, you had to be of good character, impeccably honest, and a leader of men with a willingness to work seven days a week from sunup 'til sundown, for very little pay.

Bob (Forrest) Rose was offered the foreman job many times, but since he was of above-average intelligence, he declined repeatedly, figuring that the few added dollars for the position never matched the added responsibility. However, his position was held in high esteem because Bob was known to hold a crew together and often get two days work done in one, and at the same time be entertaining the troops with his ever-present good humor and shenanigans!

Bob started out working for the "A" in 1914 in Miles City, Montana. He moved to South Dakota with the outfit in 1919 and rode for the brand until he retired in 1961. He spent a great deal of this time on the Circle P, just on the north shore of the Cheyenne River, and also at Rudy Creek, the 24 Ranch, Mossman, Ridgeview, and The Farm which was located on the banks of the Missouri, just up river from old Fort Bennett.

This man, Bob Rose, was the backbone of the labor force for the Diamond A Cattle Company for forty-seven years. Standing on a firm foundation, he watched an endless stream of cowboys, horses and cattle come and go. He served as mentor to many a young fella wanting to be a cowboy.

From what I have learned from this cowboy, he had three basic rules:

No. 1 No matter what the boss tells you, do it, even if you think its wrong.

No. 2 If you can't take it, don't dish it out!

No. 3 No booze in camp.

In those old cow camps, if someone wouldn't invent a little entertainment, I guess there just wasn't any! Many a young man fell prey to old Bob's trickery, and oh, how they enjoyed getting even!

Some of these boys that worked for the Diamond A in later years under the capable foremanship of Len (Fat) Bringman, were Jerry Till, The Deal Boys, Tommy Maupin, Charles Smith, the

Fischer boys, Willy, Leo, Jimmy, Eddy, and Andy, plus many more. Some of them have gone to meet their Maker, but the ones that are left say they wouldn't trade their experience working with old Bob and Fat for a seat on the New York Stock Exchange!

There was talk of 17 little log cabins near the site of Fort Bennett, and legend has it that upon discovering them in the late 1800's the cabins were in a state of deterioration and were occupied only by corpses, which were thought to be Caucasians. There were no apparent survivors in the settlement. One can only imagine the fate of the occupants. Perhaps they died of the smallpox virus or typhoid fever.

Whatever the case may be, old Bob, come a dark spooky night, would set the cowboys' hair on end making up stories about the ghosts from that little settlement looking in the windows and dancing around the yard in skeleton form! So, the young cowboys were on their toes for any strange sound in that creaky old house, to the point that they never even wanted to go outside to relieve themselves! To make matters worse, the old house at The Farm was an officers' quarters that had been moved up river on the ice from Fort Bennett. That, in itself, offered a ghost-like setting. (This particular camp was called The Farm because much hay was put up on the fertile river bottoms for winter feeding, and haying to the older cowboys was considered farming. Some of the "died-in-the-wool" cowboys refused to hay because it was demeaning to their occupation of making pony tracks!)

On one rainy night Bob was really getting a lot of mileage out of his ghost stories. It was especially having an effect on one little wirey cowboy by the name of Willy. Willy had a pistol, and decided it would be comforting to just sleep with it under his pillow.

Bob decided, since he was having such a good effect with his story, that maybe he should put his boot on the end of a broom handle and punch the floor below Willy's bedroom for more effect. The boot goes, "thump, thump, thump" below Willy's bed. Willy grabs on to his pistol, about half scared out of his wits, and fires three rounds through the floor before Bob gets him shut down!

Willy isn't much on revenge, but Andy sees opportunity to get even by snitching a pair of Bob's long underwear (which he wore year 'round). Andy took needle and thread in hand and just did a pretty neat job of sewing the trap door shut in the back! Now, this means, if you really got an emergency, your shirt has got to come off so that the long underwear sleeves can be slid over your shoulders and pulled down below nature's exit. Bob has really got to go, and before he figures out all this new procedure, well---he didn't make it!!!

Bob came roaring to the house, exposing his predicament and mad as a wet hen! He relieved his tension by unloading a few cuss words and calling the whole bunch little S.O.B.s! But, he had said, "If you can't take it, don't dish it out!"

I don't know if Fat Bringman ever slept, but I do know it never took him long to stay over night! Early one morning, Fat came roaring in to the Circle P where Bob and Leo Fischer were having breakfast. He made the announcement that they were going to butcher hogs that day. Bob asks how many they were gonna butcher.

Fat answered, "All of them," meaning eventually.

Bob took his 22 out to the pen while Fat finished his coffee. Upon hearing numerous shots, Fat makes the comment that ole Bob sure better get a new gun if it took that many shells to kill one hog! Fat and Leo go to the pen with their skinning knives only to find 38 dead hogs lying there!!

Fat says, "What the heck did you do?"

Bob says, "You said all of them."

Fat yelled, "Not all at once!"

This event sort of turned into a neighborhood butchering that filled Naeve's locker plant in Eagle Butte to overflowing with pork, and some even going across the river to Gettysburg as well!

Do what the boss tells you, even if you think he's wrong!

The Diamond A always wintered a good-sized herd of cows at The Farm. After the majority was calved out, usually some time around April 15th those cows would be moved to summer grass at Ridgeview.

One particular year, Fat told the boys to gather and bed down the herd in a near corner for an early exit in the morning, which they did. They unsaddled and had their supper after which they were discussing the difficult task ahead. It was going to be hot the next day, and the younger calves were going to play out, making it difficult for the skeleton crew of three, Shorty Deal, Jimmy and Leo.

It was a moonlit night, and Leo asked, "Why don't we just move them tonight?

Shorty replied, "I'm game!"

So they followed that plan and did it with very good results. When those cowboys all rode into camp at Ridgeview the next morning, of course, old Bob asks, "What the heck are you little crappers doing here? You are supposed to be moving cows!"

Old Bob was quite pleased with their successful drive of 18 miles in the dark, and rewarded them with a fine breakfast.

The boys just got nicely bedded down in their bunks and here comes Fat, the foreman! He's a little more than upset, and asks "What part of trailing cows didn't you understand?" Old Bob simmered Fat down by explaining the events of the night, and Fat is supping his coffee, trying to figure out what he's going to have his hands do the rest of the day.

Old Bob says, "You know, Fat, these boys did their day's work. They need the rest of the day off !"

Every now and then, the boys got Sunday off They took advantage of this by going to town on Saturday night, and usually went to see their folks. These young cowboys played just as hard as they worked—maybe harder—usually staying up all night Saturday night, and all day Sunday, with no sleep.

When they got back to camp Sunday night, they were tired, and not so willing to get up at 3:30 Monday morning!

Everybody is up, dragging around, on Monday morning except Eddy. Eddy likes to sleep and is hard to get up, anyway. The boys are getting worried that ole Bob is going to give him a butt chewing. But, all of this time Bob is encouraging all to let Eddy sleep. Finally, Eddy wakes up and keeps staring at Bob wondering how come, all of a sudden, he's being so good to him!

Bob breaks a few eggs in a dish for scrambling and gets the meat sizzling for Eddy. A good breakfast! The lad gets up to prepare for the feast. Eddy sort of pushes the chunks of meat around on his plate, and compliments the chef about how good the meat is — but what kind of meat is it? Bob explains that this is a new kind of sausage that old Dot Naeve has on special at the store. Eddy says that it probably was very good, but why did he season it with so much pepper if it was sausage? Old Bob told him that the shaker was plugged, so he took the lid off and he got carried away.

All is well until Eddy walks out the door and spies a partially-skinned rattlesnake in his path! He immediately put 2 and 2 together and lost his breakfast!

Now Eddy is looking for recruits to help him get even this time, and employs the help of brother Leo and Charles Smith. This kind of commotion is right down Chuck Smith's alley, and right away he says,

"Let's replace the glass of alcohol that Bob plops his teeth in at night with kerosene!"

Bob had a certain routine and was predictable. He reaches in his glass in the morning to retrieve his false teeth, slips into his bedroom slippers and goes outdoors for a pee and a look around.

Leo thinks it might be sort of funny if they would nail his slippers to the floor. He only finds one nail—a big 20-penny spike, and he sinks her to the hilt right in the heel of one of Bob's slippers.

Leo knew that the crap was gonna hit the fan just as soon as Bob got a taste of that kerosene, and he's waiting with his door open a crack for observation purposes!

Bob is regular, and on time, when he undunks his false teeth, plops 'em in and starts gagging. He grabs his slipper and puts it on. Slides his foot in the other one for a quick exit! But, the one slipper doesn't move. He slipped and straddled the partially-opened door with one arm on either side, and smacked his head square on the edge of the door! He spits his teeth out and shouts, "You little S.O.B.s!" He grabs the bucket with the wash water in it and dumps the whole shebang on Jimmy and Ray Deal. They were pretty much innocent bystanders, but had been informed of the conspiracy!

It just went on and on with Bob, and he embarrassed all those young cowboys to the point that they knew better than to go into a public place with him. One time Bob pulled up to Austin's Store and asked the boys with him if they wanted to come in.

Two out of the three declined the invitation, but one new recruit, George White Eagle, said, "Yes, I'll go. I need some "tailor-made" cigarettes."

The store was nearly empty except for two elderly ladies that were in for early morning shopping. When George and Bob got within range of this one poor old victim, Bob let a ripper, putting forth his very best effort! He then turns to this very bashful Indian boy and says, "George, I thought I taught you better than that!"

Bob has passed over to the other side and is not here to defend himself but everyone knows that no one ever got ahead of him in the trick-playing department. A lot of the things he pulled on his young recruits were so embarrassing to them, that they hold them secret. You are hearing mostly from the defense.

On those cow camps, beef was the staple of the day, and those growing boys weren't bashful about how much they ate, because there was a steady supply. The butchering was just finished on this one occasion, and Bob instructed Jimmy to go get rid of the paunch and guts. "Load it up in the Jeep and haul it out somewheres for the coyotes," he says.

The innards were contained in a big wash tub, and probably weighed in at 200 pounds, at least. Jimmy came back for help, and asked for Leo to give him a hand. Well, to those two Fischer boys, the temptation was just too great! They unloaded the tub right smack dab on top of Bob's old Jeep! He had mentioned going to town to get the mail, and it seemed logical that he should haul a load of paunch and guts along with him. Bob never noticed, or suspected, and he pulled right up to the post office with a paunch that had doubled in size by then, due to the heat!

Joe Schneider walked up and asked Bob, "What you got there?"

"Them little S.O.B.s!" He had to drive out of town and tumble it off the Jeep. Did they go too far this time? Nooo, not for Bob. He had to get even!

The whole crew was bunching cattle for branding on spring along with Kitch Lavender, who had just bought a brand new pickup at the Ford Garage at Eagle Butte. The garage, at that time, was owned by Joe Schneider.

It was getting close to noon, so Fat asked Bob if he would ride on ahead and get some dinner going, because Bob was, by all standards, a good cook. Bob was expecting company because he had been informed of the delivery of Kitch's new pickup.

The menu was spare ribs, which was Bob's specialty. He had a big old kettle going full steam with the spare ribs cooking by the time the rest of the crew came in to unsaddle for dinner. When they were all washed up, in came the company, Joe Schneider and Tony Niegle.

Bob asked Andy to take the dish rag and wipe the table off and set the plates. Andy looked around a little and asks Bob, "Have you seen the dish rag?"

Bob says, "No, get a clean one." Bob has this look in his eye! He's using this two-tined meat fork to rotate his ribs, and, when nobody but Leo is looking, he drags the dish rag out of the meat kettle, all clean and white!

Leo never ate any ribs because he had seen Bob mop grease up off the floor with that dish rag just that morning! There were probably a few mouse turds in the mix, too! The company complimented the cook, saying that those were probably the best spare ribs they ever ate!

Leo Fischer could very possibly be the youngest living Diamond A Cowboy. He is 65 years old at this writing, and has many stories of his own to tell. Fat Bringman, the last living foreman, died only a short time ago at the age of 81.

When Leo started working for Fat, he was very young. His first day on the job was to follow behind a herd of cows and calves to pick up the young calves that played out along the trail. He also packed drinking water, minced ham, a loaf of bread and a jar of mayonnaise for sandwiches.

Brother Jimmy comes loping up to the Jeep informing Leo that Fat says we're not going to stop for lunch—that we're just going to keep going. "Fix me a sandwich," demands Jimmy.

Well, Jimmy is a little hard on his younger brother, Leo, what with all his teasing and picking on him all of the time. So, Leo sees a little window of opportunity to get even! He remembers seeing an old inner tube in the back of the Jeep, so he cut a made-to-order chunk of rubber to fit between the two slices of bread. He places it, along with a generous spattering of mayonnaise, between the slices. He hears the horse loping up to the window, so he handed the sandwich out to which he thought was Jimmy. It was quickly snatched up, and as the rider loped away, he could see that it was not Jimmy!!! It was Fat, the foreman! Leo says to himself, "My days are numbered on this outfit!"

Fat takes a big bite, and with a fair amount of pressure, pulls the two slippery slices of bread out from around the rubber, which was still in his mouth! Fat spits out the rubber and turns his horse around, pointed at the Jeep and says, "Whoa!"

He gave Leo a rather unfriendly look, and rode off eating his two slices of bread!

Leo, in talking about his old partner, Bob, said that there was never a more loyal man. When he was getting up in years, Bob and two of the boys were relying on the post driver, each driving 10 steel posts a shift, building a line fence. When it came Bob's turn, he would jump right in for his turn. Those two young, strong boys told Bob that he didn't have to take a turn at the driving. He was insulted and said, "If I can't hold up my end, I'd just as well quit drawing my pay!" There never was a harder working man that ever walked, and he is my idea of a true cowboy!

Bob had his favorite cutting horse. He called him "Babe." There was this kid showed up in cowboy regalia, and Bob told him to go catch up a horse. Babe was the only one that the kid could wake up to, so here he comes leading him out with chin strap in hand and saddle slid back so the cinch was about dead center of ole Babe's belly.

He shows the chin strap to Bob and says, "This don't fit." He had the bridle mounted on the poor old pony backwards, and thought the curb strap was supposed to go over the nose.

Bob says, "Go catch a different horse.!"

One of the boys with a little more know-how dabbed a loop over a different horse, and gave him his very first lesson of the right and the wrong way of introducing his horse to tack.

The boy didn't stay long, and I suspect he might have changed careers!

The old house at the Diamond A Farm was moved up from Fort Bennett and was thought to be haunted, or occupied by ghosts. Casper Fischer traveled down river to visit his boys and shoot a deer. He was accompanied by Tom Creek, an old Indian friend, who was also interested in a little fresh venison.

When Casper and Tom arrived at camp, Tom got very excited and said, "I know that house, and it ain't supposed to be here!" He remembered the house, which was an officers' quarters at old Fort Bennett, and he said that there were two men killed inside that house. No amount of coaxing would convince him to enter the premises!

Willy Fischer was a wirey little cowboy that I spent a great deal of time with. He was at one time ordered to go to The Farm to tend to the business at hand. Willy, on this given night, thought that he saw shadows at the foot of his bed in the silhouette of a man. He tried to pull his gun from under his pillow, but was numbed and couldn't move. Willy departed from there the next day, and told his boss the story. Willy, from that day forward, was excused from going back there!

This old house was offered to Leo Fisher, but he had no use for it. However, he did salvage the old table, the platform rocker, and a dresser that came up the river in the house from the fort.

This ground is all flooded now, as the result of building the Oahe Reservoir, but it was, at one time, prime hunting ground.

One afternoon Leo was stalking a very large mule deer buck, and while putting the sneak on, he parted the grass and stared head to head with a skull! The skull had a hole in the side of it about 1 ¼ in. long by ½ in. thick. Some distance away the reminder of the skeleton was found, right up to the finger bones. Leo notified Eldon Russell, a state trooper, of his find, and Eldon came down to retrieve the remains. Later, a prairie dog hunter told Leo that he knew of the remains and had removed a very nice spear head from it.

Mr. Fischer and his wife, Lois, are fine folks. Along with raising their own children, they took in foster children and gave them the opportunity to live and learn about nature in the country. They adopted all of these kids that they could afford to, and became attached to all to the point that it was very hard to give any of them up.

Once Leo told me the first thing they want is $3000 when you adopt a child. He told them, "I want to adopt these kids, not buy them!"

One of the Diamond A holdings was the 24 Ranch. This place was acquired by purchase from an Indian lady that was always referred to as Old lady A Bear. Cow outfits were always short on water, and this place attracted attention because of a very good spring feeding Bear Creek.

Also, this location held access to thousands of acres of tribal land that could be leased for 33 cents an acre. No doubt the spring is why Emanuel and his missus settled there. It is also possible that this location could have been their allotment, which had been issued to them. (When I was a young man, every enrolled member of the tribe was issued an allotment of 160 acres on their 18th birthday. This eventually stopped because they ran out of land.)

I was told by Robert Blue Coat that the A Bear Family was very enterprising. They had large holdings with a fair accumulation of cattle, and herds of fine horses. Most Indians of the day had only the wagon the Government issued them. These wagons were referred to as "squaw wagons." But, Emanuel and Mrs. Abair rode on a fine fringe-top surrey with the fringe being bright red in color.

On one fine, sunny day late in the fall, Emanuel made the trip to Lantry for supplies. He evidently fell victim to a bootlegger and strong drink, which he couldn't resist.

Late that night, Emanuel's team came home at a rapid clip with loose lines flying, but no driver! A search was made the next day, and Emanuel was found lying face down in a muddy wagon rut, dead. It was assumed that he had smothered in the mud and water, because of the thawing of snow that fateful day.

Mrs. Abair retrieved the body and prepared it for burial the Indian way, up on a scaffolding. It got very cold, and the ground was frozen, making it impossible to dig the four holes in which to place the crotched poles in the earth for the main framework of his final resting place. Old Lady A Bear figured if she would take the insides out and replace them with salt, she could put him in the smoke house where she cured her hams, and he would keep pretty good 'til the digging got better.

The last words ole Robert Blue Coat spoke about Emanuel's parting were, "She sure cured him!"

My sister and brother-in-law own that place now, establishing a new identity called The J D Cattle Company. I remember helping feed little chickens in the smoke house. This was a warm and cozy shelter for those baby chicks.

The boys were haying at Ridgeview at a day camp. They had to haul their own drinking water. One depended upon the other to do that on their way back to camp from the Saturday night frolic. This one time, however, everyone forgot! Bob asked if anybody had drinking water, and the answer was "No." Bob jumped into his old Jeep and went to the nearest stock dam and dipped out a good ration for camp use.

The water was stale and very green with the process of nature at work. Bob figured those boys would get a little squeamish at the looks of this substance, and would want to go some place else to get some drinking water that they could see through! Bob had the idea that if he made a pail of green lemon-lime kool-aid they wouldn't complain about the color.

Leo and Jimmy came in for a thirst quencher, knowing that old Bob had gone some place for water. They saw the bucket of kool-aid and each took a big cup full. One drink and they both knew where Bob got that water!!

Leo said, "We got to get even!" They followed Bob's Jeep tracks over to the stock dam and found a little turtle and a good-sized green frog. They spiked the kool-ad with their little cold-blooded friends. They were still thirsty, and Bob kept on drinking.

Fat, the boss, came wheeling in that evening and asked, "Have you got anything to drink?"

Bob answers, "Yeah. There's a whole pail of kool-aid on the wash stand."

Fat stepped up with his cup and proceeded to dip out a batch. Right then, old Mr. Kermit, the Frog, peeks out at him. Fat never said a word, but set his cup down, probably thinking that he wasn't thirsty after all!

No doubt Bob discovered the little live creatures in the bottom of the kool-aid, but he never let on because those boys would get too much satisfaction from that! He drank every bit of it. This was nothing, for that old Tuff! He would shoo a bunch of cows out of a mud hole and jump off his horse right in the middle, take his hat off and dip it full and take a good, long drink—mud, ?????????????, and all! The boys said that he was never sick a day in his life, hardly.

One time when there was a crew working down on The Farm, Tommy stopped at Ridgeview and bought a pint of whiskey, not knowing the rules about booze in camp. Tommy pulled out his snake-bite medicine when he went into the house, and Bob said, "Let me see that!" Tommy, being a generous man, gave it right up, thinking he would probably take a little sip. Instead, Bob popped the seal and went chug-a-lug until she was nothing but glass and label with no use for the lid! The boys claim the old boy was about as green as his kool-aid the next day, and pretty easy to get along with! Other than that they never ever saw the man sick.

Bob was very intelligent man, probably, because he read a lot. He would read by the kerosene lamp on the table with his 22 rifle, loaded with shorts, close at hand. For sport he would set another lamp on the floor. He would peek over the top of his paper with his spectacles to see if he could get a good shot at a mouse. If the opportunity was promising for a good shot, he would carefully set his paper aside and take aim, blasting ole Mr. Mouse to kingdom come right there on the kitchen floor! Heavenly days! It's no wonder those cowboys were so jumpy! You know? Every cowboy that spent time with that man had high esteem for him. He could keep the crew motivated and working as a team.

Chapter XV
Dago Kelly

Toad Webb had a little herd of registered Herefords that he sort of herded like sheep—all over the country, depending on which way the wind blew. Cows, when they moved, always traveled against the wind to keep the horn flies off their faces. He never really had a place of his own for cows, and he'd turn loose and go home to the folks at night, returning to the herd the next day for the same routine. Eventually the free range was claimed and fenced, so Toad was forced to sell his little herd of Herefords to Myron Mayor. This generated a small fortune in cash and accumulation of a fine, new 1949 red Ford pickup. I had grown to recognize Toad and his little herd of Herefords and often rode to his holdings for a chat. I got to know him pretty good. At the time he purchased the pickup I was more than willing to accept the invite of a ride.

Toad had polio as a youngster and only had partial use of one arm. He walked with a limp, but only seemed slightly handicapped by his affliction. He was hired out by Frank Giesinger, who lived and farmed over north of Ridgeview. Frank asked Toad to recruit someone to drive his little Case tractor and pull a 4-section harrow over the planted ground. Frank was a very good farmer, particular about the smoothness of the ground. This job was very high paying, and I took it. The job lasted six days, and it paid $48!

This is where I met Dago Kelly. He looked like a bum that just climbed out of a box car. He rode in on an old grey horse, which was sporting a workhorse bridle with the blinds cut off. His saddle was the most beat up I ever saw, having patches of boot top on the swells and cantle nailed on with galvanized shingle nails.

Dago's real name was Mario Bonassio. He branded a triangle double bar, on the left hip of his horses. Dago had stowed aboard a ship bound for the United States when he was a mere seven years old. He was secretive about how he got to South Dakota, but was proud of the fact that he was raised by a Lakota woman and a black man. He was wise in tradition, and could speak both Lakota and Dakota.

Dago was visiting the Giesinger spread for the sole purpose of a good home-cooked meal by Mrs. Giesinger, who was an impeccable housekeeper and a fine cook. He also liked to trade tales about the activities in the community because he loved to gossip.

It was raining a steady drizzle on a June day when I ran in to this old gent just west of On The Tree Church. He thought we should shelter up in the church, and maybe build a fire if there was kindling available. We were both pretty soaked and chilly. I always had a jacket tied on the back of my cantle, but never a slicker. I never owned one.

The wood box was full, but there was no bark or small stuff to start a fire, and no matches. Dago pulled a small jar from his pocket loaded with matches. He went for a hymn book to tear up for a quick start of the

fire.   I had this little disagreement with about
destroying church property. He came back at me with
"If that was a song book and if the songs were any
good, anybody with any smarts would have them
memorized, anyhow!"

Dago never attended school one day in his life,
unless it was to bum a meal, or whatever else he could
get off the school marm, and he deemed it totally
unnecessary to read or write. But, just try to beat him
out of ten cents in a poker game!!

We finally enlisted the help of our jack knives,
and made a pile of shavings to put in the stove. We
soon had a hot fire going, and we shared the warmth.

Dago reached in his pocket and pulled out a
small handful of coins. He began to show me coin
tricks, one right after the other for, probably, the better
part of an hour. He often used a double-eagle gold
coin. No trick was the same as the one before. I sure
would have liked to learn some of those tricks because
some of them were totally mind boggling and amazing.
I'd ask him to please show me how he did this trick or
that trick and his answer was always, "If I show you
this trick, then you'll be as smart as I am!"

Not at the church meeting, but at another time,
he showed me a whole new bunch of tricks with cards.
He could double the deck, or make them disappear, or
pull eight aces. He never taught me one single solitary
trick! I'm sure Mario Bonassio went to his grave
without showing anyone how to entertain with his
many tricks.

I was curious about where he lived and I questioned him about it, and if maybe, he had a wife. I never did find out if he had a place of his own, or if he held up with someone. I once thought I would get the opportunity to find out when I agreed to break two horses for him. I told him I'd ride up to get them and lead them home so that I could get a look at his outfit. That would also give me the opportunity to ride by the crossing where I had met the freckled-nosed Indian girl. No dice. He told me he would just bring them to me because he wanted to test mother's cooking!

Those two little cherry-red sorrel geldings with the triangle double bar on their hip were absolutely two of the nicest horses I ever rode. I tried to buy them. He said, "If I sell you the horses, you would have my horses and all I would have is your money. I would spend the money, then I would have nothing and you would still have my horses, and you wouldn't give them back!"

Dago was riding the grub line when he fell into camp at Mossman just as the Diamond A was preparing a shipment of steers to be loaded by rail at the stockyards there. The "A" was under the foremanship of Nels Babcock who was overseeing the whole South Dakota operation at the time. For a trick, Nels told Dago to go count the steers in the shipping pasture so that they could order the railroad cars at the depot in Eagle Butte by telegraph. It was pretty common knowledge that Dago could only count to 10, and there were about 2500 steers sorted for shipment. Dago left camp early in the morning, packing a lot of

178

rope along.   He came back to camp in the late afternoon with his ropes knotted about every three inches. He threw the ropes at his boss's boots and said, "10 to the knot. You know how to do the rest!" where there is a will, there's a way!!

Andy Fischer worked for my dad one summer, and Dago Kelly stayed over night with us because he had heard talk about us making a big circle north of the river in Red Dog's and T.O. Traversie's outfit.   He wanted to tag along to check for his brand.   Mother was always one to pack a lunch to tie behind the cantle in our jacket.   When she anticipated a long leave of absence, sometimes she would wrap a pint of milk neatly in a newspaper to keep it cool.   That wasn't to my liking because the cream on the milk would turn to butter from the jouncing and I never liked to drink the lumps.

Andy, Dad, Dago and I holed up in the shade under the bridge on Highway 63 to eat lunch in the shade.   There was also water there for man and beast. Dago looked at his sandwich and refused to eat it because Mother had put a generous helping of butter on it.   He refrained from eating butter, but he would put a slice of bread on his plate and drown it in bacon grease!   He'd eat it like it was a banquet.   He informed me that Italians never ate butter.   I questioned him about how he could know so much about Italians if he left home when he was seven.

Some people make an impression on you that don't allow you to forget them! I will never forget this very hungry Italian that would rather starve as eat a sandwich with butter on it!

The man had no birth certificate, and if asked the question of his age, he would always say "40 something." I'm sure he was in his 60's when I first met him. Can you imagine a man without wife and children, and no extended family to depend upon in your later years? Dago had nobody that I knew of.

My Aunt Esther and Uncle Vernon attracted people in need like they were magnets. No one was ever turned away from Esther's table, and it was huge! She and her daughters would begin preparing for the noon meal right after the breakfast dishes.

There would be pans of peeled potatoes and whatever else they could scrape up. This usually involved butchering about 4 or 5 chickens. My aunt and uncle lived in the northwest corner of town, and come noon, one could see all the freeloaders headed in that direction for a position at the table. No one was ever turned down, no one ever was charged, and no one ever offered to pay.

Several older people and one young Indian man that was confined to a wheel chair took up permanent residence at that already-crowded home. George Frice, after he aged to the point when he was no longer able to run Vernon's ranch operation, moved close by and stayed near Cousin Jo Ann Martin until his passing.

Charley Hamilton, who I know had a nephew that he had contact with, moved in, too. There was Bill Peck, and of course, Dago Kelly and others. When Dago was freeloading at the Andersons' he became unmanageable and ornery. He was unkempt and unruly. Esther would scold, but would never think of asking him to leave, even though he was an embarrassment to her and her family. Dago was considered to be poor, but I often wondered, and still do. The man would absolutely not spend a dime on anything, not clothes, not food, and certainly not on foolish things like saddle blankets, or the like. He would bum smokes and chew or a good shot of whiskey, but was never in the market for these items.

Dago spent two winters and a summer at my Uncle Rusty Anderson's over near Timber Lake. My Aunt Mary was kind hearted, but ran a tight ship. In no uncertain terms she told Dago to clean up if he was going to eat at the table with her family. He accepted the criticism, and took it for the truth. He ran into Rusty and told him about having about 100 cows that he wanted someone to run on shares. Rusty agreed to run them for 50% of the calves. He wanted to use his share to get his sons started in the cow business. Dago was younger then and could still hold his own, no matter where you put him, whether on a pitch fork, or horseback or at the dinner table.

Dago and Rusty's boy, Dick, made several rides up in the Goose Creek County, and would throw their gather in on Bill Ewing. It was bitter cold and well into the −20 degrees range when they finally decided to trail the little herd to Rusty's. They were still short about 40 head, but gave up, for the bitter cold. They hoped for better days ahead. Dago stayed on with his cattle and worked for his board and room, this being a very friendly and desirable environment.

The first morning the Andersons' new guest hollered out, "Get up dairyman," referring to the milk cows Rusty had in the barn. After the second morning of this, Uncle said, "Dago, I got a clear conscience. I can sleep 'til six!"

Dago was an early riser and would sit on the slop pail and braid ropes. There were ropes around that place that he manufactured for years. He was a good braider and could tie every kind of knot imaginable.

One time he decided to follow behind his little shipment to Sioux City in the caboose on the train. Everybody was reading a paper, so he decided to be fashionable and take up a paper for himself. The conductor tapped Dago's paper and said, "It's upside down! Dago snapped back with, "Anybody can read right side up!"

Rusty was crowded for pasture and was no longer able to handle Dago's cows. Therefore, the cattle were trailed from Rusty's place to 25 miles south of Eagle Butte. Dago and Dick undertook the job of trailing them. It was a long way, and took 5 days. This is how Dago managed to get involved with Uncle Vernon and my Aunt Esther. He divided his time between working at the ranch to watch for his livestock and staying up town where the good cooking was, always working for his board and room. Dago had a stroke on the ranch south of Eagle Butte and wasn't found for two days. He lived for about another year, but he was never the same, understandably so...

Dago gave me his old saddle, which seemed to be his prize possession. I accepted it with a great deal of gratitude, although it was totally worthless! At that time he revealed to me that he did, indeed, have a home that consisted of a house and corral on 320 acres. He had sold it to a young lady that he deemed special. Her name was Patricia Miller, daughter of old Pat Miller.

Old Dago had total mistrust of banks and carried his money in a Bull Durham sack in his shirt pocket for emergency purposes. He had time to dispose of his livestock before he passed over to the other side. But what he did do with all the money he hoarded those past 70 years? I'm thinking there is a very large stash in safe keeping somewhere on the Moreau River, including four double eagles.

Chapter XVA
Dynamite

Several of the young men from the Eagle Butte area traveled to Moab, Utah to look for work. Charley Steen had discovered uranium and that little Mormon town became a boomtown pretty much like Deadwood did when gold was discovered in the Black Hills. If one was lucky, he could get a good-paying job in Moab. I, myself, traveled there with Buck West and Steve Joachim, but could not get a job because I was too young and had no skills at running machinery. After about two weeks I returned home. Andy and Willy Fischer, having found good-paying jobs, were among the several that stayed on. They also staked claims and worked them in their spare time. No drinking was allowed in that state, so steady as she goes with the work, because that was about all there was to do in those parts.

Andy became very skilled at setting charges with his dynamite, knowing how much to use and how long the fuse should be, and all such things as that. When he came back to Eagle Butte it was just natural for him to bring back three or four cases of those slick brown sticks of powder so that he could show off his skills, don't you know!

Dad had the school land rented on the little flat just south of the Green Grass School. The creek had dried up so he and Andy went down there with a willow crotch in order to "witch" for a likely spot to dig a well for the test auger. They got down six four-foot lengths and hit a rock, or some sort of obstacle. That stopped the progress of tapping into the good vein of water underneath. Andy hauled down a few sticks of his trusty powder and cleaned out the hole, but good! They set up a pump and tank there for the purpose of watering a bunch of our horses. I don't think that they drank there hardly at all. There was too much traffic with the Indian kids at the village below for the horses to stick around very long. Also, the case being, range horses were very territorial, and wanted to go farther west onto higher ground where the flies and mosquitoes were more easily avoided.

One Sunday afternoon Andy and his brother, Leo, myself, and a couple of other boys were driving around our little town looking for a little excitement. Someone in our group wondered what would happen if we threw a stick of dynamite in the old cinderblock toilet behind the Masonic Temple.

Just for laughs and giggles Andy put a cap and fuse on the stick and pitched her in the outhouse hole. We got back in the car and circled the block kind of slow awaiting the results. It was then that we spotted old Palmer Horseshoe limping over in that direction with a sense of urgency! We were all saying, "Oh no! We gotta warn him or he'll think there was something really bad in the beans!!!" About that time she goes Ka-Boom. Palmer was a hundred feet away and stopped in midair. It looked like that toilet lifted up in the air about 14 inches with cracks in every cinder block, but it settled down just pretty as you please!

The local residents came scampering around, but not too close to the toilet for fear of another explosion. Of course, there was much speculation about whether it could have been spontaneous combustion, etc. This mystery was never solved until just about right now!!!

Andy was working for my folks about the same time Dago Kelly was hanging around there. One Sunday Andy invited me to go fishing. Not having any luck with a pole, I suggested that maybe his blasting powder was getting old and we should try fishing with a big bang. I don't remember for sure how it went, but I think the first time he tied three sticks to a board and floated it toward the middle of the pond. I do remember a geyser of water shot skyward about 30 feet! I also remember about five bullheads floated to the top of the water. Andy was more than just a little disappointed with the results, so he went back and got six sticks, I think, bound them together, affixed the cap and fuse and gave the bundle of sticks and pitched the package out into the water.

Andy and I were standing on the fill of the dam when the spark hit the powder, and I could feel the earth move like a California earthquake!

We sure depleted the population of bullheads! No big ones, though because there were thousands of little bullheads in this small stock dam causing overpopulation. The water was stale and smelled terrible. Cows would walk right past this water in search of a drink. Later on the fishing was very good in this old stock dam, and the livestock readily drank from it. Our devilish prank turned out to be of much value for both man and beast---and fish!

Chapter XVI
Johnson Family

Curley is my friend. He has hundreds of friends. There were six children in the family, and Curley was the only boy. His sister, Edie, said that the 5 sisters would all go to the river to swim every day. When asked if Curley swam, too, she replied, "If we could have caught him at the river, we would have drowned him!"

Curley's full name is Anthony Lamont Johnson. His dad said if he didn't settle down by the time he was 33 years old he was going to throw up his hands. His mother said, "He's my only son. I've got to stick with him!"

On Saturday nights the sisters watched their clocks. They figured by 10:00 o'clock he would probably be in jail, and they could quit worrying about him, and have fun at the dance! Curley was very little sugar and a whole lot of spice. Some people ran to him. This one thing I know for sure---if he shakes his hand in friendship, he will be your friend for life.

> A hundred miles to town and back
> I'd hurry if I could
> I've got an awful headache
> The booze was too darn good!

The first time I remember laying eyes on Curley, I was about 7 years old. I was riding in the back seat of the old black sedan while my dad was driving around up on the big flat near Fox Ridge. We were looking for horses just east of the Art Schrempp spread. We spotted a lone rider off in the distance, so Dad drove in his direction. It was Curley riding a piebald bronc with a bosal hackamore.

Dad asked if he needed a drink of water. Curley said, "You got any beer? It was during prohibition, and he was all of 14! The answer from my Dad was "No!" and the conversation lead to the horse. The old piebald had the hair rubbed off under the jaw from rough handling, which usually meant that the horse had just one or two rides on him. Dad asks, "How old is he?" Curley replied, "He's just a two yearling!" that response stuck in my memory for all time, as the normal answer would have been "two-year old."

Curley was 15 miles from home, which in this case was his front yard. His door opened on the south side of the house. He rode horseback more miles backwards than most people did frontwards, and we bumped in to each other a lot in our travels. We traveled together at times, and were business partners at times.

He was mischievous, and always a prankster, so even though he raised his share of the dickens, everything that happened in the entire country that wasn't taught in Sunday school, was blamed on him. He just took the rap for everything.

Halloween was a time when kids could pull all sorts of stunts without getting into too much trouble. It was just expected. We would hear about things our folks did on Halloween, like put the school marm's buggy on the roof of the school house, and the milk cow in the school house, etc. We inherited all sorts of tricks from our folks that we heard them talking about on the QT.

The biggest sport was tipping over the "outhouses." Some of the "men" in our little town of Eagle Butte would get together and move the toilet ahead of the hole so the would-be obstructers would "fall in" in the attempt to push it over. This would be done on the darkest of nights. One can only imagine what the smell was like if, heaven forbid, they were trapped in the outhouse wastage.

On one Halloween night a friend, Lee, and I decided it was too far to town, so we decided that we would just go down to the little Indian camp at Green Grass and tip over a few outhouses there. On the way down, we got to thinking that if we tied our throw ropes together, dallied them, and rode, one to each side of the toilet at a dead run, we could make quick work out of a whole lot of toilets in a hurry.

We hit the very first one at a pretty good clip, with our ropes flipped high to allow for leverage. Down she came! Instant kindling along with one screaming squaw pulling up her pants! We headed for home, not sparing the horses. I don't think that my heart started beating again until we got back to our barn!

To this day, or until they read this, they think that Curley Johnson did it! Who else would think of such a thing? What I'm saying is, everything got blamed on Curley.

Most all French-blooded Indians either went to Cheyenne Agency or a Catholic School. Curley being 1/8 Indian, belonged to this group. He made friends fast because he was highly sought after to entertain the troops.

He was attending school at Stephan Mission. He was running low on cash, so being an enterprising young man, he went to the kitchen and "borrowed" a couple loaves of bread and some peanut butter to supply his new found enterprise which was selling sandwiches to the other students! Some of the students didn't have the 25 cents to buy one of those delicacies, and surely it was one of them that squealed on Curley to Father Casber!

Curley did his penance and he was warned that his punishment would be severe if he got caught doing anything underhanded and Unchristian again.

Curley and 43 other boys were sent to mass, but the priest hadn't showed up yet. Curley thought that it would be a shame to waste the confessional! It just so happened that there were two brothers, George and Ed Wolf that certainly needed to get something off their shoulders. So Ed, unsuspectingly, unloaded his sins on Father Curley's shoulders! Sometimes Curley doesn't talk real plain, and when Ed got done with his confession, Curley said, "Say 10 dot dam our Fathers and 10 Hail Mary's." This sort of "gave him away." Ed left out of there with a grin, and in came George. George is just getting into clearing his conscience when the warning was given, "Here comes the priest!"

Somebody has always got to ruin Curley's fun. He got sent to the big round table where Father Casber and six other priests were waiting. Father Casber said, "Tony, (the name the priest preferred to use) We're going to send you home. You are a bad influence."

Well, Tony, having no money, no phone to use, or any way to reach his folks, went to the music store and "borrowed" a spoon-shaped mandolin. This he sold for $15, which he used to buy a bus ticket, which cost $9. He traveled to Gettysburg where he ran into his Uncle, Tommy Claymore. Tommy was headed for Yakima, Washington. Tony told his uncle of his dilemma, and Tommy took him all the way home to his parents' home on the Moreau River.

Chauncey and Edith were very disappointed in their little Tony. Grant Iron Lightning and Chauncey had a band of sheep on shares. They were wintering the flock and had a wagon on Pretty Creek. A 17-year-old boy was the camp tender. Chauncey thought it would be good penance for Tony to just go up there and help out.

You know, things get pretty dull around a sheep camp in negative 10-degree weather where the cramped quarters barely allow for one man to turn around. Tony was the dishwasher and Butch was the woodchopper. Well, Tony, who had just finished the dishes, opened the Dutch door of the sheep wagon to throw out the dishwater. But, he just can't quite resist the temptation to dump the water on Butch instead! This kid is tough, and he ain't about to let nobody dump dirty water on him on a cold morning! He picked up a fresh ax-cut piece of firewood and pitched it right into the center of Tony's forehead, sort of exposing his skill. This, of course, caused much bleeding.

Now Tony was seeing red and he decides to select from one of the three firearms in the wagon so that he can blow Butch's head off. There was a 30-30, a 410 shotgun, and a 22. He loaded the 410, aimed at Butch's head and squeezed. Well, Butch had become older and wiser by the minute, and he ducked his head. Tony hit him in the arm, and the buckshot followed the sleeve of his sheepskin all the way up his arm to his back. When Tony shot him, he made two summersaults uphill!

Tony had a change of heart, and, forgetting about the blood running off his forehead, he saddled Nigger to strike out and look for his dad. Chauncey went up to Bernard Anderson's and asked him to haul Butch to Dr. Cramer. The doctor proceeded to dig buckshot out of Butch's arm and back. The whole cleaning and patching cost Tony's dad $1500.

As a result of the fracas, there was a hearing with Judge Burns presiding. Judge Burns ruled self-defense. The family will hereafter call the site of the incident Cuckoo Ridge.

A different incident occurred when Curley was tending to 1500 ewes. This was the historically severe winter of 1949 when the roads were all blocked with snow and transportation was limited to saddle horse, work team or airplane. It was 31 degrees below zero, and Chauncey rode into camp to see how things were going. Curley was still snug as a bug in the sheep wagon. Chauncey inquired as to why the sheep were still bedded down with no shelled corn having been fed yet. Curley said he hated to get them off the bed grounds because they were still bedded down. Chauncey took the broom handle and broke the thermometer and said, "There, you don't have anything to look at!" Curley was soon to graduate from sheep herder school and look for bigger and better things.

(Note: Curley gave me his old bobsled, which was in need of repair. My purpose was to teach his son, C.L., how to harness and drive a team. This was never done. I still have that sled. Mel)

During the never-ending blizzards of that year Curley helped his dad feed the cows and sheep with a good team of horses and a bobsled. Every other day Curley would travel nine miles to highway 65 to pick up ten 100-pound burlap bags of cow cake. In order to have drinking water and water for cooking, Edith would take her washtub outside and heap it with snow to melt. That water yielded about 2 inches of water to the tub full of snow. It had to be strained with a dishtowel to get the sediment out of it. This was a never-ending and tedious task. Edith would promise Curley "waffles" if he would take the cream can and go by the well after his cake run. After an eighteen-mile round trip for his ten bags of cake and loading a cream can full of water, a warm house and waffles must have been pure heaven!

An airplane equipped with skis flew around to area ranchers to deliver mail and check to see if anyone was sick, or if there was an emergency. Very few people took advantage of this service unless there truly was an emergency.

Other than sending the message to the trucker to haul more cake and stack it along the road for a continued supply, the answer to the pilot of the little Piper Club was, "No, we don't need a thing."

All things come to pass and Chauncey made his mark at Marty Mission at Wagner. He boarded with Billy Rittenhouse at Timber Lake to finish educating the teachers along the path to higher education!

Curley has a record of surviving 25 car crashes, caused mostly by very high speeds. There was maybe only one fatality. In September of 1950 Curley, Jim Brooks and Curley's sister, Betty, were riding to Dupree with Norman Hennigan in his new model '98 Oldsmobile. They hit a steel bridge head-on. Norman was killed. Jim Brooks was badly injured. Betty was bruised and shaken. But Curley's army of guardian angels worked overtime!

One time Curley ran under a gravel truck in his new Chevy. No Curley – nobody at the scene! It was unbelievable that anyone could live through such a wreck! A search party was formed and relatives were panicking. This occurred at about 2:00 am. Well, Curley had just walked away from the wreck, crossed the road afoot, went to Homer Brook's house, climbed the stairs, found a bed to his liking and went to sleep. He came down stairs to greet the Brooks family at 3:00 pm, ruffled, but rested!

On the third drunken driving charge, he was brought before Judge Hershrude. The judge said, "Tony, I've got to do something with you before you kill somebody! Thirty days in the county jail and a $100 fine!"

Rusty Anderson was the Dewey County Sheriff at the time, and he never locked the jail cell. He gave Curley special privileges to eat with the family. Although his career was colorful, and he "borrowed" a few things, this is the only time I remember Curley "doing time".

The ladies were chaining up their dogs and hiding their daughters when Curley came to town, so he decided to do something honorable and patriotic like joining the Marine Corps. Even this started out on shaky ground. A busload of recruits was headed for Aberdeen for induction. Curley, the self-appointed entertainer, offered to share his ever-present fifth of good Canadian whiskey. The warrant officer suspected that the resulting boisterous behavior was due to drinking. So he heads to the back of the bus for inspection. Curley sure didn't want to be seen with no bottle, so he opened the window a crack and gave her a good toss – right through the window of a highway patrolman's vehicle!

This wasn't a good deal, and there were all kinds of repercussions too numerous to mention. This was in 1951 and this little marine probably was just a little tougher from all the calisthenics he did because of the whiskey toss!

Anthony Lamont Johnson was picked for automatic weapons and was an A4 machine gun specialist. He was also a gunner instructor.

He was wounded in battle and on his way back to the hospital aboard the ship, a cute little nurse bent over to give a wounded comrade a shot. With that tempting target at such close range, Curley just couldn't resist the impulse! He reached out and pinched her right on the back side. The nurse let out a scream and said, "He's crazy! He's crazy!" – more trouble for Curley. The commanding officer gave Curley an ultimatum, "You can go back to the front lines or I'm going to give you a Section 8!"The easy way out would surely have been the Section 8, but not the honorable way. Curley is a man with a great deal of pride. After a 40-day rehabilitation, this tough little marine from the Cheyenne Reservation went back to the front lines for 12 months and six days of pure frozen hell. He and his fellow marines lived in foxholes with high humidity and 35-degree below weather. Cockroaches and mice huddled around the little oil heaters.

Curley was responsible for hundreds of enemy casualties. Donnie Livermont testified to the fact that he would leap out of his foxhole with his A4 and scream "Tum and det me, you dot dam dukes!" and he'd actually pile them up like cord wood.

When the troops would take position to "dig in," they would dig on the frozen ground until their hands bled, but there was no way and they would entrench themselves with dead bodies.

When the U.S. 155s would fire their bursts for support, they would cover themselves with dead bodies to avoid being hit by shrapnel. At one critical point in a pitched battle, 3800 in Curley's unit were ordered to take a hill that held 5 divisions of 20,000 enemies. They took the hill, but 3,420 marines were killed or wounded. Curley's army of guardian angels was at work again. He was one of the 380 that came off that hill alive and well. He had a calibration device that was supposed to afford great accuracy for his A4. He detached it. In his words, "If you took time to calibrate, you were dead!" Anthony Lamont Johnson was awarded with a purple heart. It later burned up in a house fire.

Curley made himself a promise that "If I ever get out of that war alive I am going to drink whiskey 'til I can't hold no more." He kept his promise!

When Curley was discharged, he was enjoying a little rest in a large hotel on Market Street in San Francisco. There were several large swans swimming in a pool. Being a little "full," he decided to have a swim with the swans – uniform and all! He jumped in with his famous war chant, "EEEE Ha! Bawl and squall, let the maggots crawl up and down the wall!" No problem. He was greeted with applause and a helping hand out of the pool. He was a marine!

Curley's father said that if he didn't settle down by the time he was 33 he was going to throw up his hands and surrender. Curley married Joyce Hill when he was 32. He hasn't touched a drop of liquor since.

His famous quote was, "I'm gonna get a tase of tuarts, a pink Tadillac, a blonde cutie and tut out for Talifornia!" He got the pink Cadillac, but the rest never happened.

Curley lost his daughter, Bobbie, his wife, Joyce, and then his son, C.L., who was killed in a car crash. C.L.'s funeral was one of the biggest ever held in South Dakota, with an attendance of 2400, plus 183 horseback riders who waited outside the large auditorium. They were there to escort C.L. to his final resting place. There were dignitaries in limousines and people from every walk of life at his final farewell, along with hundreds of American Indian friends.

C.L. was a world champion bull rider and had appeared in 21 movies. Kevin Costner helped to get his stunt license in 90 days because of his superb performance on his paint horse in the movie *Dances with Wolves.*

Chuck Norris was a personal friend of his, and C.L. appeared in several episodes of *Walker, Texas Ranger.*

Curley's daughter, Frankie, is also a master horsewoman. She trains horses and has been in several suicide races. In one of these races, her sign language spoke louder than words! It was at the Fort Pierre Stanley County Fairgrounds during a suicide race. She slid off a 300-foot shale bank far in the lead of the pack by about 7 lengths. One of the obstacles on the course was a deep water hole through which all horses were required to ford.

Frankie was unable to check her mount, and he lunged in head first, taking in some water and throwing his head up to smack Frankie right in hers. When a horse breathes in water with hard breathing such as in a race, they tend to faint or pass out. In her dizzy state she had to jump into the water and hold her horse's head up. She and her mount finally splashed their way out of the water. She leaped back on and finished the race. This, by the way, was done bareback from start to finish! When she crossed the finish line the announcer made the big mistake of asking her how the water was. In front of a grandstand full of people, she gave him the famous "hand signal" in reply. The race was good, but this was the highlight of the day. I'm not sure who the announcer was, but I think his first name is Don!

Curley and I did quite a lot of business together as partners. Sometimes we were trading horses, sheep and hogs, but mostly haying together, or buying hay for resale. Curley had a big New Holland baler with a Wisconsin engine in it that would really eat up the hay. It made nice heavy bales. We would buy surplus stands of hay from ranchers up and down the river, and hire a crew to pitch the hay from the big loose haystacks into the baler by hand. There would be someone stacking the bales on the truck as they fell from the bale chamber. This was beautiful green hay that had very little exposure to the sun except for the sides and tops of the large stacks.

Truman Parker worked for us at that time and was a good, dependable hand with the machinery. He was in charge of the hay going into the front end of the baler with the help of Oliver LaBlanc, Jerry and Johnny Thompson, and others. It took at least four good men—two to the team pitching into the baler. This work was extremely physical because we would work steady for 5 or 6 hours to the shift, unless Truman shut the baler down for service or repairs.

Gus Clausen was in charge of taking the bales that dropped out of the back end. He and Jacky Fischer and myself would stack seven high on the trucks. We did this all one winter long, until there was no more hay available to purchase. The demand was so good for this high quality western wheat grass hay that we could get a very good price for it. Most of it went to North Dakota, and the balance was sold to the Sioux Tribe for their beef herd. This was hard work, but we kept a lot of people in spending money, and made a little for ourselves.

Curley acted as agent both in buying and selling the hay. He also collected the money after sales. He never ever beat me out one red cent. He was a good partner.

We were having to haul some of this hay through Charley Peterson's pasture where he had around 250 appaloosa mares. There was just no grass left for them to eat. Those old mares would follow me on the run in hopes for getting a bite of hay, until I would out distance them in the truck. On the third trip through there, I couldn't stand to see them go hungry any more, so I pulled my ropes off the bales that secured the load and made a "sharp left turn," tumbling the bales from the bed of the truck. One day's feed for 250 horses, compliments of the Cheyenne River Sioux Tribe!

Our hog enterprise was not good. Curley ran his on the Moreau River, once in a while dumping a load of screenings out for them, and I ran mine south of Eagle Butte on my Uncle Jim's place. We found out the hard way that one couldn't run hogs like cattle! They would just keep wandering off away from where they were supposed to be fed, and would end up in someone else's frying pan or checking account. I was down south one day putting oats in a feeder for my hogs when I heard a shot fired. Then I saw a tractor with a loader swinging a hog dangling by its hind legs off the bucket. I don't know who it was, and I didn't want to know. It went west.

Antone and Fred Kost helped me haul sheep home from Gettysburg. I added this to the three hundred ewes I'd bought at Faith. I had a good start building my band of sheep, which now totaled about 460 ewes. I was sort of burning the candle at both ends at that time, covering quite a lot of ground, so I asked Curley and Gus Clausen to help eye and tag these ewes. This was always necessary before lambing. This took place at night in a big shed. About that time we were hearing rumors about stolen sheep! The neighbors were driving by my pens real slow-like and also a sheriff and then a Stock Grower Investigator. My Aunt Betty heard a rumor in Naeve's Grocery Store that I was stealing sheep! Two days later my old friend, Slim Berndt, the Dewey County Deputy Sheriff, met me at the corral gate and says, "I sure hate to do this, but I got this search warrant, and I've got to go look through your band of sheep. Two of your neighbors are losing sheep and we are checking everybody's bands for strays."

After looking them over carefully, he says, "Sorry for the inconvenience, but your band is clean. Have you sold any?" "Nope," was my reply, "I'm buying, not selling. Haven't sold any."

The law went up to Hansmeiers Wool Warehouse at Newell and cut open the sacks containing my wool to check the color of paint on the wool. It was impounded for that purpose. Sheep brands were registered with the Stockgrowers and a specific type of paint was used to dab onto the wool with the owner's mark. Everybody in a specified area would agree to use a certain color so as not correlate with the neighboring flock in case of a mix up. The sheep could be run through a sorting gate and sorted in short order just by glancing at the color. My brand was Heart Open A, and my color was orange. After examining my fleeces, whoever was doing the examining never found any color but orange, so I guess I didn't steal any sheep!

A year after that incident with the law, Marvin Mortenson was working for me. I had made a deal with him to get a share of the lambs over 100%. He worked very diligently and ended his count with 155% because there were a lot of twins. The day he turned the sheep out to summer pasture, a bunch of coon dogs got into them and killed 191 head of ewes and lambs. Sometimes the mother, sometimes the baby lamb. This was a terrible day for me.

I had to ride all over the country and shoot the maimed sheep that had not yet succumbed. We ended up with 76 bum lambs that we had to bottle feed from that mess. On the very morning that this happened I spotted a bloody coon hound bitch loping off toward the direction of town. I was riding my good horse, Rickles. I took my rope down and roped the dog. I was very angry and had no wits about me. I was loping up the road with the dog dangling behind. She got wrapped around a guard rail post and jerked my horse down, breaking the tree in my saddle, as well as the dog's neck. I was well acquainted with the owner, and I drug the dead dog to his door, pitching him the end of the rope.

The man who owned those dogs was a very good man. He was deeply saddened about what happened and did his share about taking care of the problem. I have no animosity toward him.

There was also a very large German Shepherd dog that I suspected was in on the slaughter. The owner of this dog must have somehow heard about what happened and just as I rode up to his trailer, he grabbed his dog and went inside with me right behind him. My temper is still at the boil. He said, "Mel, I don't let my dog run. He's tied to the clothes line at night." I had leather gloves on and grabbed the dog's collar. I reached to his jaw and pried his mouth open to find wool stuck between his teeth. The man took his big pet outside and tied him to the clothes line and told me to shoot him. He walked away and started to cry. Mister, there was no way I could shoot that dog. I left with instructions for him to keep his dog at home.

This big German dog may have been the ringleader of the whole bloodthirsty ordeal because he was caught killing sheep in another band south of town. The owners of these sheep had a little housedog that came around cycle. The man tied his little Innocent to the corner of his truck and when old big German came around to investigate, he was shot dead, at close range. The dog was so big that the man couldn't load him by himself, and had to get help. He gave me his restraining halter for my birthday.

Sheep are bad news for Melvin. I never owned another. Pigs are no better!

Just days before Lee gave me the collar that he took off the dead German Shepard, I was greeted with another German Shepard running around in my yard. From a distance it looked just like the dog that was in my sheep. German Shepards pretty much all look alike. I shot it. It went home. My neighbor lady, Casey Keller came to call. It was her dog. She didn't bother to knock. She saved the dog. I'm in the doghouse!

Chapter XVII
Work Teams

In 1943, my dad bought a hay sweep that had Montgomery Ward stamped on the main frame. It cost $125 and came unassembled. Included were wrenches at hand and instructions. It took him two full days to make it look like a piece of haying machinery.

Shortly after he had the teeth polished, he turned the hay bucking job over to me. I was 7 years old. I was so proud to hold the lines in my little hands and buck hay. The bucker, as dad called it, was 12 feet wide, with a tongue and single tree on each side. This meant that the horses were about 14 feet apart. In order to hold their pattern, a rope was tied to the ring of the snaffle bit from one horse to the other. Our old team was composed of Tony on the left, and Dan on the right. Dad would get the team hooked to the bucker and get everything adjusted. He'd take his three-horse hitch, hook on to the 5-foot mower and rake. He'd proceed to mow nearby so that he could keep an eye on his apprentice son.

The bucker had a steel pipe running full length with steel wheels attached on either side. The little wheels were 20 inches high and 5 inches wide. They ran steel on steel on the pipe, which served as an axle. Much oil was required to keep things lubricated. Part of the original equipment was a clicker squirt oil can that rested in a saddle especially made for the purpose of holding the can. I was cautioned to oil the wheels every few bucker piles, or they would get hot and possibly start a fire.

When you are a boy of seven, you just have to learn how to whistle! I was doing my best, but not mastering the art enough to be recognized as a tune. Here comes Dad across the hay field at a trot, with the rake and sickle bar both in transport position. He drove right up to me. The first thing he does is start to lecture me about oiling more often. I'm all worried and tell him that I just did oil the wheels. He looked at them and says, "They sure do look oily!" he screws the lid off the squirt can and says, "It's only half full of oil. I can't figure out why the wheels are squeaking!" I think that it took him 4 or 5 days before he figured out the squeaky noise was his young son learning how to whistle!

After a steady diet of about 10 days of pushing hay into piles, I began to get bored with my job. I tried to think of ways to make it more exciting. I figured out that if I would climb up on the steady accumulation of hay on the bucker teeth, I could ride the pile to great heights! Boy! This was fun! It also presented a problem. I made the piles so big that when I backed the team away from the hay, the rope tied between the two horses would not clear the pile! The horses were just the same as tied there! If the team was so inclined, however to make a huge effort to back up, the rope would drag over the top and I would be free to go again. In my frustration I decided to try getting by the horses' heads and push back on the bridles. Tony backs up pretty good this way, but Dan stays planted!

I walk over to Dan and he squints at me like, "I ain't doing nothing for you, you little squirt!" I see that look of defense in his eyes, so, I spit on his nose! Boy! Did I get action! He flew back and almost broke out the tongue, scattering hay about 30 feet! This went on for the rest of the day, now! This ain't for making neat bucker piles, and it also ain't good for horse manners.

The next morning when my dad was harnessing, he touched old Dan's nose. The horse flew back in the stall and broke the halter rope! Dad never could figure out why that horse was so sensitive around the nose, and even though I decided to never do that again, it was my secret!

All the stacking was done by hand. We had a system that we used to roll the hay up into a huge stack with ropes. Four 100-foot x 1-inch ropes were laid over hay that was bucked up to make the base of the stack. The ropes were attached to the hooks on sawed-in-half single trees driven flush with the ground. Then, four good-sized bucker piles would be brought in from the field and positioned on the ropes. The last pile was pushed hard against the others for compaction. The four ropes were then unhooked, and the braided ends were joined with a clevis on a cable where a separate team at the far end of the stack would pull the big roll of hay up onto the stack. This team had to be calm and good pullers because when this process was repeated over and over again, the horses had to pull the hay up off the tapered end as high as 25 or 30 feet, causing leverage to pull them off their front feet. Once these stacks were completed and topped out, they would "keep" for 10 or 12 years without much spoilage.

In the winter time this hay was hauled home, as time permitted. This was also done with a team, hay rack, and the mighty pitchfork. The hay in these big stacks was packed so tightly that it could not be pulled apart with a fork, so a hay knife was used to slice about four feet off the end until you reached the bottom of the stack, allowing a fork to be used.

If a person was cold when he started filling his wagon load, it was a guaranteed cinch that he'd be warm after he got done! It was a comfortable ride home burrowed down in the load of hay.

My dad always had a green puller (young unbroken horse) on his mower. His method was unusual because he worked three abreast, hooked to an evener that calculated the leverage he needed to subdue the unbroken horse. The ranker the horse, the more he made him pull. Dad was a great teamster, and it didn't take him long to get one of those old snorts' number on a mowing machine. The extra horse power was needed because he sawed the tongue off the rake and attached it to the pedestal of the mower that the seat was bolted to. Along with the three horses he was driving, he would reach behind him and set his hand on the pedal that dumped the rake. This was a very modern system for the time because raking was normally done in a separate operation, with a man driving a team hooked to the rake, sulky style.

We were usually at least four miles from home when we hayed because the breaks along the creek did not yield like the big flats off the creek bottoms. So, my mother had to pack a lunch, complete with a canvas water bag or a jug with a gunny sack tightly sewn around it. This would be dipped in water for the purpose of keeping the drinking water cool. It worked—barely!

We would always end our lunch in the shade of the hay rack, and Dad would take his fifteen-minute nap "so the horses could rest."

Dad had two misfit horses, which he called Noname and Stinky. One was a stag and one was an original (had a testicle in him that could not be found). Those horses were not of much value, and couldn't be sold, so Dad made slaves out of them. The only way Dad could harness Noname was to wire his ears together with baling wire and put a screen nose basket on his nose. The stag he called Stinky could not pull his penis all the way in and when he got mad, he would discharge urine all over the place. This was the meanest pair of horses I ever saw, but my dad got more work out of those two horses than any four good ones.

When Dad left home with this team, Mother always worried and asked him to please be home before dark! This team was used to slide many a Fresno load of dirt over dam fills. The madder they got, the harder Dad worked them.

One morning Mother never got the lunch bucket strapped in the wagon, and Dad never noticed. He had the wagon tongue pointed at a snubbing post so he could tie Noname and Stinky to the post while hooking them to the wagon. I suppose he was preoccupied. He got in the wagon and pulled the slip knots. He was circling the wagon in a tight circle at a pretty good clip when Mother came running out to deliver his lunch. It looked to Mother like if you got within a hundred feet of that dust cloud you were dead! Dad just kept hollering "Throw it in! Throw it in!" She threw the gallon syrup pail full of his lunch in the general direction of the wagon and went back into the house! Dad left without his lunch!

We had some really pretty grey draft colts, and Dad had a couple stalled in the barn. He had actually ridden them both some, but his intentions were to break them to drive. They were really look-alikes and of about the same size.

Dad left for town for the weekend and left myself and Bennett Cook with the responsibility of feeding the cows and calves. This amounted to pitching on and unloading two big hayrack loads of hay. Then the hay would be pitched down along the feed rack for 80 heifer calves. When we watered the team and stalled them, we untied the two greys to lead to the water tank. We got to thinking that maybe we could entertain ourselves by hooking the colts up to the wagon to relieve the boredom for both us and the horses. On the way back to the barn Bennett spied the old cow hide hanging on the corral gate on the west side of the barn. He suggested that maybe we could make a toboggan out of the frozen hide. This is going to take some time, but I agree that it's worth a go! So, we take the stiff old hide down and nail a 2 x 4 to one end with the hair down and the frozen fold pointed up to sort of serve as an end gate. We wired a single tree to the 2 x 4 and we were all set to go sledding in our one-horse toboggan! We harnessed the seemingly tamer of the two greys and led him out of the barn and hooked him up with Bennett promising to hold fast until I was mounted and had the lines in hand. I learned that day why people used blinders on the head gear of a work horse! I'm sure if that horse could have seen what was going on behind him, we would have never got him hooked up to that dead thing!

I gave the signal and popped the lines across the back of ole grey. The race was on! Out south and a big circle over west to the dam and across the Green Grass Road and back home through snow banks across draws over snow banks, uphill and down hill at a dead run! The fold in the hide caught the snow and bent my end gate down so every now and then I had to "take a new seat" or get covered up. The snow was most definitely an improvement to the ride because those frozen cow chips felt like they were coming through the hide and biting my backside!

Bennett saddled up Tuffy and came to join the chase, but he couldn't get that horse within 500 yards of me! After about an hour of this, ole grey just plumb ran out of gas and quit me right in the middle of a deep snow bank. I had to let him blow a little before he could be coaxed out of the snow bank and head back to the barn. We unharnessed a very tired and sweat-soaked broke-to-drive grey horse! Dad rode home on Sunday afternoon to check things out. We had to explain to him what we had done. Did he scold?

Nope. As long as we didn't have to go anyplace to be entertained or it didn't cost anything, he didn't care, and he was actually amused by it!

The grey toboggan-pulling horse turned out to be one of the best horses that I ever drove. Dad named him Dick. The mate to him, Dumpy, was slow and lazy, so we split them up because they wouldn't pull together as a team. We teamed Dick with Captain, a horse that worked at the same pace, and was able to pull his fair share of the load.

Dad pastured a white mare for the Catholic priest at Eagle Butte, Father Golden. She ran with a big Percheron stud and his bunch of mares. In two years she had two horse colts from the mating. Dad asked Father Golden if he would sell the two bay colts out of this mare. He was thinking that the priest would probably give them to him for running the mare all that time. After the horse trading was over, the two bay colts cost Dad $50, which he really hated to pay. It turned out to be a very good investment, however. Those two little full brothers weighed in at about 1450 pounds each, and could pull more for their weight than any other team in that country. They were named Cap and Dan and my dad was very proud of them. They broke more double trees, tugs and hame straps than any two teams on our place put together.

The winter of '49 was a doozy. Dad ordered cake form his brother, Vernon, and Bobby Dupris hauled it down from the east road. The north road was totally blocked. The snow in the creek was so deep that Bobby missed the crossing and was just sort of sitting on top of 6 feet of snow, which filled the creek. We unloaded six of the eight tons of cake off the truck and onto the bobsled—20 bags at a time. We hauled them to the barn for unloading. We left 2 tons in the front of the truck box. Dad said, "I'm going to try to pull you out of there." I am only 14 years old, and I think to myself, "Dad, you're nuts!" Bobby, the big, tall happy-go-lucky Indian boy just drops his head and laughs!

Dad pulled the pin on the double trees and held them in one hand while backing the little team up to the truck. He hooked on to the front bumper of the truck, and gave the shrill whistle that he had manufactured from his own lips. This he used when he really needed to have his team pull hard. That whistle prepared the team for what was expected.

Dad was a firm believer in swinging his team on a dead pull to allow for the advantage of forward motion. He whistled and hollered, "Cap! Dan!" The little team got right down on their bellies and dug their toes in, swinging the front of that truck sideways over the snow bank and out came the red Ford. Dad was so pleased that one would have thought that he'd pulled it out with his own two hands!

Dad and I batched during the winter for three years because Mother had to stay in town with the kids so that they could go to school. We had this ongoing contest to see who could unharness his horse the fastest. The loser was always rewarded with the job of doing the dishes! He could sweep the collar and harness of a horse in seconds, and I don't think he washed a dish for 3 years! I know I was faster than he, but I was just always a split second behind him in hanging the harness on the peg.

The only new saddle Dad owned was an E.C. Lee, which was made in Fort Pierre. I bought his old saddle, which was also made by E.C. Lee, and was nearly worn out.   Both these saddles were single-rigging saddles. Dad thought that a back cinch was a total waste of leather and hardware. Besides, it took twice as long to saddle a horse. He was always racing me to see who could saddle and mount first, with me, being on mostly cold-backed, humpy broncs. Seems that he should have allowed for a 5-minute handicap, but no sir! He would mount up and ride off, leaving me with a bawling, pitching bronc in front of the barn. He would never look back, but I could almost see the grin on his face as he looked straight ahead. The loser of this contest got to mop the floor! I got pretty good at mopping the floor!

The threshing crew came to our place on an annual basis. This was a very exciting time for my brother and me because we were allowed to listen in on the wild conversations among the teamsters and spike pitchers.

Dad only had 38 acres, but it seems like we spent half the summer in that field. He would plow with a two-bottom sulky plow pulled by four horses abreast. I think that I was only 8 years old when I followed up with the two-section drag, walking along behind Scotty and Tony, our old faithful team. They knew more about the operation than I did. I sure got

216

tired of walking, but it was not at all safe to ride on a harrow. I was warned over and over again never to do that.

I remember that Dad sent all his broke teams to Iowa leaving us with only our old team and several halter-broke broncs. He hooked up a red roan and a black and ground drove them for 15 or 20 minutes. A trip was tied to each of their front legs, and with a little help from Homer and Sam Blue Coat, he managed to get them hooked up to the 7-foot McCormick drill. Away he went, driving those never-before-worked horses to the field, every once in a while tugging on the trip ropes to slow them down and keep them from running away. Homer and Sam followed up with the wagon, which was loaded with seed oats. They managed to get most of 20 acres planted that day! The first couple of rounds sort of went in a zigzag pattern, but after that, it went pretty well!

I don't remember ever having a crop failure. It seemed that we lived in that field, binding and shocking bundles in rows to cure for preparation of the exciting day that the threshing crew came to do our little crop of oats. There were several machines around, but the one I remember best is the machine operated by Raymond and Leif Moland.

When I was 13 I asked Dad if I could graduate from being a spike pitcher to having my own bundle rack. Dad bought a small bundle rack from my grandfather, Joe Fischer. I had already used it to haul hay in for $1 a load, and I was pretty stout for my age. Since the rack was only 8 x 14, it only held about half the bundles that the big racks held. My dad said that if I would take care of my own team, and could harness and unharness them by myself, I could go ahead. I felt like I was 10 feet tall! I was always a little short of stature, so I positioned two feed bunks in such a fashion that allowed me to lead my team between them, as I stood in the bunks to harness and unharness them. The teamsters took pride in their teams and curried them until they shined, making sure that their manes and tails were free of burrs and foreign matter.

I worked hard at my new responsibility and never missed my turn at the threshing machine throwing in every other bundle head first into the feeder house, keeping up with the man on the opposite side doing the same. I hauled 9 loads of bundles that day, causing me to get overheated and very sick.

The hardest job, I believe, was by far, the feeding the usual crew of 15 to 20 hungry men. They ate 3 meals a day, plus a morning and afternoon lunch, which was taken to the field by Mother and sister, Betty. I can still remember helping them and the hired girl, Nina Heffernan pick 10 chickens to fry for the crew. Usually about 20 baked-to-perfection pies and many dozen cookies came out of the oven of the old wood-burning range.

Gallons of coffee to wash down stacks of buttermilk pancakes, bacon and eggs by the dozen waited for the crew for the breakfast rush. Mother often made four big batches of pancakes. Greg Woods would tout the others by saying that he could probably eat more than anyone else. That he could! Palmer

Horseshoe said to Mom, "Rose, you make burned penacakes—just the way I like um!"

Fast and furious roared the big engine flywheel turning the belt that set the thrasher in motion to separate the grain from the straw. Dad and Valentine Joachim hauled the grain away to be stored in the granary.

One day, and it's over for me, as the crew moved on to the next neighbor. The routine would be repeated over and over again until all threshing in the neighborhood was done. Remaining in the fields where the crops had grown would be huge yellow straw piles to supplement the winter feed supply.

My dad was not one to waste an unnecessary motion, so to make unharnessing a quick job; he took the pole strap off the harness completely and snapped the back strap to the square on the market tug. He used a chain with a common slider to hook to the neck yoke so that when it came time to shed the harness, all that had to be unfastened was the buckle on the hame strap, the buckle on the belly band, the snap on the breast chain and the buckle on the collar. Only four places that could be reached without as much a shifting position.

This was really handy except when one came down the long hill going into the ranch on the Gerald Berndt property! This hill is steep, and without the pole strap hooked to the back straps there just weren't any brakes! When the bottom of that hill was reached one would be going flat out like one driving a stagecoach with a bunch of holdup men after you!

I only remember one wreck, all the time we were on the Starkey Ranch breaking teams to drive. I was bringing a load of hay home from over south of John Curtis's. I was nearly home when a rainstorm was closing in on me. I was going at a pretty good clip through a draw, figuring that my team couldn't pull the far side if it rained because the trail had a hardpan spot that would be so slippery the team would stall out on it. There was big gully wash at the bottom of the draw, and in my haste I misjudged my turn and dropped the back wheel of the hayrack into the gully. The hayrack tipped over into the gully with me pretty much buried underneath the hay. The horses went home with the running gear! I suppose if I hadn't panicked so much about getting out from under the two tons of hay, it would have been easier. That hay was heavy and I was pawing like a badger to get out of that dark, airless place. To make matters worse, I was 500 yards from the house and was darned good and soaked by the cloudburst that I was trying to outrun with the team!

Moisture-wise and crop-wise, 1950 was a good year. We spent so much time shocking grain and picking corn that we failed to get enough hay in, although we had quite a lot up in bucker piles. We had topped them out and left them in the field. Although the winter of 1950 and '51 was not as severe as the winter of '49, there were huge snow banks all over the countryside that had to be navigated around. Billy Maupin worked for us that year. Dad traveled three miles to the west and just south of where George Webb lived with his three-horse abreast hitch to haul hay from the bucker piles that had been left in the field.

The first two horses of the hitch were hooked like one would hook a regular two-horse hitch, with double trees, and the third horse, always one that he was breaking to drive, was tied hard to the left-hand corner of the hayrack to his own single tree. In this way, if the bronc decided to act up, dad could hold the gentle team back and let the bronc pull the whole works until he decided to behave himself. Those green horses didn't know how to handle themselves when they were pulling in deep snow, and would often flounder around until they went down. If this was the case, and you stopped, you were stuck and that meant a whole lot of shoveling to get unstuck. There was a very good chance that the runners on the bobsled would freeze down because they were at least warm, and sometimes even hot from friction. My dad's solution for that was to tie a good-sized rope around ole bronc's midsection with a Bowlin knot, through the bellyband and under the middle horse to the eye of the tongue of the sled. This way, if the horse went down, he would just simply pull him through the snow bank and stop long enough for the downed horse to get to his feet, and off he'd go again!

Hauling hay this way was a very hard task, and it took its toll on Dad. The snow was so deep, that the location of the bucker piles was sighted only by the mounds in the snow that had been caught by the hay piles. The piles were completely covered up. He would pull up to one of these snow mounds with the

221

team and hayrack mounted on a bobsled, take the scoop shovel and shovel the snow off the hay, then pitch on all he could reach the rack with. Then he'd pitch the balance of the hay out of the hole onto the snow and then pitch it again onto the hayrack. He would usually get 8 bucker piles of hay, which amounted to about 2 tons to the load. That heaped the hayrack up high in a huge pyramid.

The cane in the long ricks at home were no picnic, either! No matter how dry the cane bundles would be when stacked, it seems like they would sweat, and any snow that landed on them would melt and then freeze. These 10-foot bundles were carefully stacked, two bundles wide, butt end out, with the heads in the middle. They were almost impossible to get out of the stack with a pitchfork. I would help Billy jump on them to break them loose. Most of the bundles were loaded by hand. By the time a fellow would get a load of them on the rack, he would be soaking wet from sweat and the handling of snow-soaked bundles. I'll bet that Billy was very careful not to ever again take a job where the rancher had cane bundles!

The winter of '50, because of the hay shortage around the place, Dad decided to sort off 2 bunches of cows, forty head to the bunch, and put them out with the stud bunches. There were two different bands of mares. One bunch of about 80 was on the east side of Highway 63, and the other bunch of 65 was up Green Grass Creek, about 1 ½ miles southeast of the ranch. I went out and gathered the far bunch and brought them home to break trail for the cows, and then this band of 80 mares with 40 horned Hereford cows were taken back across the highway. This was a distance of 5 miles with the mares, anxious to get back to their home range, outdistancing the cows. My feet and hands were both frost bitten trailing these cows that day, and there was an eeriness about the weather, what with a ground blizzard going on, but the sun shining above.

I remember so well my dad sorting those cows. The stronger, younger cows carrying the most flesh went with the horses to fend for themselves. This included two cows of mine. I thought that I would never see them alive again. Those old horned Herefords survived by taking advantage of the horses pawing the snow off the grass. They would push their way in amongst the horses and steal the grass they uncovered. Those old range cows made out pretty good. They followed the horses around all winter, licking snow for water and eating whatever grass the horses would uncover for them. The cows actually made out better than the horses. The mares got pretty slab sided, but I don't think we lost any.

The days were getting longer in early March, and warmer, too. I rode out across to visit Russ Curtis and to see if my two cows were still alive. I spotted the horses and cows sunning themselves on the east slope of a high ridge. I picked my way around on high ground to avoid the snow in the draws. The horses seemed to be in a trance, barely acknowledging my presence. I counted 39 cows—one short! My two, branded on the left ribs with the big No Heart, were still there. On the way down the long ridge to the Moreau, I ran into a set of tracks—one cow, one pony! The tracks went right up to Madison's log house. George must have been hungry!

The river hadn't started to break up yet, and it was easily forded on solid ice. Russ was so glad to see me and was anxious to catch up on the goings on because he had not been to town for seven weeks. His only communication to the outside world was his old battery radio. He still had a big slab of side pork and potatoes, and he offered me up some. This along with hot coffee and fresh sourdough biscuits made a meal for a king, if the king was hungry!

Russ was insistent that I go to the barn with him to water my horse in the water tank. All the time he had a big grin on his face, like something was up! He says, "Come here!" and he opened the walk-through door on his horse barn. All I noticed at first was his fat, sleek team and his old saddle horse, Lucky. Then I spied this breedy little blood bay in the far stall with his mane and tail all combed out just so. There was my Tuffy horse! He was all fat and sassy. Russ knew I had been looking for my fine little bay saddle horse for nearly a year, and recognized him because he had seen me ride him. Tuffy had been running with a bunch of Bill Ewing's horses, and Andrew Dupris recognized the Bar Lazy S brand. He took him to his place with some of the Dupris' horses. Russ went down to pick him up, and had had him since December. I can't imagine anyone pitching hay in one end of a horse and cleaning manure out of the other all winter unless there was need for the horsepower!

Tuffy was out of one of the hot-blood mares that Dad got from Orbeck. This gelding showed his breeding and was very pretty, but also high lifed and a handful to break. Dad didn't get along with this horse at all. When Dad was halter breaking him he had to lead another horse in the stall along side of him so he could even untie him to lead him to water. If he didn't do that, little Tuffy would pull back for all he was worth and lunge at his human adversary with ears pinned back and teeth bared! I don't have any idea why, but I got along good with him, and my dad agreed to trade him to me for two young geldings that I had started.

Thinking back about Tuffy, I remember that about ten years earlier, Dad had come home late, and in the conversation with Mother while he was eating supper, he said that he was sure tired, but he had to lead that little devil of a bay horse to water before he could go to bed. The creek behind the barn was running, and that being the closest source, was where we were watering our horses. I said, "Daddy, I already watered him." And, I had! I was a little boy 5 years old at the time. Horses have such an instinct about them. If a person is afraid, it is passed on to the animal in the same degree. This is especially true if one is holding something, which is attached to their mouth or head, like driving lines or bridle reins. Believe me, they can sense your tension and will act accordingly. As a little boy, I had no reason to fear this horse and he could sense that. He had absolutely no fear of me because I was no threat to him.

I had had no trouble untying the bowlin knot on the big halter rope, leading the horse to water and back and in to the barn stall. My dad just couldn't believe that this rank little bronc would let me walk in beside him to untie him. Dad lit the lantern and went to investigate. The proof was there! I hadn't yet mastered the bowlin knot that Dad always tied, and there was good old slipknot in its place!

Russ really wanted to buy that horse, but although he was 10 years old by then, he was still a bit of a handful. Russ always rode his old Lucky horse at a fast walk. This was not at the gear that Tuffy used. This was one of those horses that one had to "ride the hump" and be careful with, or he would sure as shootin' buck! Some days were just good days, but this was one of the best! My bay gelding was in good hands.

Russ talked me into letting him keep the horse just a little longer because he wanted to try riding him later in the spring when the ground wasn't so slick. By the time I got home that night, my chocolate-buckskin gelding with the mud-splattered belly was tired. I slept well that night.

Chapter XVIII
Blank Check

My folks had a program in place for us older kids to help us get our little herds started. It went like this. Dad gave us a heifer calf when we were twelve years old. If we were lucky, we would possibly have an increase when the heifer was two or we were 14, that is, if she had a heifer calf. If it was a bull calf, it belonged to Dad to help pay for the keep of the heifers. If your cow had bull calves three years in a row, you just had no increase, and vice versa! By the time I was in the ninth grade in school I had a "herd" of 4 cows. They all had bull calves! I had been working from sun up to sun down right along side of my dad all summer, and I finally got up enough nerve to ask him if he was going to let me keep those 4 calves. "Nope! Not 'til you get out of school." Well, that's easy—I just quit school! The absolute dumbest move I ever made in my life. I ran those steers until they were 2 years old. I shipped them to Sioux City by rail, and they weighed 914 pounds. They brought $210.22 apiece, to total about $840.

This is good! I later bought a nearly new straight-8 Pontiac for $725. The bad part was that I worked at home for $1 week for 4 years!

The horse deal was my mother's. She had a little pacing mare, which was just the sweetest thing. Her name was Lady. It seemed that she could just look over the fence at a stallion and get with foal! She just never missed. Mother gave each of her children a foal from her mare as soon as we were old enough to recognize that it was a gift. She usually had two or three mares or fillies to pick from and let us choose what we liked best. We were obligated to "pay back in kind" one horse. This was difficult for each of us, because, we hated to give up our increase, and we were usually attached to every one of the horses. Linda, my youngest sister, had such a hard time deciding which horse to use to pay back her debt! All her horses were light duns with bald faces. They had roan-tinted legs and underlayment. She informed my dad that she wanted to wait until I got home to help her pick, because probably he would get the best one if I wasn't there! I was gone from home by then and was not able to help her make the choice.

Arthur Anderson riding "Lady" holding nephew Perry. No bridle. This photo was taken at The Green Grass Picnic. Lady was Mother's mare. She gave each of her children an offspring from this mare.

Mother never wavered from the contract! This was a good experience for us because it helped teach us responsibility and discipline.

Dad had a black 1951 Ford pickup that he was so very proud of, (despite the marks of the shotgun blast on the passenger side door)! He had built a high stock rack from oak one-by-fours. He was able to haul cows, bulls and an occasional saddle horse or two in it.

I think that he realized that he was using me for child slave labor, and offered to let me take his pickup and go to Fort Pierre and buy a couple of cows. Of course, I accepted and took to the road one early Friday morning. I had with me a signed Dewey County check blank in my billfold!

West Texas was dried out, and David Yak had leased the Diamond A24 Ranch, which was willed to Dartmouth College by the previous owner, Leon Williams, in his last will and testament.

Dave shipped about 800 head of the saddest-looking, poorest-quality drought-out southern cattle I'd ever seen. My brother-in-law, Dick Schrempp was in Dave's employ at the time. The cattle were mixed-blood Brahma, shorthorn, and Hereford crosses with a few outcrops that could not be distinguished. There were a lot of brockle faces, roans and brindles that carried a small hind quarter and big ears.

David went to Fort Pierre with the whole kit and kaboodle the day I went to Ft. Pierre to make my big purchase of two or, maybe, three head. I had been over helping Dick work Dave's cattle, doctoring for screwworms and such, so Dave knew who I was. He took me over to the Chateau to wine and dine me. He gave me my first lesson on how to skin the rabbit without getting your fingers full of fur.

I'm telling him that I have this check and I came to fill my load. He volunteers to show me a pen of his choice cow-calf pairs that he could probably sure make me a good deal on.

I'd done quite a bit of horse trading and I began to dicker—me being 16 years old 5′ 6″ tall and about 150 pounds. This big 6′6″ Texan weighing in at about 260 pounds reminded me of a banty rooster (me) taking on a vulture. The asking price was $125 a pair, and I offered $80. He came down to $100 and he told me what a good kid I was and that he would only do that for me in order to help me out. I offered $90. he said, "$91 a pair and you can have them!" This was in the fall and the calves were big enough to be weaned, so I said, "Sold!"

It's about 200 miles round trip from home to Ft. Pierre. I got home about 11:30 that night and Dad came to see, maybe, if he could help unload the pickup. He holds the lantern up so that he can see in the box and says, "What's the matter? Didn't you see anything you liked?" I said, "Yeah. I bought 90 pairs----180 head. The two semis will be coming in the morning to bring them home." You'd have to know my dad to appreciate the reaction I got! I thought that he was going to expire! Very few people even had $8190. I know he never slept a wink that night, and when the trucks came and unloaded, he was physically ill! I don't think the thought ever entered his mind that these cattle only cost $45.50 per head when one figured in the calves. It didn't take much of a cow to be worth that.

He made me split the herd with my sister and brother-in-law, Betty and Dick. Sort of making his odds better in getting some of his money back.

Dick and I sorted off 8 cows, which were so skinny that we didn't think they would put on enough flesh to make the winter. Cal Smith hauled those 8 old shells to Mobridge for $25. The check, minus the trucking was $263 for a grand net of $32.87 per head. That's more than a dead cow would bring, but not much!

Dad just hated those cows even though some of them raised decent calves. In those days, if your herd wasn't straight Hereford you were considered not much of a rancher. The next year I sold every cow, yearling and calf on the anniversary of their arrival for $8493. After I proudly paid my dad back I had $4378.71 left in the bank. I made good use of that money! This sort of made up for the $4 a month dad had given me for the past few years. I don't have to tell you this do I? He never ever again offered to give me a signed blank check!

Betty and Dick purchased the 24 Ranch from Dartmouth College and advanced their share of those cows to higher and higher levels, improving on their quality with good bulls and good management, not to mention hard work. Their family keeps adding acreage to their spread, and although no one ever offered to let me take a head count, I believe you would have to tie enough knots in your rope to count out 2000 head, figuring Dan and Rick in the mix! The Schrempp outfit is now known as the J.D. Cattle Company.

Chapter XIX
Mischievous Boys

Mother was living in town with the younger kids so that they could attend school. Dad, the Curtises, Berndts and George Webb rode the caboose to Sioux City to ship cattle and sheep to the Rice Brothers' Commission Firm for the once-a-year pilgrimage and sales of livestock. I suppose some of the boys went out on the town just a little bit seeking the "spice of life" so to speak.

I was left with the chores so I talked Jr. Smith and Billy Davidson to come down to the ranch with me to do chores and also to see what kind of mischief we could get in to. At that time there were literally thousands of prairie grouse scattered through the heavily-timbered draws. Of course, the big straw stacks where those meaty little birds would scratch their way through the chaff in search of grain were a big drawing card for them, too.

Billy decided that we should take the '48 Ford up to the field and shoot a few birds with Dad's old J. C. Higgins 12-guage shotgun. We couldn't find the keys so Billy gave us a fine demonstration on under-the-dash-positive-to-negative wiring. He had that old maroon Ford going in a matter of minutes. Now we are about to fulfill the old adage, "One boy is a boy. Two boys is one-half a boy, and three boys is NO boy at all!"

Now we're quite a threesome, let me tell you! One boy daring the other and each showing off how much nerve he had by showing that he wasn't scared of nothing at all!

We took the old Ford up to the straw stack and got off a round with that old cannon. All the birds took flight and away off into the gumbo breaks to safety. Our level of mischief was not nearly spent, so we headed back home to eat lunch. I'm thinking that since we were all pretty good cowboys, we should, maybe, try our skills out by riding cows. I was pretty good at that and sure would like to give my buddies a little schooling on how it's done. Of course, the milk cows were handy because their calves were in the barn and the cows had tight bags, so they were waiting until milking time and some relief. We let the calves do the milking chores and ran the cows over the hill afoot and into the narrow runway we called a chute and drew lots. Three milk cows (the term was used lightly because anything that had milk that we could tie to a post was a milk cow — usually a roan or brockleface or anything that had some milking shorthorn blood in her).

I got the red-eyed cow, Billy got the roan, and Jr. drew the brockleface. Billy is liking his draw, because she is small and not very intimidating. Our chute never had a side gate, so we just held our feet up and rode straight ahead until we were clear. Then we buried our spurs and hoped for the best!

Right outside the chute was a barbed wire gate, just on the left side, with no clearance at all. If it was left open, it gave access to the hay corral and from there Katey bar the door!

Billy calls for the outside and Jr. swings the gate. Ole Billy rides roany like Jim Shoulders at the Garden. He steps off with his loose rope in his hand, all professional-like with his chest stuck out in the stud rooster pose.

Old red eye is next and I climb aboard in confidence that I could show the boys how to really stick it on one. Jr. unfastens the latch on the gate and Old Red Eye jumps as high as the snubbing post and goes into a spin! This okay, and I'm having fun—until my pant leg got caught on that barbed wire gate. I always rode right handed and ole Red Eye crashes the gate post and leaves me dangling on the gate with my left hand all bloody like with a good three-cornered tear. I can still show you the scars today. Now, Jr., who's little more sensible says, "I just paid $2.98 for these Lee's, and I'm not about to get them torn off on no barbed wire gate. You can just turn Old Brockleface out, and I'll give the contest to Billy!"

We, Blackie Johnson, Homer Blue Coat, Dad and I had been hauling hay, so we had eight real good Percheron pullers in for that purpose. I asked the boys if, maybe, we should exhibition one a piece of these big prancers. Jr., again being the sensible one, threw his handkerchief and said, "You go right ahead. I know your dad. He'll skin us alive!"

Billy volunteers to ride one, but I have to go first. Okay! We run all these big prancers in the pole corral and I've got a plan! Dad rode this one grey horse called Thunder a lot. I could probably saddle him and ride him off and he wouldn't, maybe, even buck. My equipment wasn't the best—the hand-me-down, E.C. Lee that I'd bought from Dad, which had a 13-inch seat with wide swells, and just the halter rope for a buck rein. But I got good Jerry Ambler spurs with turned in shanks that I can get a good hold with. This old Thunder weighs about 1650 and I got to let out a lot of latigo to get the cinch to fasten. I pet ole Thunder on the neck and say, "Good boy! Good boy," and step up.

The old horse just walks away as nice as you please. That is until I hit him in the belly with the spurs! I don't know how to describe what happened next! The word "astronaut" was not in existence yet! I rode him all the way around the shed before he bucked me off. Mister! Did that horse buck! I got launched straight up out of there. You talk about a helpless feeling coming down out of the air at a height of about 15 feet without a parachute! I don't think either of my comrades saw it.

We got old Thunder caught and unsaddled. I asked Billy, "Which one do you want?" His reply was, "The hell with you!!"

Art Moran spent a lot of time with me. He was a true and faithful friend who was always willing to get into a little mischief. Joe Bush, an old bachelor who lived south of Eagle Butte, had a horse he wanted me to ride. So, I borrowed Dad's pickup and we went down to Joe's to load the horse. He was nothing special—just kind of a jug-headed sorrel with a bald face and an abundance of fetlock hair like a Clydesdale. The horse put up quite a fight as we loaded him, but I finally backed up to a bank that was almost level with the bed of the pickup. I let the end gate down and threw a trip rope over his hind end so we could load him. This is all working out about average, but it's Saturday night, and there is a dance at the Legion Hall!

We got the bronky horse in the back of the pickup to show that we were pretty salty cowboys. Between us, Art and I had $8, and we decided to look up the bootlegger to get us a six-pack of malt liquor. (This bootlegger, made us swear that we would never reveal his name. I never will!)

We parked up close on the south side of the dance hall. This way we could drink our little cans of 80-proof and listen to the piano music that Agnes Rousseau was letting escape out the open window. We entertained ourselves for about 1 ½ hours outside the dance hall when instinct and self preservation told me that I'd better get that pickup home and put it to bed where it belonged.

All you have to do is give an Indian a couple of cans of that malt liquor, and he's got more guts than brains. Art was no exception. My mother never did tell anybody that I was overly smart, either! On the way home Art got a little vulgar about how that horse thought he was tough and he didn't think he was going to load for us. He'd say, "He ain't so tough!" and with that he'd reach across with his foot and step on the brake and sort of bounce the poor old unsuspecting pony off the front of the stock rack. By the time we got home the three cans of malt liquor were hard at work. Maybe we would have been all right if my folks had been home, but they were uptown doing their Saturday night stuff.

Art recommended that we ought to just tie up a foot on that skim-milk-fed son of a farmer's plow mare and show him who's the tough ones around here. Well, of course, I had to agree!

There was a walk ramp in the chute, or runway, that we used to work cows, and we unloaded "Joe" and saddled him right there so that when we sprung the gate he would be in the pole corral. Art asked, "Are you going to ride him, or am I?" I said, "Well, Sir, it's your idea!" Art is really on a roll now and with his speech a little slurred, he says, "You ride him and I'll tie a scoop to his tail!" Oh, heavenly days, I agreed to that, too! I'm a little dizzy, too.

We got all tied together and I climbed over the boards to do the get on. Art springs the gate and hurries to find the scoop shovel. The horse just crow hops across the corral until he feels the tug on his tail and the race is on! Of course, Art is in no shape to stay with the scoop. Maybe he never got on for all I know! I was busy! All I could think of is waking up in Hell with a rope around my neck with the scoop shovel! Old Joe was tearing around that corral with the scoop shovel bouncing and clanging behind him. I had set the snubbing post about five feet from the corral, and the rope finally wrapped around the post and jerked out the tail hair! He had a pretty short trim!

How did Joe Bobtail turn out? I ain't saying!

I broke a sharp-looking blue roan gelding and pretty much camped on him all fall turning cattle back to our range. I really had him riding good and watching a cow. I was planning on getting a good price for him. I turned him loose that fall, and when I went to pick him up that next spring, I couldn't find him.

I knew old Posey Moran rode every day, and I would ride up the bluff overlooking Chauncey Johnson's outfit and back to the southwest, looking through bands of horses. Then I'd head back to the northeast to the river where Posey had his outfit.

Posey was getting old and never rode much off his home range, but he sure knew what was going on in his locality which was about 5 square miles. He had such a squint you couldn't see his eyes, but he could see like a hawk and could tell you who went where, when, with what, and how many! Posey was the step son of Scotty Philip, and was in charge of a large lease in the northwest corner of South Dakota where Scotty grazed a huge herd of cattle bearing the Seventy-three brand on the left side. When Scotty died, Posey moved to the Moreau where his in-laws lived. He had the fattest Hereford cows I ever saw. Those cows had huge gobs of fat on their hipbones that made them look like there was something wrong with them. His bulls were huge. The horns were never weighted, so they pointed straight forward. I'm sure he saved back bulls from his own herd for the purpose of getting his cows bred. Posey used a cottonwood log to picket his horse, and would dally the stake rope and pull it a little every day so his horse would have fresh grass both winter and summer. The reason he rode every day was to herd his little herd of about 70 or 80 cows back to his cabin and kick all the strays off his range. His herd was always clean and no one really ever expected to find strays when riding through them. They were so fat that when riding through them, they would be bedded down under the big cottonwoods, barely shifting their weight, chewing their cuds and grunting.

Posey was selfish about his grass because he never ever put up a forkful of hay, bought a block of salt or a sack of cottonseed cake. He knew what a cow needed and what she was going to do 10 minutes before she did it. He may have gone to town some, but I only saw him there, once. He was sitting in the shade of the old abandoned lumberyard, puffing away at his Bull Durham cigarette. I assume that he had caught a ride to town with one of his boys, Donovan or Stanley, and was waiting for them to take him back to his stomping grounds.

My folks usually had a box or carton of Bull Durham stashed in the closet because the hired men would run out of smokes and would use that for an excuse to go to town. Dad would drag down a couple of sacks of tobacco to dole out, and then take it out of their wages. He did the same with the little packets of cigarette papers. Dad never smoked, and Mom only did on the QT.

When I figured I was going over to see Posey I would swipe a bag of Durham to give him. So much, in fact, that when he would ask me to step down and have a drink from his water barrel, he would sort of stand close in expectation of his gift.

Posey was not a full-blooded Indian, but was married to one—a Larabee, I think. He lived the Indian way. Indians never had three squares a day like white people. They ate when they were hungry, or when they had something to eat.

It wasn't their custom to invite you to eat or drink from their water barrel. If the pot was on the fire with boiled beef, or the contents thereof, you were supposed to go help yourself without any to-do. They were actually flattered if you would sharpen a stick and spear yourself a nice chunk of meat from their pot. Those old women would actually look at you and give you a big smile! (You could count how many teeth they had, which was usually about six, or sometimes, one!)

Posey broke that tradition, probably, because he was around cowboys and cow camps all his life. He was always hasty to ask if I was hungry, and to help myself to the water. I graciously accepted the water because I didn't want his missus to go to any bother of sticking a chunk of pispisa (prairie dog) in her fry bread for me. She would offer up wojape because she knew that I liked that.

After all the formalities, I'm still looking for my blue roan gelding, and prying Posey for information. He said, "Only one blue roan—you don't want him. Boog Edson rides by three day ago. Bed tarp tie on back. Packing iron. Bad mood. Crazy mad. Not your horse. His horse old. Hair on face and legs turning white. I'll watch. Let you know. Bring more smokes!"

It was customary to run all the cattle thru a dipping vat in the fall to kill parasites, lice and mange. This photo was taken at The Lee Robley Ranch, later purchased by my friend Russell Curtis.

Chapter XX
Saddle Horses

I've ridden a lot of horses in my time, and am still looking forward to riding the best one, ever. Horses are just like people in personality, disposition and stamina. The horses I rode as a young man were from foundation remount studs with Morgan and Thoroughbred blood. They were bred back to range mares, mostly from mixed Indian ponies. Although they never had near the brain power and the quickness to learn, or the willingness, they had the heart and stamina that the horses today, in my mind, do not have. There are exceptions, of course.

Today's horses, if ridden like the old cowboys such as Ed Lemmon rode, would be crippled on probably just one ride. Ed claimed to have ridden one horse from the Grand River near the North Dakota border to Lame Johnny Creek in 16 hours nonstop. Lame Johnny Creek is on the Nebraska line, so this would be 7 ½ miles per hour. Horses today are bred for speed and athleticism rather than stamina, which is just fine. If a horse travels 120 miles today, he is going to do it in the back of a horse trailer.

My father had business at the state capitol in Pierre, which is about 90 miles, as the crow flies, from the home place. This also involved swimming the Cheyenne River at a narrow point on the Sonenshine Bottom. He left home at 3:30 on a Monday morning, did his business, which involved a hearing concerning an accusation of him stealing C.B.C. horses that were found in St. Paul, Minnesota. He was cleared of all charges in Federal Court, and he rode into his own yard on a fast running walk at 4:00 pm the next day. The horse he was riding, named Moses, was a steel-grey four-year-old gelding that was half Percheron and half thoroughbred. That horse came in the yard heads up and proud after 180 miles in two days. He didn't look any the worse for wear.

That aforementioned hearing, in which Dad was cleared of all charges, is to my knowledge, the only time the law ever pointed a finger at Dad. After that incident, he had no use for Ike Blasengame. None at all!

Our saddle horses usually found a new home soon after they were broke to ride. Barney Downing would probably have a home for them, or one neighbor or the other would trade Dad out of a horse. This might occur right out on the prairie. His horses were always for sale, and he taught us kids to never become attached to one, because he would just jerk the saddle out from under us and sell them every chance the got. He would say, "You will never ride the broncs if we have gentle ones around!"

There were a few good horses that stayed around long enough for us to at least get to know them. Spider was a beautiful chocolate-brown gelding with four stocking feet and a wide strip. He was good at cow work and could run right up on a calf so that it took very little effort to rope it. He proved this time and time again when screwworms invaded the herds of fresh-branded calves in the late 40's and early 50's.

we had to ride every day to rope calves and put "smear 62" on the brands that had loose scabs on them from the peeling brands.

Several different outfits pooled together to ride up and down the river to detect and doctor those poor calves. When smear was applied to the wounds, the screwworms would exit by the thousands. These maggot-like little worms could bore into flesh and literally eat those calves alive. The roping of these calves was pretty pathetic. Most of the northern cowboys couldn't catch cold standing on a slab of ice, let alone catch a calf!

Mark O'Leary was pretty good, Lee Robley was fair, but Slim Berndt couldn't catch much of anything. I wasn't very good, either, but the Spider gave me such an advantage of getting up close, that I could practically drop the loop over a calf's head. Dad and the Curtis boys were terrible ropers, but did most of the groundwork, and that was good. Mac McGillicuddy was from the South, and he was a wizard with a rope. He very seldom ever missed. He tried to buy the Spider from Dad. Dad wanted $225. The going price for a good saddle horse at that time was about $85. Mac didn't have that much money. He was working for Bill Ewing and only made $125 a month.

One day I was riding down Green Grass Creek, and a man was standing on what was left of the fill of a washed-out dam. He was waving and hollering, so I made a hasty run to the rescue. It was Francis Curtis. He had tried to ride around the big washout in the middle of the dam, and, although it was dry on top, it was full of silt and had no bottom. His horse was stuck plumb up to the D rings on his saddle. He was just plumb tuckered out from struggling and lunging to free himself. I volunteered to try to snake his ole pony out of the muck. I'd had some experience pulling cows out of bog holes. Ropes weren't very stout in those days, and mine was old. Francis had a brand new one tied on his rope strap. He could stand on dry ground to get it off, and I told him to tie a bowlin knot around his horse's neck, and I'd give the pull a try.

I didn't know where to put my horse to get the most leverage, but I chose high ground. The Spider set into that rope with a vengeance, snaking the old pony right out. John must have told Francis what Dad wanted for the horse because he dug out his checkbook and pencil and wrote her out for $225. I was worried that he wanted to trade saddles right there to take advantage of his new investment, but he handed me the check telling me to give it to my dad, saying that he would be around tomorrow to get his horse. We lost a never-to-be-forgotten horse to our neighbor there.

Spider the Trick Horse---This is the good saddle horse my Dad sold to our neighbor Francis Curtis.

Then there was Tuffy. He was a one-man horse, me being the man. I sold him to Pat Dieter for $165 plus two horses in trade. This horse was left with Russell Curtis to try, but he was just too high-lifed for him. I went down to Russell's place after him on April 14, my brother Lawrence's birthday. The sun was shining and the grass was peeking through with a hint of spring in the air. My mother said the air was heavy, and the chickens never came off the roost. She was worried about a storm. I argued, "Mom, the sun is shining. It's not going to storm!" She grabbed Dad's big heavy sheepskin coat and chopper mitts and insisted that I tie them to my saddle.

I almost left the extra baggage in the barn because that big bundle was sure going to take away from my brand new red bat wings that I had ordered out of the Fred Mueller catalog. These chaps had black trim and the letters MEL sewn on the wings. They cost $65 — a lot of money---and I wanted to share them with my friend, Russell, to admire. I suppose it was about 12 miles across there to Russ's place, but the river was bank full, and I wasn't about to try to swim it, and for good reason!

I was riding a horse I owned called CheeChee. He was the product of the mare that my mother gave me. I really like to show off on this horse. He would buck every time I got on him, but it was like riding a rocking chair. I could practice my spur lick and could really get in time with him. He would just buck when I

247

first got on him, and no matter what, he wouldn't buck again until the next time I got on him. Then he'd buck again, but just once a day.

When I got down to Russ's, he was pitching on a load of hay for the next day's feeding. He was getting ready for the storm that was coming. I tied CheeChee to the corner of the hayrack and helped Russ finish loading his load of hay. I then followed him home. He was really worried about the weather. He pointed skyward to explain to me that the expanse of clouds above were called 'fish ribs." This, he said, was a sure sign of a heavy moisture accumulation.

He went to the back room to get his side pork while I hauled in some wood to the wood box behind the stove, then peeled some potatoes. We visited some about weather while the side pork was dancing around in the hot skillet. It started to snow and Russ invited me to stay at his place until the storm blew over. I knew that Mother would worry and figure that I'd tackled something I couldn't handle if I didn't show up at her doorstep!

I ate a hurried meal and put on my new red chaps and headed for the barn to switch my saddle to Tuffy for the trip home. Tuffy was aggravated by the tight cinch around his girth, and I had to walk him around a little until I got the hump leveled out in his back, making the saddle sit flat. Russ said, "By garsh, I hate to see that horse go!"

He suggested that I leave my spare horse there, but I declined. I would not have been better on my horse count than I was when I left home, so I left riding one and leading one. The wind started to pick up and it began snowing hard. I pulled the slip knots on my saddle strings and retrieved the sheepskin and choppers' mittens. I said to myself, "Thank God for Mothers." as I slid that big coat over my shoulders and put up the high collar to hide behind. The snow was hurting my eyes and when it hit my face, it stung. I rode straight west against an increasing northwest wind in what had become very poor visibility.

The snow began to blow into drifts and I had a hard time judging the lay of the land to stay out of the gullies and big drifts in the bottom of the draws. I had always heard that one should let the horse "have his head" and he will take you right to the barn door. You wanna bet? I had to work pretty hard to keep my little pony from turning, and make him go northwest into the prevailing wind. If I would've let him have his way, we would have ended up some where in Northeastern Nebraska!

I finally got to Green Grass Creek and could switch directions from westward to a more southerly direction. Boy, that was sure a relief for both horses and rider. My little Tuffy horse was covered with frost and ice sickles hanging off his nostrils. He was getting tired. He was sleek and fat, but standing in the stall all winter had made him soft. I just let him bide his time because we had only three miles left to go. I actually rode into a horseshoe-bend in the creek where there was a big plum thicket, so as to let my horse blow a little, and for me to get my bearings. I rode on home in a full-fledged northern blizzard to a very relieved mother.

PeeWee was little bay Indian pony that I had bought from Elk Heads' boy, Raymond. He was broke when I got him. The little Indian kids started riding him when he was a colt. He was what we called Indian broke. Very gentle but with not much heart. Several times I tried to run horses on him, but if he had to run up hill, he would get a little winded and just quit me. I mean, he would just stop and blink his eyes and no matter how rough I would get with him, he just refused to take a step forward. He was a pretty fair cow pony, but I wouldn't saddle him if I wanted to go out to bring in the wild ones. He was raised right down on the river and those kids would take him into swimming water. They'd get on him while he swam around, usually down river with the current. Swimming was old PeeWee's cup of tea! He was the best river horse I ever rode. I'd ride him up to the water and he just took to it like a duck.

One time when Dad and I crossed the river to retrieve a little bunch of cows over on the O'Leary side, the river had come up a bunch while we were sorting out our cows. The cows had pretty small calves following them. We pushed the cows up to the water's edge, and no matter how hard we tried, we couldn't get them to take to the water. Dad was riding a high-headed black and white pinto. He rode over to me to explain to me his plan of execution. "We'll back them off the river a quarter mile or so, and come at the river with them at a dead run." In order to take my mind off the coming ordeal, I think, he told me to count the cows. There were 27. We followed the plan and put the scare on those cows with Dad swinging his rope and whistling with that shrill built-in siren he had between his teeth. His paint horse, with his head up in his lap was prancing up and down. Over the river bank, and into the water we went with the whole kit and kaboodle, me included! Old PeeWee is swimming high with my feet barely getting wet—just raised out of the stirrups a little.

PeeWee—The Indian pony that we depended upon to swim The Moreau River. He loved to swim. Mel sold him to his father for $25.00 so he could buy a new pair of boots.

Dad's horse is taking on more and more water, and all I see is his horse's head, and Dad from the waist up. I'm scared. The cows are paddling for all they are worth for the far side as the current was pushing them down river. Every calf pressed in alongside his mother on the off side of the current, just like they had their own little guardian angels.

Dad swims his horse up as close as he can to me and shouts, "Are you all right? Don't look at the water! Look at the tree on the far bank!" the whole world seems like it's tipping upside down with me, and I'm getting dizzy. I answered, "Yeeeeesss," in a quivering tone. PeeWee sure did his part. He could swim like a beaver, and cows, horses, Dad and a scared kid all scrambled out on the opposite bank behind Moses Bad Male's house. My Dad proved to me that day that he had no fear of high water on the Moreau, even though his brother Chick, had drowned in this very same river only 4 miles down stream from where we crossed. Come to think of it, Dad had no fear of anything! About 25 years later, I had another river thrill while crossing the Cheyenne when the ice was going out. I was riding a good little horse that we called Alkali Pete. I jumped him up onto a portion of ice that seemed to be set firmly in place. Our weight caused a chunk about 30 feet in circumference to break off, and we went floating down the river like we were on a ferryboat. But, that's another story!

Cattle swimming The Moreau River late fall after a big rain.

The black and white paint horse that Dad was riding was named Scout after Tonto's horse on the radio show The Lone Ranger. He was a real honest-to-goodness knot head. I always figured Dad would kill him or ride him to death or, that he might kill Dad. He would stick his head up in the air and run through washouts, lakebeds, trees---just anything, acting like a freight train! Maybe Dad thought something of me after all. He never would let me ride him. I never asked to, either! The harder you ran him, the hotter he would get, and he would just catch another gear and go faster!

Dad walked with a limp. I know ole Scout was the cause of it. Those old E.C. Lee saddles had a high cantle and wide swells without a dish for your legs. Just straight down to the skirts. Ole Scout bucked and bucked with Dad. He pulled a groin muscle, and dislocated a hip. Of course no doctor or hospital for Dad! He walked with a stoop and limp from that moment on, but without complaint.

The last time I saw Dad ride that horse, he brought in and penned a bunch of horses on him. That horse was so high headed that it looked as though his reins only needed to be two foot long! Barney Downing was there to shut the gate, and Dad, without dismounting, to my astonishment, tossed the reins to the ground! The old paint had had it. He just stood there and blew air with his sides heaving in and out. Dad must have made quite a run on that bunch of horses.

Barney was a little unsuspecting, and asked Dad if he would sell Scout. There was a shipment going by rail to Chicago, and he needed to fill an order for a real heads-up parade horse. Dad sold him to Barney for $85---big money! I overheard Dad say to Mother that Scout would probably start running and be back in South Dakota within the week! The report dad got back from Barney is that the horses took to the parade route with a shiny new silver-mounted saddle with all the trimmings. He was a sight for sore eyes. The trip on the train took its toll, and the horse had his "sea legs." After that he was pretty easy to get along with.

Slew Foot was the horse I rode to school when it was too cold or slippery to mess with a bronc. Not pretty, wouldn't watch a cow, and appeared to be clumsy, but he was a great night horse, meaning he could see in the dark, I would give him a small forkful of hay and two gallons of barley. If the folks would head for town at the same time I did, we would all arrive at the same time. He did nine miles, in 45 minutes, day after day. During the dog days of winter, it would be dark, or near dark, when I would leave the stockyards for home. Old Slew Foot would be very anxious to get to the stall hat home for his bait of barley and he would lumber along the whole way on a lope. I'd be home in 45 minutes.

The trail was hilly and rough. Some nights it would be pitch dark before I got home. I would catch myself holding on to the horn with my eyes closed, hoping my horse wouldn't fall into a hole or something... I rode a lot of miles just going back and forth to school. A round trip of 18 miles a day times 5 days a week is 90 miles a week, or 360 miles a month. Take 5 months times that and it's 1800 miles per school year, less about a month for bad weather in which it wasn't fit to ride.

Blackie was a great cow horse. I'll swear when you were working a herd that old black horse could read brands! When one would ride into a herd and he saw the big Lazy S on her, he would lock in on his own accord, pin his ears way back and take the cow out of the herd towards the cut on his own. Dad really liked this horse, and very seldom ever let anyone, but himself use him. He kept a close eye on him, and never put him up for sale for a long time. At the age of 10, Blackie started to stiffen up in the joints from all his ducking and diving while sorting cattle. Frank O'Leary had spoken for the horse, so Dad told him if he wanted him he could have him. He must have thought a lot of Frank because this is the only time I ever saw him give a horse to an adult as a gift. Frank accidentally shot himself about a year after Dad gave Blackie to him.

Frank was afflicted with polio and had a crippled arm and hand as a result. I don't know if his handicap had to do anything with it or not, but a bunch of geese were flying overhead. He grabbed a rifle to gamble on downing a goose, but the gun accidentally discharged, striking the fatal blow.

Chapter XXI
Mother's Refrigerator and Dad's New Tractor

We put up ice in the wintertime and stored it in the icehouse for warm summer days. Even though it was placed underground, covered with straw and heavy logs, which, in turn, were covered with earth, the ice only lasted until just after the Fourth of July.

The ice was used to put in the icebox in the kitchen. The icebox resembled a refrigerator in size and looks. The top compartment was made to hold two ten-pound chunks of ice that would melt down into drain tubes and into a holding pan on the bottom. This was an effective way of keeping things cool as long as the ice lasted. Then another trip would be made across the draw, a distance of about ½ mile, over to the icehouse for more ice.

Keeping things cool was not only inconvenient, but also inefficient. When the ice was gone, everything had to go back in to the root cellar. Mother would always coax her children to clean everything up at the table so that it would be "a nice day tomorrow." She didn't like leftovers because of poor storage, and no food was ever thrown out.

In 1951, Ervin Linstad started selling Serval bottle-gas refrigerators for $66, installed. Mother persuaded Dad to buy one. The day Ervin came down and installed the new appliance was happy one for Mother. Finally there was a place in the house to keep milk, cream and butter cool, and to store eggs and leftovers. There were ice cubes for the kool-aid and lemonade, and trays for homemade ice cream.

My brother Larry, and I would get down onto the floor and peek at the blue flame underneath that marvelous appliance in bewilderment. We would ask each other how in the world could a fire possibly make ice? Mother had already refused to go down into the root cellar because a big rat had jumped on her and nearly scared her out of her wits. Although the cellar was still used extensively to store our winter supply of food, she didn't have to ask one of us kids or Dad to go down as often.

We still had to carry water dipped from the cistern behind the house, and Mother still cooked on the wood range in the kitchen, but little Rosey, Mother, was a very happy lady to have that refrigerator.

Dad was bothered by the Curtis Brothers putting up volumes more hay with their tractor-driven mowing machines and their almighty jayhawk stacker, than he could. He finally gave in and sold a big bunch of spotted Poland China feeder pigs for $8 each, and bought his first tractor. It was a 26-horse Ford-Ferguson with three gears forward and reverse. Third gear was considered "road gear' and at that high rate of speed it clocked 8 miles per hour.! The tractor cost $755. he bought a No. 5 John Deere mower that was driven by the power take-off shaft on the back of the tractor. He could lift the seven-foot sickle bar with the three-point hitch. He also bought a new 10-foot John Deere dump rake with a holddown that would keep the teeth from bouncing and skipping over the hay.

The rake cost $125, the mower $192. Extra sickles ran $6.25 each. Dad was in business! In second gear, one could cut and dump rake into windrows at the rate of 160 acres in five days.

Curtis's turned an old Oldsmobile car into a hay jeep. They took the body off and somehow turned the transmission around so they could mount a hay bucker to the back, as far from the radiator as possible. Boy! Could they ever push hay! I tried very hard to get Dad to get a rig like that. All he would say is, "We got horses."

The mowing outfit never stopped that first year, and the windrowed hay far outdistanced the horses. Dad cut everything standing, and we had much hay in windrows going into the winter. We bucked all our hay with horses and hauled it in for two more years with our steel-wheeled hayracks pulled by horses. By this time every outfit around there had tractors, and Dad's work teams that he had for sale were no longer in demand. He was one of the last ranchers in Dewey County to buy a tractor. Times began to change rapidly.

Still there was no running water, bathroom or mail service going to Green Grass and the Anderson Ranch.

Chapter XXII
The Minneapolis Girls

My Aunt Dorothea lost her husband at an early age. She had two children. The oldest was a boy near my age, named Duane. Gail was her little freckled-faced daughter that just loved horses. Dorothea would bring her children to South Dakota so they could stay the summer with their numerous Anderson cousins at the homes of her brothers, Rusty, Art and Paul Anderson. She had all the modern conveniences of the big city at her fingertips, but wanted her children to get a taste of country living where there were barely the affordable necessities of life. Not once did I hear complaints from those kids about no indoor plumbing and having to go to the toilet behind the house, or even having to use the big tub in the storeroom to take a bath. Sometimes, maybe, they'd be the third or fourth in line to use the water. Mother was the final word on when the water was thick enough to change. She'd rinse the tub for round two, and so forth. Water was so precious that she would dump the bath water on the two elm trees in front of the house that eventually afforded good shade.

The work on the ranch, however, was quite difficult for Duane. Working in the hayfield was dirty and dusty and hot. It required much muscle, and he was always thirsty. Duane would take the cork out of the canvas water bag and peer into the opening like he expected something to jump out at him!

The Eagle Butte celebration and rodeo was coming up soon, and I was flat broke. So, one morning I got up enough nerve to ask Dad if he would give me $1 a load to haul hay from up on the flat. He agreed to that, but he said I had to partner with Duane, and it would sure do my city cousin, some good if he went along to help pitch the hay onto the rack and back off the rack when we got home with it. This, of course, meant that I had to share in the profits fifty-fifty! We had to haul the hay across the creek, up a steep hill and over to the hay corral on the flat at the Joens' place.

The round trip amounted to 10 miles—one load in the morning, and one in the afternoon. That's twenty miles a day for the team and two arguments a day for me to convince Duane that when the hay was level with the top of the rack it wasn't yet loaded! He would just hate to put another fork full of hay on the rack when it reached that level and would argue that a load is a load and the rack was full! "We won't get paid for any more if we pile it to the stars!" he would insist.

By all codes and standards, the rack would easily handle twice as much hay, or more, as when it was level full. That is when I would get up on top and tromp the sides and build the walls of hay straight up until it was time to top out the load to tie it all together for the trip down those steep breaks toward home.

Nope, Duane just wasn't cut out for country life. We finally got twenty-eight loads hauled, and I got my hard-earned fourteen dollars to go to the big celebration at Eagle Butte. I saddles up old PeeWee and headed out to the shindig with a brand new silk satin shirt with snap buttons that my mother sewed for me for the occasion. I had fourteen dollars in my pocket. Boy, was I proud!

Now Gail, the little freckle-faced horse lover took to country living like a duck to water. Without being asked, she would put things away and help my sisters, Linda and Betty, with the dishes, etc. She was quite a helper. Mainly, she would help so that she could get outside to be with the horses, or rather on a horse. This was her passion, and she was good at it. I suspect after about the second year she began to dream of someday marrying a South Dakota cowboy and roughing it in the country just like we were doing. She grew to love that ranch and still does today.

Gail had friends at home that liked horses, too. I don't know how this happens, but horse lovers gather like sparrows in a loft. Gail began to bring her girl friends along with her for the summer. The two I remember are Kit Turner and Carolyn Maurine.

The Anderson boy cousins and brothers started changing shirts a little more often and checking to be sure their socks weren't sticking out of the soles of their old worn out boots.

Carolyn had a way about her that took a boy's mind off his work and the competition at our house was fierce for her attention. My brother came out way on top unless she went to Uncle Rusty's and a whole new audience with Buck, Boyd, Gordon and Richard. The hand soap disappeared faster there than it did at home. The laundry piled up faster, too. I always thought Carolyn would marry one of those Anderson boys, but it took too long for her to make up her mind, or, maybe, she plucked too many sunflowers reciting, "He loves me, he loves me not."

Gail got her cowboy, Buck, but they quit the prairie and went back to the tall timber to live.

Then there was Kit. She would sit across from me at the kitchen table and take her shoe off and rub my leg. My face would get so red and I'd be so flustered that I plumb missed my plate and poured syrup on the dang table!

Now, my dad could read sign. He took a quick look under the table and with a huge grin on his face said, "Now, Melvin you cut that out!" Knowing full well that it wasn't me that was doing the toe dance.

She would take her warm little hand and hold mine every chance she got, and once invited me to go out and sit in the old car next the house. We played kissy face in the old car until about 12:30 when my sister, Betty came out and ordered me to "get in the house and go to bed!" Those orders came from the big boss himself!

The next day we figured out a tactical strategy that called for horses and "you go up the creek, and I'll sneak around the big hill and come in from the east and meet you at the dead cottonwood; that strategy seemed to work just fine, and we were sort of picking up where we left off the night before. Kit was more emotionally generous than any other girl I'd ever known. All of a sudden we hear a war whoop and over the hill comes a sorrel horse headed right toward us at a gallop. Jerome Schwan had been helping us break horses, and Dad sent him post haste to stop the parade. Jerome relayed the message from Dad. It was rather precise and not repeatable. "No more monkey business." And the flame flickered and died.

Kit Turner—one of the Minneapolis girls riding Frog Legs the horse that won all the races at the Green Grass picnics.

At the time, the city girls were decorating our horses, by making short rides on them. I traded Fat Bringman, the Diamond A Ranch foreman, out of a beautiful quarter horse stud that was shipped up from Wagon Mound New Mexico. He was a red dun with a dorsal stripe, carrying the foundation bloodline of Peter McCue. This was pure, fine horseflesh. He was only halter broke, but gentle to handle on the ground. This horse, with a long slope to his powerful hip, a body standing on strong legs with long pasterns, was fit for a Persion General. He stood 15.2 hands tall and his pretty head was attached to a thick neck with high withers. He was just at his 4th birthday when the title was turned over to me.

I tied up a hind foot on him and put a sack on a stick to "sack him out," and in just a few minutes he was confident that I was his friend. I had pretty much given up on my E.C. Lee saddle, and had traded Morris Egna out of his Association that he'd bought with his "Sioux Benefit." So, I was about to ride a fancy horse with a new saddle. A new saddle with sheepskin sewn to the skirts tended to roll until the wool flattens and forms to the leather. So, the first couple of times it's used, there is no need for a blanket, especially in a bronc. One might take a trip over the head of the horse, saddle and all, if things aren't quite conformed to the horse's back.

The horse's registered name was Mac's Traveler, so I just shortened it up to Traveler. I saddled him and grabbed the feador on the hackamore, and stepped on and off several times, getting him used to my weight. I petted him on the neck and hindquarters with much movement to get him used to me and then I stepped down to take off the Scotch hobble.

He settled his leg to the ground and I stepped back on, knowing he wouldn't immediately know that he was free from his one leg restraint. I flopped aboard him and petted and talked to him, in hopes of getting him used to his human intrusion. He just stood still and sort of turned his head to see what kind of nut was sitting on his back.

Since I had his right hind foot tied up, he should be soft on the right side, and give his head to me if I put pressure on the bosal for a right turn. I tried it. Nothing. To the left. Nothing! The horse refused to untrack. I don't wear spurs the first few times I ride a horse because I like to kick as hard as I can with my bare heel and put them in a tight spin if they try to buck. It takes their mind off it, and I, for one, sure don't like to have a freshly-started horse buck! That's just one more thing one has to work on if they buck!

I'm putting the boot heels to Traveler and he his still locked up. I got off and lead him in a tight circle to the right then a tight circle to the left. I got back on and asked him to go right. He flexes his neck and pivots to the right, big as you please! I'm not a horse, but almost! That horse thought he was still restrained by the Scotch hobble. I was soon loping him around the pole corral going in both directions.

I rode Traveler for only about 30 days, and could get good response from anything I asked. I roped some good-sized studs off him at stud-cutting time. He was a stud, so I had to turn him out to "stud stuff." He never got rode much after that initial time. I had no idea what I had within this horse! We got a lot of good dun and roan colts out of him that broke out real fine and made good saddle horses. My dad had taught me well. Never fall in love with one horse! A man, Jerry Sheridan, from Huron offered me eight

Hereford cows and three mares. It looked to me to be a good trade at the time, but it was not worth a fraction of what that stud could have made, had he been in the right hands and put on registered mares.

Mel and his Diamond A Stud Traveler

Chapter XXIII
Freddy Kills First

Freddy Kills First lived alone on his allotment in an old frame house just north of the river above where the Green Grass picnic was held each year. (An allotment was a 160-acre parcel of land given to each individual Indian on his or her 18th birthday. This was fee-patent land given by treaty.) His living alone was very unusual because Indians are a close-knit people, and are usually cramped for space.

I never saw visible signs of smoke coming from his chimney, so I know not how he cooked or kept from freezing to death in the winter time.

Freddy seemed sort of odd, but appeared harmless. He would go to one rodeo a year and enter himself in the bull riding to prove his courage. He would get a contestant number splashed on an oil cloth and pin it to his shirt for all to see. He would wear that number wherever he went for the rest of the year to show everybody that he was bull rider. I pulled his rope at the Days of 1910 Rodeo at Timber Lake, and it took all the courage he had to get on that bull! He had no business riding. He was so scared that he shook all over. But he thought it to be an honorable act, and entered for several years, never once getting his bull rode, but not getting hurt bad, either!

One winter in late February, Freddy came walking in to our place, all tuckered out. Dad and I were batching at the time, and I was alone in the house.

I had just baked a new-fangled "box cake," and had scrubbed the floor that had been neglected for at least a month. Freddy said that he had run out of shells and that he sure was hungry. I asked him if he wanted shells or food. He said, "Food."

I never asked, but I believe that he had been living off cottontail rabbits and grouse all winter. I don't think he would butcher a beef because he was deathly afraid of being locked up in jail. The one time that he had been thrown in jail down at the state capital, his cellmate hung himself in the night while Freddy was sleeping. All he could think about since then was "Homer's ghost" whenever he thought of jail.

I started cooking coffee and went in to the storeroom with the meat saw to cut a huge steak off the hindquarter that conveniently hung there. Now, this steak was probably fourteen inches in diameter, weighing about 3 pounds. It was too big for the frying pan, so I put it on a big cookie sheet and stuck it in the oven. He was looking on like it didn't even need to be cooked at all—just thawed out!

I got out, and sliced a loaf of homemade bread, fried eight eggs, and opened up a can of pork and beans. I gave him a soupspoon and told him to go ahead and start with the beans while I went to the root cellar to get a quart of peaches for dessert. I was thinking all along that he couldn't eat all that beef and I would wrap up what he couldn't eat to send home with him.

Say, it wasn't one of those little 8-oz. cans of beans that I left with him, it was double that. By the time I got back in the house with the peaches, he was clanking the bottom of the can with the soupspoon, cleaning up the liquid!

The steak was still rare, but "just the way he like it." The beans had really built a fire under his taste buds. He tied into his three-pound round, tied into the eggs and dunked his bread in his coffee. The man is a cannibal! He ate everything! A loaf of bread, a can of beans, three pounds of meat, eight eggs and the whole quart of peaches! I'm just a little afraid that he's going to kill himself or at least founder. He could have ate more, but I shut him off.

By the time he got done eating it was about 3:00 in the afternoon. The warm house was starting to take affect on him. He was sort of nodding off, and he was starting to smell a little ripe! I sure didn't want him to stay over night!

I said, "Freddy, you had better go. It's going to be dark soon and you got almost five miles to walk.

He said, "Yeah! Can't find my horse.

I asked, "What horse?"

"I got my horse tied up but he get away."

"How long ago?"

"I go to Fort Yates Christmas and he's got away. NO halter, but still got saddle, maybe."

"What color is he?"

"He's a black mare."

"You got anything to eat at home?"

"No, just eat snow. No shells."

I fixed old Kills First up with 4 quarts of Mother's canned beef and all the pork and beans that we had left in the house, and sent him on his way.

I asked, "Freddy, where is your rodeo number?"

He answers, "On my shirt. Get ready for practice bull riding in spring!"

I was pretty curious about the black horse with the saddle, and I have yet to find my big blue gelding, so I decided to make a circle to check cattle and see what I could find. I rode through the Elk Head, Bad Warrior, and High Elk horses, and didn't see a black horse with a saddle.

There had been a pretty good blow two days back, and usually, when there was bad weather, both cattle and horses would drift into the Looking Horse breaks. If I rode west until I got to Hay Draw, and then came back north to the river, I would bump right into the rugged terrain that offered the protection for livestock in bad weather. No matter which way the wind blew, there was a spot in this ice-age-made formation for the stock to get out of the wind, and to graze a little.

No blue roan, but I ran into the little black mare with the saddle on. The stirrup leathers were both torn off and the bare tree was showing. The single riggin was attached and the cinch held fast around the girth. I dropped a loop over her head, thinking I would just drop that piece of junk saddle right where she stood, and turn her loose. The little mare was awfully thin but was very gentle. I undid the latigo and attempted to pull the saddle and blanket off. It offered a lot of resistance and she just quivered with pain. I did manage to get the saddle off, throwing it in the snow, and leaving the blanket alone. But now what? That old wool blanket has just grown to her back! I had no choice but to lead the poor beast all the way home, which sure slowed me down because it hurt her to walk due to the sores on her back.

When we got home, I watered and fed the horses, and went to ask my dad what I could do about the stuck blanket. He said to put a pail of water on the stove to warm and to add a little Epsom salts. Then I was to take it out and pour the water on the top of the blanket, over the withers and kidneys. I was to just leave it and let it soak over night.

Dad went to the barn next morning, and after he had milked, he went into the pathetic little mare's stall where he grabbed the far side of the blanket and gave a mighty pull. Off came the blanket, hair, hide and all. And oh, the smell!

It was easy to doctor the mare because there are no insects in the winter, and it didn't take long before white hair started to grow in the raw spots on her withers. I fed her six quarts of barley a day and kept her manger full of hay. Dad never said a word about the time and feed spent on that little mare except for one morning, while we were eating breakfast he looked up at me and said, "She ain't yours, you know!" I had already thought of that, and I'm wondering why Kills First hasn't got hungry again!

Freddy never did come back, and I'm thinking he probably ate all four jars of Mom's canned beef and killed himself from over-eating! I went over to have a look-see. I ran into Pete Fast Horse, and he told me that Freddy was home — that he had company from Wakpala.

I rode across the Kills First's shack and there were two skinny little kids hitting a deflated basketball with sticks. My horse surely didn't like the sight and sounds of that! Freddy came out of his shack with his "wife," and seemed glad to see me. I told him I had his horse in the barn, and although she had sores, I'd give him $25 for her, but that he would have to sign a bill of sale. (Which I already had prepared!)

He said, "No sale."

His new-found friend said something to him in the native tongue, and pushed him, about knocking him off his feet!

Freddy said, "I take it."

Now I own a $15 mare that has big white splotches of hair on her belly and back that cost me $25 plus all the feed and care I had given her! Ahh! My horse-trading image has really suffered a setback today!

One day Pete Fast Horse was loading wood in his wagon at the river and I stopped to ask how he was getting along. Pete always seemed to do good, or at least, have something for his family to eat. He was a friendly guy, and always seemed to know what was going on at Green Grass Camp.

He asked, "Why you go see Kills First?"

I told him about the black horse and he said, "Oh, ha! Kills First go to Fort Yates Christmas and leave horse tied to tree—no grass. So I turn him loose.

I asked, "Why did you leave the saddle on?"

"He's skinny—keep him warm with saddle on."

I gave him the sign of approval with my right hand and started to ride off when he said, "Hey, Malvin, you buying horses?"

I asked, "What you got?"

He said, "My roan team horse, he slip on ice. He die—got no mate. Sell mare and two colts for $100."
This is looking good because I know that Robert Blue Coat has a roan work mare that I could probably buy, and then I would have two "team" horses. One problem---I only have $77 in my pocket! I asked Pete if he would trust me for the $23.

He said, "You take horses home. Pay me next time.!

The winter was pretty open, with not much snow, so the cows could graze, giving me more time to see my fiend, Bob Blue Coat about his roan mare. She was pretty snorty, and a huge mare for being four years old. But, I had seen my dad hook and drive a whole lot worse! Bob sold her to me for $45, and I herded her up the creek to home. I put her in the hay corral. She stuck around for two days and then got homesick. She broke the gate stick and went back home. You can bet that a horse will go home to their herd mates if they get a chance! So, I go back down to Bob's to see if she came back.

Bob said, "She came back yesterday, but Sylvester is jealous 'cause I sell her to you, so he take her to Timber Lake and sell her to Guffy." Bob went on to say, "Sylvester, he no good. Turn him in. He's my son-in-law, but he steal everything. Bad one. He needs to make license plates. Go to school in Sioux Falls."

I'm only 17 years old, but I knew better than to get involved with sending one of those guys to the pen. I would have to contend with his relation, and they are ALL related! He'd come home, some day.

The Hawk Eagles all sort of live in the same house. Tom, the old man, was smart, and he owned more land than any other Indian I knew of, or at least his family did—four sections.

I rode up there like I had good sense, and just asked Sylvester how he wanted to pay me back for the roan mare. He said, "She's mine! Bob stole her from my wife!"

My play, "If you don't come up with something worth $45, I'm going to turn you in."

This got his attention! Let me tell you. He said, "I sold all my cow to Glen French. Got no more horses. Got black car---runs good. Can't go---no clutch. Bring me 6 cans malt liquor when you get your car, and it's a trade. I got title for sign now. "

My dad was not a drinking man. When I asked him if he would buy me a six-pack of malt liquor for trading purposes, he looked very disdainful. Even more so, when I asked if he would harness the team and go with me down to Hawk Eagles to pull the car home.

He bought the six-pack for me. The one and only time that he ever bought booze for one of his sons. I'm putting money on that.

Our old high-wheeled wagon didn't have a spring seat, and it seemed like a very long way riding down to Hawk Eagles' with my dad. He was skeptical, and a man of few words. He made the comment, "You dealt with him before," meaning that that should have been enough dealings with Sylvester! About 30 minutes later, into the bouncy ride, he said, "The tires will all be gone off the car, and we won't be able to pull it."

Now he's really got me worried. I just wouldn't put it past Sylvester to sell the tires if he could find a market!

When we got near Thomas Hawk Eagle's house, we found that the car had been pushed down into a little draw south of the house. I suspect that he had some of his relatives help him push the little car over the little incline so his brothers wouldn't see him retrieve his six-pack of malt liquor. I hope he waited a spell before he opened the can. If he didn't all he would have retrieved was a mouth full of foam.

The ride home for me was cushy on the seat of the car, but I had to be so careful about getting too much slack in the chain, because Dad said that a hard jerk would be awfully hard on the horses' shoulders.

Going in to the river was a little hectic. There were barely enough brakes left on the old Chevy to hold it back. I was so afraid of running in to the wagon. The reach (what holds the back wheels to the front wheels with a bolster pin—a hardwood 2 x 4, usually 12 feet long). Stuck out the back about 3 feet, and I was sure that it would poke through the radiator if I got too close to it.

We finally got home with the new piece of trading stock. Oh, yes. It would sure enough run, but it wouldn't go anywhere. For the life of me, I can't remember whom I sold that old car to, or for how much.

The little black mare was really a honey of a little horse, but in those days if you rode a mare on a roundup, you would be laughed and teased. Mares always caused trouble with the "pecking order" of the geldings. There would be lots of biting and kicking.

I sold her to a drifter called Sunshine who was working for John Curtis, for $75. We took a ride up to John's one sunny winter afternoon to pick up 8 cows of Dad's that John had on his feed row. I rode along side of Sunshine and the black mare for a little visit. She didn't like the looks of my gelding, I guess. She kicked me in the leg a good one. That's gratitude for you.

Chapter XXIV
Trapper Bohers

There were men in our little town, which made such contributions with their services that they are never to be forgotten.

There was Jerome Payne, with his innovative method of making his own light plant to generate electricity for the city. He did most of the wiring and setting poles at every block corner for street lights. He even ran around town with a note pad to jot down the kilowatts used by each household for billing. The man, classified as a genius, never slowed down.

Cliff Ralston, with his forge at the blacksmith shop, could heat his metal to shape into plow lays or whatever else was needed.

Hank Arends and Chris Mortenson, with their garages, were always selling gas and repairing automobiles.

Fred Peterson, always with a cigar in his mouth, ran the drugstore and all that went with it.

There was Dot Naeve and her grocery store, and Austin's where you could buy groceries and dry goods.

Cal Smith did all sorts of trucking, including moving houses, with his old Diamond T trucks. He was a very strong man.

But the one man who made the biggest impression on me was Carl "Trapper" Bohers. He was the drey man who hauled loads of coal and freight from the railroad cars at the depot to all the residents in town that needed such services. He had a matched team of huge white horses of which he took very good care. Trapper had a horse-drawn water wagon that he pulled around town to deliver water from the Spiel well for domestic use. When my mother lived in the Fischer building before she married my father, she said that Trapper would carry two five-gallon pails of water up two flights of stairs to fill her 50-gallon barrel. The charge was 1 cent per gallon. Trapper was a willing worker with much strength.

His old wooden stay water tank seeped water if left empty because the stays would begin to shrink, so he liked to leave water in it at all times. This created cause for much mischief from the kids in town. They thought it quite daring to open the valve and cop a drink from the unsuspecting owner.

Trapper lived in a peaked roof frame house just across from the jail and firehouse. When I delivered papers around town, I discovered that Trapper ran a game in his little house. He would admit certain people into his dwelling for the purpose of shooting crap (dice), and playing poker. For this he was allowed to "skim the pot," for the use of his facility. Players would also bet on big events like presidential elections and boxing matches. The favorite was to bet on basketball tournaments, especially during the period that Pete Zacher's boys were playing for the Eagles. Bill, George, Sylvester, Red and Francis were instrumental in putting many a trophy in the case at the Eagle Butte School!

It was rumored that Lee Garrett and Mike Keller even bet their ranches, one against the other, on the presidential election when Eisenhower won over Adlai Stevenson. I don't know the results of this bet, or if it was, in fact, really done, but Trapper told me that at one time those two gentlemen had each laid 10 one-hundred dollar bills on the floor of his dwelling, "winner take all" in a dice game.

I usually stalled out at Trapper's house when delivering papers, if he invited me in to look at pictures. He would get a huge chuckle out of showing me his cladless pinup girls. I would get very embarrassed as this was not the order of the day.

Trapper had three sons and a daughter. Ernie took over the drey business and later hauled sand and gravel. He had a daughter, LuAnn, who was in my class at school. She was a brilliant girl, and always received good grades for her work.

Johnny was a talented carpenter and rancher, and Swede was by all standards a gentleman, a state senator and a national war hero.

Swede was a survivor of the Bataan Death March. On April 9, 1942, 6300 Philippines and American forces were taken prisoners by the Japanese. These sick, starving, wounded survivors were forced to march to Camp O'Donnell, over 100 miles away. Not only were the survivors robbed of all their belongings, and denied food or drink, but the soldier that could not hold the pace was shot, bayoneted or beheaded. This horrible event numbered ten thousand dead. Only the mentally and physically strongest survived.

This loss of the Philippines to the Japanese was the largest single defeat of American Armed Forces in history. Swede spent over three years as a prisoner before he was liberated. When he finally returned home, he was barely recognizable as the same man who had left to serve his country. This poem was written for the survivors of Camp O'Donnell:

The battling bastards of Bataan
No mama, no papa, no Uncle Sam
No aunts, no uncles, no cousins, no nieces
No pills, no planes, no artillery pieces
And, nobody gives a damn!

When Swede was discharged and came home, he did quite a bit of drinking, probably to block the smell of death and the sound of suffering from his mind. His drinking partners were Stoney and Buster LaBlanc. They often held up at May LaBlanc's house near the northwest corner of town, just one house down from my uncle's house.

May had a son, Happy, that I had association with, so I entered May's house several times. There was very little furniture in the house, no linoleum on the floor and no visible food or drink for nourishment.

One evening I passed Swede and Buster at the corner streetlight by Swede's sister, Laura's house, and I heard, "Whoopsie!" I looked back to see Swede being helped off the ground by Buster. Swede had fallen down, probably due to his unstable condition caused by consumption. They examined the contents of a brown paper bag, and were pleased to find no broken bottles. Away they went towards May LaBlanc's house.

The street light shone bright where he fell, and I saw shiny objects. I went back to investigate. There was a handful of change that had fallen out of Swede's pocket when he fell. There was about two dollars and a coin that looked cone-shaped and not of familiar vintage. I took change in hand and followed the fellows to May's house to reunite the money with the rightful owner. I knocked on the door and May answered. She was polite and asked me to come in. I handed Swede the money, and he was very grateful. He sorted out the cone-shaped coin and handed the rest back to me, insisting on making me a gift of it. He showed me his cone-shaped coin and said that that coin was of great value to him. A bullet had hit it while he was carrying it in his shirt pocket during the infamous march. It had saved his life.

Swede, being of good character and strong will, completely quit drinking and was a great diplomat for the state of South Dakota. He married and raised a fine family.

He left a legacy. He was more than a son, more than a husband and father. He was a hero who returned home, back to what he remembered so well— the liquor store or saloon with the horseshoe-shaped bar and the smell of cigarette smoke, stale beer and brass spittoons. A place where it was more common to see up to three fist fights going on at one time, and where one was more apt to get kicked out for spilling his drink on the bar than it was if you gave somebody a bloody nose.

He had taken with him the memories of The Legion Hall on Saturday night being the place to be if you had nerve enough to ask the girls to dance the two-step to Frank Zacher's accordion, or to run outside when you heard the words, "Fight! Fight!," to watch the young "toughs" blow off steam and get their shirts torn off.

Ellen Marshall's rooming house which was always full, and, if that old building could talk, very few of its former paid occupants would not be safe from gossip!

The cafés run by Wally Maupin and Pat Dieter were where you could get a hamburger for a quarter and a cup of coffee for a nickel.

He was not dreaming—just remembering renegades on the Rez.

Swede was home.

Chapter XXV
Sparky

1949 was a terrible winter with much snow and wind, which caused misery and death for both man and beast.

My dad bought his first new car in 1948. it was maroon in color, had a flat-head V-8 engine, and a Ford emblem. Our family was very proud to ride in such luxury, even though the travel was usually limited to going to town on Saturday night.

One of the Iowa cowboys that came to South Dakota to work for the Holloways. A quick learner, and a good hand---Bruce Baird, riding one of Mel's mares. Note the brand new 1948 Ford car in background. Our family's pride and joy.

We traveled home from town for Christmas vacation in this fine vehicle, enjoying the comfort of the warm heater. This ten-day break from school was most exciting because of the upcoming events of exchanging gifts and gorging on the fine foods prepared by Mother and my sisters for the occasion.

On January 2, 1949 it started to snow, and it turned out to be a full-fledged blizzard that lasted 78 hours. Oh, how my parents worried about the range stock in that never-ending storm.

I was mostly worried about my dog, Sparky. This dog was given to me as a pup from my loving fifth grade teacher, Dianne Dunbar.

Anderson dogs were never allowed in the Anderson household, no matter what the weather. There was no way for him to enter the barn with all the doors closed. I was thirteen years old at the time. My dad asked me if I would mind bundling up and hauling in as much wood from the wood pile as I could to store in the storeroom. The ranch house was barely a shell, so the wood was in much demand. Although the visibility was poor to none, at best, I completed my difficult task. I had much difficulty breathing from the blowing snow and wind. I never saw Sparky.

Dad ventured below the hill to the barn to tend livestock, which were confined in that sanctuary where there was hay and protection from the drifts of swirling snow and wind. I don't think that anyone in the household worried about Dad because he had proven so many times his triumph over adversity. He, it seemed like, was gone a very long time for the task at hand. He only had to milk the cow, feed her calf and the horses—the two work teams, Sandy the stud, and Blackie, his favorite saddle horse.

After what seemed a long time, he showed up with a pail of fresh milk and eggs from the chickens that had laid their eggs in the barn. He looked like an iceman with eyelashes full of snow and ice formed around the scarf that he had wrapped around his face and nose.

His remark to Mother was, "Its pretty rough out there! I've been down to the straw shed, and all the calves are in. I suppose they could sure use something to eat---nothing to feed!"

Mother scolded and asked, "How did you find the shed? Don't you know you can get lost?"

He said, "I know, Rose. I followed the barbed wire fence around to where it neared the open door of the shed. Sometimes I had to hang on to the fence and go hand over hand. I couldn't see because my eye lids kept freezing shut. If this keeps up one more day, no range stock can possibly survive. They'll be so hungry that they will begin to come out of their sheltered spots in search of food." He feared that they would become stranded in the huge drifts of snow and perish. We kids, all listened in silence as he painted this grim picture of death on the prairie. With very little hope, he speculated that all that would be left of our holdings may be the calves in the shed and the few horses stalled in the barn. Hell had frozen over. I dared not ask about my dog.

After seeing that Dad was "all right," Mother asked him to please go the root cellar and get some canned meat, canned peaches and potatoes because she was getting low on food. She was afraid that the cellar door would cover up with snow. Dad was glad to oblige. Oh, how we appreciated that old root cellar!

Mother had to wash clothes, and would hang them on a small rope across the living room to dry. It doesn't seem like we had many clothes those days, so what we had, had to be washed often. In times such as these, the water used was obtained by melting snow in a tub on the woodstove.

After three and a half days of snow and raging winds, the snow subsided and the sun came out to reveal an eerie Arctic-like landscape. Snow swirls were still dancing defiantly over the huge drifts.

Dad left us kids to handle the chores at home as best we could. He saddled his strong sorrel stud, Sandy, to go look for livestock. Thankfully, my dog, Sparky, showed up in front of the house, very hungry, but very much alive. He surely received a great deal of attention from us kids.

Dad was back home before dark with only 18 cows. We were outside doing some chores when he arrived. Those cows appeared to be in such bad shape that we were sure that the rest had perished. He put his horse in the barn and was harnessing the team when we kids cautiously entered the barn, fearing bad news. Dad was jubilant with news that many horses were still alive and had shaken the snow off. They were pawing the snow, looking for grass and seemed to be none the worse for wear. The best news was that he had found 88 cows all in one bunch, and alive! He said that he tried to bring them home, but the deep snow had gotten the best of them. He planned on going back the next day with Sparky. He asked me, "Can you help?" (A nice way of saying, "You are going to help me.") I said, "Yes."

Dad pitched on a big load of hay with me placing the hay in the rack to build the load straight up for acquisition of all the hay that could be hauled on that rack. I helped him feed the calves that were in the shed and the 18 cows that had made the trip home with him. This left a good share of the hay on the hayrack to feed the 88 cows when we returned home with them the next day.

We awakened to a very cold morning. It seemed an impossible task to drive cattle through those huge snow banks. It was 14 degrees below zero when we went out to saddle our horses. A man, a young boy and a dog left over the hill to the north to rescue the 88 cows. Without that dog nothing would have happened. The cows were barely 2 ½ miles from home, but in a weakened condition. My instructions were to, "bring up the rear."

Dad was always thinking, having me ride the stud that had had a hard workout bucking drifts of snow just hours ago, and I was less weight on his back than a grown man would be.

Faithful Blackie was Dad's mount. His job was to go ahead and break trail through the huge drifts, lunging through chest-deep snow to break a path for the cows to follow.

Sparky went to work lining the cows out, single file, going back and forth along the line of cattle, nipping and threatening in such a manner as to keep them moving. Had it not been for that very well-trained collie dog, we would never have been able to move those cows even a half mile that day.

Blood was oozing out of the cows' nostrils from taking in so much snow and breathing the frigid air. My face was frost bitten, my feet were numb, and my fingers were freezing inside my choppers mitts. Dad's horse was played out from lunging through the snow. The dog's feet were bleeding. We still had ½ mile to go, and Dad threw up his hands. He called me to come to him. He had an astonished look on his face when he saw my face with the grey ash look of frozen flesh. He told me to get off my horse. I got off, discovering that I had no feeling in my feet. He took some snow and put on my face to thaw it, and cupped his hands and blew on my face.

I said, "Dad, my feet feel funny."

He asked, "Can you walk?"

"I think so," I answered.

We left the cows and headed towards home --- the whole bunch of us being a sorry lot.

Thirty minutes or so after we got home, here came the cows, slowly walking in single file. Some wise old bossy decided that she should check out the feed ground for hay, and she followed our tracks step by step to investigate.

When we finally got to the barn, Dad said, "I'll take care of your horse. You go to the house."

Mother took one look at me and went to work undressing me to check for frost bite. The three fingers on my left hand, the ones that held the bridle reins, were swollen and blue. My feet were giving me much grief and both were frost bitten. The walking probably is what saved my feet from being totally frozen. Some doctors said that snow doesn't work to thaw frozen flesh. Snow does work.

My dad had frost bite on his face, but his hands and feet were fine. The activity of his lunging, jumping horse as he bucked the snow banks increased his circulation, affording him a much warmer ride than that of mine riding behind the weaker, slower line of critters.

I was so very tender in the spots that were frost bit, and as I healed, huge chunks of black skin peeled off my face, feet and hands.

Although Sparky was undisputedly my dog, Dad had trained him. He was a very good dog, loyal to the end. I never did think my dad was good to his dogs. He never petted them unless they performed amazing feats. (He never petted his boy children, either.) I always thought that his treatment of his dogs a bit unusual, but they trusted him completely and would perform human-like tasks for him when called upon.

Sparky could be sent a long way, all on his own, after the milk cows if they were in sight. I could point and say, "Go fetch." He would jump up and down and hop around, looking at me like I was an idiot. Dad would point and give the same command, and he would travel as far as ½ mile to bring in the milkers. I sort of resented the dog not taking orders from me. He was MY dog. I asked Dad one time how come I couldn't get a dog to do the stuff he could. His response was, "You have to be smarter than the dog to teach him anything."

Mel with dog "Sparky" left. His fifth grade teacher Mrs. Dunbar gave this dog to him. Great Cow Dog.

We lost that good dog to a "getter." A getter is a device set into the ground with a piece of rawhide attached to cyanide device. This deadly contrivance was designed to attract coyotes. When a coyote tugged on the rawhide, the shell would explode the poison into the coyote's mouth. Death was instant.

Dad had another dog---an Australian Shepard that was just as loyal as Sparky. His name was Obediah—Obie for short. My cousin, Gail, raised these little cow dogs to sell. She picked Obie from a litter for the purpose of giving a gift to her Uncle Art. This dog was pretty much a natural, and required very little training.

When dad was diagnosed with cancer. He was told, by his doctor that he only had six months to live. In typical fashion for him, he told the doctor that he was not quite ready yet, and that he could probably cure himself with vitamins. He lived six more years with much suffering and agonizing pain, but every day thinking he was probably going to beat his affliction.

He continued to work nearly to the end, doing chores around the ranch and feeding his cows with his old two-banger John Deere tractor that he had bought in 1953. That was the same year that my little brother, Eddie, was born, as well as the year when we finally got electric power.

Faithful Obie was about the only help that Dad had. He had the dog trained to watch the gate into the hay corral while he made numerous trips in and out with grabs of hay on the loader. If there wasn't a guard at the gate, the cows were sure to enter for bites of hay from the stack. If this happened, it was almost impossible for one person to persuade them to depart from their feast because they would just circle around the stack.

Obie would lie in wait beside the gate just daring those cows to enter. Every now and then Dad would let a cow in the hay corral just to give Obie a tune up.

On one very cold, miserable day, Dad got sick and went to the house forgetting to close the gate. It can get very cold right down there on the creek bottom where our little ranch is located. That night it got down to 24 below zero. That dog, Obedia, never left his post. He stayed at that open gate all night. The next morning when Dad went to retrieve him, he was nearly frozen. Dad felt so badly about neglecting him, so he asked him to come into the house. The dog refused to enter, having been taught that he didn't belong indoors. He had to be drug into the house, but would only lie close to the door on a rug, as if he was ashamed to be in the warm shelter. This dog had a rightful place in our hearts for his loyalty. He went to God's Happy Dog Heaven before Dad finally gave up the battle to cancer.

Chapter XXVI
The Bob Sled

The winter of '49 will go down in history as one of the worst ever in western South Dakota. Every day the wind blew and the snow drifted into drifts that were impossible for equipment of the day to break through. Our road to the ranch wound through the breaks and could only be classified as a wagon trail. It was not on the priority list of the county. My father was a man of action, and was not dependent upon anyone to bail him out of a situation, if he could stand on his own two feet.

On January 9, 1949 Dad hooked up the team to the bobsled and hauled his family back to Eagle Butte so we kids could continue our schooling. He studied the lay of the land and picked his route around drifts of snow that towered over us. When we entered the more populated area up on the flats, we saw people with tractors and a homemade snowplow, trying to break a road, but with not much luck. A lot of the farmers, and even some of the ranchers, had abandoned their teams of horses for the more modern tractor to perform the task of feeding livestock and farming. The heavy equipment would simply mire down in the snow, as compared to the team and bobsled, which could simply be driven over the snow drifts, and, in most cases, having good results.

Our team walked and trotted along steadily all the way to town where we encountered our only difficulty. The snowplow had unsuccessfully tried to clear a path by the schoolhouse. We sort of ran into a wall of snow. Dad took his shovel and caved the steep drift down so that the horses could climb over the drift. This only took about 10 minutes. When Dad asked the horses to "step up" the collars slammed into their shoulders and they immediately quit trying to pull. In that short time the sled runners had frozen down. Dad took a bar, which was always carried for such an occasion, and went around to all four runners, sticking the bar beneath each one. He lifted upward to break the runners loose.

Dad stood alongside the bobsled and with a firm hold on the lines, once again asked them to "step up." Away over the bank they scrambled with him still alongside the sled, making it better. We were back in town and our education was again resumed as priority.

I was so disappointed that Dad did not allow me to take a horse with me to ride back to help him on weekends. He said that if I got caught in a storm I would freeze my feet and hands again. Maybe I would not be so lucky the next time. He explained to me that once a person is frost bit, the skin that grows back is very tender and is very apt to freeze if exposed to cold. He said that I was very lucky that I never got blood poisoning. If that had occurred, I could have lost both my legs, or even my life. I know this to be true because for two or three years after I froze my feet, hands and face I had to be so careful in the cold weather. I was forced to wear heavy socks, a good scarf around my face, and a warm cap that had large wool ear flaps.

The Milwaukee Railroad was the lifeblood of all the small communities in western South Dakota. Produce, coal, mail, passengers and livestock all arrived and departed by train. The hub of the activity was centered around the railroad depot. This also housed the telegraph office where the depot agent, Frank Heckel, was adept in Morse code. At this time all messages were sent in this manner.

When the train could not break through the massive snowdrifts with the huge V-shaped plow protruding out the front, they would sometimes literally get wedged in the snow. A message would then be sent by the conductor to the depot for all available hands to immediately come, with scoop shovel in hand, to the aid of the stranded train.

There was good money paid by the railroad for shovelers, and many a man dropped what they were doing at home, or in their stores, to go help shovel out the train. This was a never-ending task in 1949. Life itself depended upon the train getting through.

Going to school didn't seem to be much of a chore. Because of the difficulties involved in running the rural school bus, nearly all the country kids moved in to the dorm run by Mrs. Lopez. The town kids just walked over the snow banks to get to school. I don't remember the teachers postponing school many days.

The State Department didn't have equipment big enough to break through the enormous snow bank on Main Street, which extended from Kinnings Implement to the Kinning house on the far side of the street. Main Street was blocked for 93 days. Finally, a huge rotary plow was sent in by the National Guard. Nearly the whole town watched as that huge machine chewed through the huge banks of snow, blowing it skyward.

Mother was worried about Dad. We hadn't seen or heard from him for almost 5 weeks. We kids would try to reassure her that he would surely be all right. We kids all thought that he was pretty much indestructible. Mother asked me if I would walk to the post office to ask Mr. Pinell, the postmaster, if he could get in touch with J.D. Kessling, the undertaker from Timber Lake. Mr. Kessling had a plane and she wanted him to fly his plane down over our place on Green Grass Creek to see if there was evidence of life.

Mr. Pinell said to me, "Sonny, you will have to go to the telegraph office. They have an emergency base set up there. Tell Mr. Heckel what you want and he'll send a message to Timber Lake. J.D. picks up his messages every day."

J.D. and other pilots of light air craft had been flying to area ranches delivering mail and groceries, and even picking up expectant mothers to be transferred for the delivery of newborn babies. Everyone was stranded at their homes.

J.D. got the message and he did fly over the area to check for distress signal in the snow, but found none enroute. He had snow skis on his little Piper Cub, so he could land on the snow and also take off in a very short distance. Dad was doing fine. We lost no livestock in that terrible winter, but in the spring we lost six weak cows that mired down in the mud.

I overheard my dad say many times, "Any darned fool can winter cows. It takes a good hand to get 'em through the spring.

Those old horned Hereford cows were range cows that could pretty much fend for themselves. Sometimes one would miscalculate some of those old girls' age if she carried a lot of flesh in the fall. The only way you could tell the age of them was by the rings around their horns. Usually when they had 2 or 3 rings around their horns, near the base of the head, they would earn a trip to the Sioux City Stock Yards. But, if the age was misjudged, they could also earn a trip to the bone pile.

The winter of 1950 started out just like 1949, only earlier, with much snow in late November and on in to December. This brought us another ticket on the bobsled to go home for Christmas vacation. This time I had a horse boarded at Danny Rice's Dairy, so I never had to ride in that slow contraption. But Mom, Dad, Betty, Larry and Linda, who was then the youngest at 7 years old, sleighed home in the bobsled. Dad came pulling in to the yard in town in the early afternoon of December 22 so he could watch the school Christmas program before taking us home the next day.

He had a generous amount of hay in the box for the horses to eat, and of course, if there was any left over, the passengers could use it for a cushion and warmth. Mother warmed up bricks to put down by the feet of the younger children, and drug out all the old, heavy homemade quilts. She sort of buried the kids in the box along with the Christmas presents (which didn't take up very much room.)

Dad was driving Tony and Dan. The going was good at a smart trot, but this also caused a draft of wind that cooled the bricks in about 15 minutes. The younger children remember being very cold, especially their little noses, feet and hands.

I was riding Dad's good horse, Spider. This was before Dad sold him, and I felt like a real cock-a-doodle-doo riding this fancy horse out of town. We just got past the old Fred Peterson farm, and Dad pulled up his team and asked me to ride up to him. He asked me if I thought I could ride on ahead and get the fire going in the house so that we could get Mom and the kids to thawing out when they got home. Boy! That was just what I wanted to hear. I wouldn't have dared suggest it for fear of his resistance to the idea, however.

This ole Spider horse knows where he's going, and he is in a hurry to get there. So, it don't take long and I'm at the barn door. I pulled the saddle and forked hay to the stock in the barn before heading up hill for the house. It was cold in that old shack. Mother had a brand new porcelain-covered wood-burning stove that decked out the living room, but it had long ago burned up the big ash log that Dad had put in it the day before. The dipper was even frozen in the water pail.

Well, I know how to start a fire. I get some dry bark from the wood box along with 3 or 4 small sticks, dab on a little kerosene and light, being sure the damper is open on the chimney so the smoke goes up instead of into the house, add a log or two and wait for the warmth to drive out the cold. I did all that.

I got hungry. I also had been taught by the best how to make pancakes. A dash of salt, ¼ cup of sugar, one tablespoon of baking powder, a splash of soda, 2 ½ cups of flour, 4 eggs and add enough milk until you get the proper consistency, then cook on a cast iron skillet, but not too hot. I figured I was good for downing about four of them.

The brand new wood stove in the living room is doing its job, and the Karo syrup is so stiff it will hardly run out of the pail. So, I set the syrup pail on top of Mother's new stove. You guessed it. The dang thing blew the lid off a brand new pail of syrup, scattering the sticky stuff all over the new stove, on the wall behind the stove and clear to the ceiling.

I kind of forgot about being hungry. I knew I was in trouble with my mama. Not much of a problem getting the goo off the floor and ceiling, but when I went to wipe it off the stove, it came off, porcelain, paint and all. My mother, today is 91 years old and she is living just so she can tell me about what I did to her new stove.

The county had two little road graders that ran together just in case one got stuck. Then the other could pull it out. These two little graders were sent down to our place to plow out our roads so that we could get back to town for school in a vehicle. That all worked out just fine. Dad took off immediately with his car loaded with Mom and us kids. He also turned around and went right back home because it was drifting. He barely made it back because new drifts had formed in the path of the freshly-plowed-out road.

The two graders were still there. They could not make it back through the drifts going up the steep hill one mile south of our house. We were not very popular. Those two graders with the snowplows attached to the front were stranded below that hill. They never made it out until we got a big thaw in February. This was the big difference in those two winters. In 1949 there was never a break or a thaw. The winter of '50, which was actually the last month of '49 and into '50, broke about Valentine's Day. We never had another storm until early April.

Cattle prices were good and steers put on good flesh.

One afternoon Dad gathered the family and told us to sit down, pointing at the table. He pulled a Milky Way candy bar out of his pocket, pulled out his jack knife and cut it in to three pieces—one for me, one for Larry, and one for Betty. (Linda never got apiece. She must have been too young to eat candy.)

He would buy 10 or 12 of these candy bars for a nickel a piece and store them in the root cellar. They were forbidden fruit for us kids, and we never dared touch them. They were only for rewards beyond the call of duty. Which was sort of like when he petted the dog—very seldom.

We're all sitting at the table with some of us enjoying our treat, when Dad told us we were broke. You could have knocked me down with a leaf off a cottonwood. He went on to say that he was going to have to go to Timber Lake to borrow $250 in order for us to make it through to shipping time. I still, to this day, don't know what the lesson was, but if it was to scare us kids, he sure got the job done. (To my knowledge, this is the only money Dad ever borrowed.)

This happened in July. He shipped 83 big steers to Sioux City in October. They brought 26 cents pr pound. He said that he would probably never get that much money for steers ever again.

In order to get the steers rounded up and to town for shipping, we would gather them the first week in October. We would put them in the little pasture that protected the oats crop from the range stock. This, at that time, was the only fenced pasture on the ranch. The fence encompassed 160 acres. A freak rainstorm came up just a few days before we trailed the steers to town. Lightening struck and killed 3 steers on top of a high hill. They were almost lying one on top of the other. This event dropped Dad's number from 86 to 83. Those 3 steers sure would have bought a lot of Milky Way candy bars.

This was also the summer that Betty and I could no longer resist the temptation of stealing a bottle of beer from the root cellar. This was Dad's annual purchase of an alcoholic beverage for the branding crew. One case—24 bottles. There were usually 36 Indian calf flankers there to vie for a bottle. In other words—never enough to go around. One could sort of figure out the "pecking order" that way.

I don't think that Betty had ever tasted beer, and I know that I hadn't. The folks were gone to town, so we robbed the case of one bottle. We were pretty careful to divide it evenly, taking it down a finger at a time. I think it was our imagination, but we both thought we got silly.

No way were we gonna put that empty bottle back in its resting place. We filled it up with good ole cistern water, and with pliers in hand, carefully replaced the cap.

Come branding time, it sure wasn't hard to tell who got the bottle of water. Rufus Crow hollered from the top of his lungs like he'd been shot with a poison arrow, "Art, you cheated us."

Art putting on the brand. Mel holding steer.

Chapter XXVII
Moving off the Reservation

The Curtis Brothers eventually split their holdings, resulting in Vern moving to the east of us on to the old Charley Hamilton homestead, and John claimed his holdings on the west, extending to the river.

Hereford Cattle---carrying the V/C Curtis Brothers--- Dewey County

John married Borghild Moland, a beautiful little Norwegian girl, and Vern married Marie, the Green Grass School teacher.

The biggest change in our lives, and in the area, was when the Curtis Brothers bought thousands of steel posts and barbed wire. Up until this time we ran on open range. There was still an abundant amount of land in the county control that was lost by the original

305

owners because they couldn't pay the taxes on their land. There were still a few tribal range units left in the control of white ranchers, but not many.

The days of all the ranchers running their cattle together were over. When Curtises made the decision to fence, it was mostly a necessity for their survival. Because of so many neighboring cattle trespassing on their range, this was the only reasonable solution for them to be able to utilize their grass.

Our range was basically cut down from hundreds of thousands of acres to 3,700 acres. We had deeded land, and also a range unit on the east side of highway 63, but without fencing it, our range stock would not stay on our holdings. They knew no boundaries and would wander on to other units consistently.

Our ranch, the Bar Lazy S, found it necessary to sell more livestock. 1954 was extremely dry and we were forced to put all our remaining stock in our small holdings. I remember so well, the horses walking the north and west fence in an effort to escape their entrapment hoping to head for their home range. But, they could go there no more.

I could see no future on Green Grass Creek, although I had by then accumulated a small band of mares and 25 cows. I went to Moab, Utah to find work, but no such luck.

While I was gone, all I could think about was my little sweetheart that I had left back home. I decided that when I got back I was going to ask her to marry me. I was 20 and she was 17. She weighed 110 pounds and had a 22 inch waist. She would graduate from high school in May, and we planned a June 2nd wedding.

There were drawbacks. Her teachers all urged her to go to college and get a higher education, thinking that she had a very bright future because of her natural ability to work out problems and also because of her excellent marks in all school subjects.

Another question faced us---where were we going to live? I told my dad we were going to get married, and in no uncertain terms he said, "Well, you ain't gonna live here." He had promised me that he would help me get started, but at that time our little ranch was far too small for two families.

Then there was the big drawback of me having to ask her father, the local barber, for her hand in marriage. This took nerve. It had to be done, so I figured out a strategy. I would go in to get my haircut and ask him. But I figured I'd better do it right away when he was pinning the apron around my neck. I remembered his procedure that when he got all done with the clippers, he would take hot lather and splatter his clients slide burns and neck with a brush full of suds. He'd then take his razor and strop it on the razor strop 8 or 10 times to take the burrs off, and proceed to shave off the desired hair on his customer for a smart look.

I sure didn't want to ask him while he had a razor in his hand! I was afraid the shock would just be more than he could bear.

307

Thank goodness the barbershop was void of all customers but myself. I sat down in his chair and gave him my best greeting while he snugged the apron around my neck. He flipped on his clippers and was about to proceed with precision. I just came right out with it. "Is it all right with you if I marry your daughter?" Everything stops. He shut off his clippers and walks around in front of the barber chair whistling this little tune, then he steps back about 5 feet and looks me over up one side and down the other. He don't say anything. He just whistles. He walks back behind me and kicks the pedal on the chair to raise me up another inch, and goes to cutting. Not a word. I'm still worried about the razor part of this operation. He gets done with the clippers and vigorously strops the razor to be sure I'm noticing how sharp he's getting it. He slops the shaving cream around my neck and under my ears. I was sort of wishing that I was maybe at the post office about now. He finishes me up without drawing blood, and I take my first breath in about 3 minutes.

Haircuts were $1.25. I handed him a $5. He gave me back the change and said, "I sure hope you've got more money than that if you're gonna marry Eileen." He shook my hand.

Now I'm thinking, "Where am I going to get the money to get married?" I had worked too hard putting together my little bunch of Herefords, and I needed them to start a herd. I had six saddle horses, a John Deere tractor and a Pontiac car that was paid for. I had

308

$188 in the bank. That was not enough I decided I had to sell my six trusty steeds.

I went up to Eagle Butte to see Pat Dieter at his café to see if he would make an offer. He said that he would be down at 3:00 that same afternoon to take a look. There was no question that these horses were broke to ride. The question was, how much were they worth? I had them all in the pole corral when Pat got there in his old gray Oldsmobile.

Pat was a short guy with a big belly, and he always wore oxford shoes. It seemed he was usually leaking a little tobacco from the corners of his mouth when he talked. Myself, being the seller, brought out all the good points, and he, being the buyer, was the critic, but not so much as to upset me.

I had one particular horse that was just outstanding. He wasn't very big but built stout, and he loved to work cattle. He was a bald-faced sorrel with four white socks and a light mane and tall. He was gentle as a dead pig. His name was Skipper. He got that name because of the way he'd pin his ears back and skip back and forth on his front end while working cows.

Pat offered $180 a head. I said, "What about the bald-faced sorrel? He's worth a lot." We went back and forth, dickering. He bought them for $225 a head, but with the understanding that I would travel to Mobridge and ride them through the sale barn for him in two weeks on a Saturday night. That would give him time to promote them a little, because in his words, "he paid way too much for them."

The time had passed when one would just simply trail the saddlers the 80 miles to Mobridge. Although there was not a horse trailer in the entire county, there were a few people with trucks that were hauling for hire, one of whom was Cal Smith. Pat hired Cal, planning to load the 6 horses early Saturday morning to allow himself enough time to pull their tails and roach the manes.

On Friday afternoon, my dad volunteered to help me go out and sort my saddle horses from the bunch. This way we didn't have to corral the whole herd. We didn't have far to ride, so we left about 5:00 pm. It was dark, and cloudy with much turbulence above. Dad said, "We'd better hurry or we might get wet!"

The horses were down on the creek, not a mile from the corral. It didn't take but a short time to sort and head for home. Dad looked back and said, "Here she comes!" It looked like a wall of water descending upon us. He gave out his shrill whistle, and said, "If we hurry, we may be able to beat the rain."

The barn was in plain sight, just across the creek. We were riding "all out," when a sharp crack of lightening struck close by. I was no more than 30 feet from Dad, and my horse lit up. The little arcs of fire were dancing between his ears, and his mane looked like sparkers on the Fourth of July! He went to his knees and I was knocked out. I woke up in the drenching cloudburst with my dad holding my horse and his. He thought that I was a goner. The six saddle horses had gone on across the creek and were standing by the barn when we got in. We went ahead and tended all the horses, and dad cautioned me not tell Mother about my ordeal. She was deathly afraid of lightening. When she was a young girl, a bolt of lightening knocked her unconscious, and it killed the dog that was lying under her bed.

I had no bad affects, nor did my horse, from that frightful experience, but I've been cautious of lightening ever since that incident.

Pat got the horses cleaned up to his satisfaction, with my help. This was the first time that I ever saw an electric mane clipper. It was noisy, and the horses were unsettled and uncooperative when Pat clipped close to their ears.

We were done with the grooming about 4 o'clock, and Pat decided that we should, maybe, ride a couple of horses down Main Street to show them off before the sale. He asked if I thought he could ride the pretty little bald-faced sorrel bareback. I said, "Sure."

He said, "You lead him up to the fence and I'll climb up there and jump on."

Well, he sort of fell on, but this horse would tolerate just about anything. I rode what I thought was the next best horse called Nute. Away we went up Main Street with a lot of conjecture and ribbing from the local residents because many were acquainted with Pat and his irresistible desire for horse flesh.

The horses sold good, and had I had the foresight to take them to Mobridge myself, I could have been dollars ahead, but the experience was worth much more.

At that time $250 would have bought a real top saddle horse, and these horses brought from $150 to $485. The little bald-face, which brought the $485, was bought by a top hand, Julius Dietrich.

I know of only one other horse in the area that brought over $400. There was a horse sale at the rodeo grounds at Eagle Butte, also put on by Pat Dieter. A good sorrel horse was consigned to that sale that I tried to buy. I went to $400 on him, but that's all my finances could stand. Albert Lopez got him for $410. he came up to me and sort of chuckled. He said, "When you see a good horse, you should try to own him. You don't have to, but you should try to." Albert had a lot of good ones, and very few poor ones.

Now I have over $1500 in the bank, but I still have to find a place to live. Eileen and I were good friends with the Lutheran minister, Jay Erickson, from Faith. He had much inside information as to the goings-on around Faith and the surrounding area. He said that perhaps he could help us to find a job. He was acquainted with an old lady that lived south of Faith. She had large holdings of real estate and some cows. There were two houses in her yard, one of which was nearly new.

We all ventured down there and this nice, but no neat lady, was out feeding a few of her pet cows. She had an old beat-up wash pan full of cattle cubes, and her mission was to feed each cow 2 cubes out of the wash-basin. After a very nice visit with her, we bid our good-byes and gave thanks to the Lord that we didn't have to move there.

Jay had heard from the man that ran the Conoco station that A. J. Marks was looking for a man to put on his place just north of the Cooper Ranch on Deep Creek.   At that time, A. J. "Bert" had ranches established in several locations, including the one that Arnold Bell managed at Maurine as well as two on the Moreau River.

We were told that the man to see was Slim Robbins, who managed one of the ranches where Bert had a little bungalow in which he stayed when he had business at his ranches.   This ranch was located 30 miles west and north of Faith on the Moreau River. Jay Took us down there and we were told by Slim's wife that the men were up cleaning out a big shed where they were going to shear sheep.

We soon found the shed where Slim was running a new John Deere tractor with a farmhand loader on it.   Two guys with garden rakes were cleaning the manure from around the walls and posts that the loader could not get close enough to. It didn't take long to get impressed with that outfit. That was by far the cleanest barn I'd ever been in, and the first time in my life I ever saw anyone cleaning sheep manure in a white shirt, and, what looked like, new polished black boots. This was Slim Robbins.

Slim Robbins in his work attire.

I talked to him for just about 12 minutes. I told him that I was getting married and needed a job. He said, "What can you do?"

I said, "The subject would be shorter if I told you what I couldn't do."

He took a rag out of the toolbox of the tractor and wiped around the gas cap of the machine where he'd spilled fuel, causing dust to collect. He said, "How old are you?"

I replied, "20."

He said, "Your boss will be Mr. Marks, and he expects his men to kick up a little dust when they work. The pay is $200 a month. We pay the electric and furnish the house, but you feed yourself. If extras eat at your house, we pay $1 per meal for extra help. If you want the job, be ready to go to work at 6:00 am on June 15th."

I shook his hand and said, "Thank you, Mr. Robbins. I want the job, and I'll be there."

I had been told that Bert Marks never allowed his help to run their own stock on his property, so I had to find a place for my cows. I rented a pasture from Harold Brewer, a neighbor to the southeast of our ranch about three miles. I had six mares and a stud that my dad agreed to keep for one year. I had a blue roan saddle horse that was still on the lost, strayed or stolen list, but I was ready to move off the rez.

At 6:00 am on the dot, A. J. Marks drove into the yard in a new Packard roadster. I met him at the yard gate and introduced myself with a handshake. I had envisioned this man of great wealth to be tall and handsome with, perhaps, a big hat and a handle-bar mustache. I'm sure that he had been told of my short stature, so he was not so surprised as I. He was barely taller than my 5' 7", was bald headed, without a hat or cap, and he was wearing shoes.

If not for the fancy high-priced rig he drove into the yard, I'd have guessed him to be a magazine salesman. I asked him if we might have time enough for him to come in and meet my new bride. He agreed. Eileen was courteous, but slightly embarrassed because we had no coffee to offer. Bert was looking the house over, probably noticing the absence of furniture. We had a lot of room in that old house because furniture didn't take up any of it. We had bought a bed and mattress and a new couch and chair with small wagon-wheels for design to hold the arms up. We were proud of that set.

Bert was always improving his ranches by building new fences, building sheds, painting, or whatever it took to make his ranches stand out. He had 1 ½ miles of old fence to roll up so that he could put in all new. He was not sparing the cash to do it, either.

Mr. Marks asked if I had gloves, and, of course, I did. The next question was, "Do you know how to roll up wire?"

I said, "You betcha."

My dad, who always seemed to have this sense of urgency about him, no matter what the task, had taught me how to roll barbed wire. He would start his roll at eye level so that he wouldn't have to stoop while rolling. Also, one could cover much more ground with a big roll about the size of a wagon wheel. Then one had to tip the roll as he went from side to side to bind the wire into place as the roll was woven along.

Bert had an old 5-gallon galvanized pail and a pair of fence pliers. He said that he'd pull the staples and I could roll the wire. I remembered Slim saying, "Kick up dust."

I had that big roll of wire right close to my new boss's rear for about 3 hours. The faster he pulled staples, the faster I rolled. Finally, he extended his hand and flexed his fingers. He looked at me and sort of waved the pliers at me and said, "Sonny, maybe you should stay about one post behind me."

He had an old blue International pickup on that ranch. When it became apparent that he was a little fatigued from me "kicking up dust," he would have me haul him back to his car. He had tested my metal.

I only had the privilege of working one-on-one with this old master one more time. I wish that it could have been more.

He had two earthen dams—big ones—up in deep draws, which ran into the river. He had built them for the purpose of flood irrigating some developed hay bottoms. He had valves installed through the fills of the dams. The stems of those valves extended upward and were attached to wheels that resembled a steering wheel on a car. When turned to the left, the gate would open and the water would rush down the draw and through a culvert under the road onto the first dike in the field. This was causing much erosion due to the swiftness of the current. So, Bert asked me to help him build a berm to check the flow and inadvertently stop the erosion. We worked on the berm for three long, hot days with forms, cement and rebar. He was proud of our job. We both put our initials in the wet cement. I was proud to have my name next to that of such a distinguished gentleman.

The next day, at 6:00 am, he was at my door again. We had agreed to let the cement set overnight,

317

and give our engineering feat a test. We drove up to the valve on the dam, and he said, "Turn it on, Sonny!"

I asked, "How much?"

He said, "Full blast." Which, I did.

The water gushed out the gate with much force, being pushed by all the thousands of gallons of water behind it. We drove to our berm post haste in fear of missing the outcome of the water hitting it. We arrived just before the head of water hit the berm. We were just in time to see the water tear the berm from its anchors and wash it about 50 feet into the alfalfa field. He never rebuilt it.

In our conversations during the time we were slaving away on our failed project, he told me that any $5-a-day hired man could do the work, but it took a good manager to make money. I never, ever forgot that.

1957 was a wet year, and hay on the creek bottoms was indescribably good. I was to report down on the river and take orders from Slim. They were still sitting around the table after dinner with the windows open in the house for a cool draft to do the cooling, when I was asked to enter.

The outside of this old ranch house was neat and painted. The yard was manicured to perfection. The inside was the same—neat and tidy. Nothing was out of place except, maybe, Ab, an older cowboy, probably 60, who had new but soiled clothes on.

The lady of the house was petite. Slim had on his pressed white shirt and creased trousers, as well as shiny black boots, like he was going to the

Stockgrowers meeting instead of the hayfield. I was wondering if this man ever got into the dirt, or if by magic, he could just keep himself clean. (Or, maybe he was one of those good mangers.)

Slim told me about the new little John Deere tractor in the shed and the mower in the stall along side. He asked if I could mount the mower onto the tractor. I sure wasn't going to say that I couldn't. I asked if I should start mowing if I got the mower on. He said, "Sure, you can start on the little creek bottoms east of the bridge."

This sounded fine to me. I was sure anxious to try all that new equipment. Mrs. Robbins asked if I would like to have a glass of lemonade. I was not that well dressed, and I was bashful, so I declined— reluctantly.

When I left the house and walked toward my old International pickup, I heard Ab say, "He's just a kid."

I thought to myself, "If I ever get you in a haystack Albert, I'll show you what a kid can do."

Slim made the mistake of not checking on me for a day and half. When he came up the creek he said, "Hold your horses. You got too much cut. You'd better catch your team and start raking this stuff so we can stack it."

Slim pulled the plunger on the grease gun to see if I was using any, and sort of eyeballed the tractor. I had wiped around the gas cap with a rag. I was wearing my go-to-town shirt, and I had certainly polished my boots.

319

I was digging in for the long haul.

Ab Woodcock and Slim Robbins on The Moreau River

Chapter XXVIII
Good Lessons

I had mostly worked around my dad, the Curtis Brothers and Holloways. Their schedules were "sun up 'til sun down," for however long it took.

The A.J. Marks ranches were on a schedule, without the stressful sense of urgency. We worked from 6:00 am to 6:00 pm on weekdays, with an hour off at noon, and took Sundays off. We got much work done. Maybe it was because of the mechanization and good machinery, but it seemed to me that we were more rested and willing to tackle the task at hand.

The only thing we did with a team of horses was the raking operation. Those tight bends in the creek bottoms didn't allow a tractor and rake enough turning room, but one could go in those tight spots with a team and sulky rake and drag the hay out where the stacker could get at it.

On one occasion, I was raking quite a ways up the creek. Eileen volunteered to bring my lunch so we could sort of have a picnic under a big shade tree. She showed up with a good lunch, and we enjoyed it much while visiting. I had unhooked this good ole team and tied them to a tree while we were eating. After Eileen left, I untied the team and took them down to the creek bottom to water. I then led them back up on top, and put the bridles on. I was just snapping the line straps to the bits when a big black horse fly buried his stinger in the rump of ole Clem. He swung his head around hard to rid himself of the pain, which the huge fly had inflicted. This knocked me into the other horse, Clyde. When I came to, I remember seeing my new $2.50 straw hat lying out yonder with the top torn off.

I'm thinking, "Oh boy." I ruined my new hat." I was a bit groggy and felt something warm on my cheek. It was blood. I felt my head and there was a good-sized moon-shaped gash in my topknot. I think maybe I'd better hook the team to the rake and head for home.

I go over and retrieve my hat, and I get everything set to go home. I'm so dizzy I can barely climb onto the rake and get my seat. When I get up there, the teeth are still rattling along the ground, so I've got to get off again to lift up the teeth and lock them into transport position.

It was probably two miles to home. The team knew where to go. I was just along for the ride. Eileen had not been home but just a little while, and she saw me pull up and swing the team up against the pen attached to the barn. She came outside and asked what I was doing home. I said, "Don't worry, honey, I'm not badly hurt." I took off my straw hat. The blood had collected around the hatband, so when I removed it, the blood just made a rush to the pull of gravity. Eileen fainted.

I opened the door to the shed where we kept our car, and it had a flat tire. We were headed to Faith for the doctor, but not before we changed the flat tire. Eileen drove. I thought I was in pretty good shape by the time we got to Faith and the hospital. The doctor grabbed my partly detached scalp and asked, "How did you do this?"

When the horse swung his head around, he drove mine into the bolt that holds the tug to the hames with such force that it tore a huge chunk of my scalp loose. The doctor had my scalp lifted, and was cleaning hair and all the foreign matter out of the wound. He asked Eileen to "come look at this." She took a peek, and down she went again. Old Doc sewed my loose scalp to the part that was still hooked on without painkiller. I've never had anything pain so much before or since. I made up my mind right then and there that if I ever had to have any more knitting done on my head that I was going to see if I could get Doc Sletten, the resident vet to do it. At least he'd put me in a squeeze chute so I could have a little help standing still. Maybe he'd put a twitch on my upper lip.

Doc said, "Go home and don't do anything for a week."

"Okay."

I took off a day.

Mr. Marks was visiting about his sheep-buying days on one occasion, and he said that he was "broke," meaning that he probably only had a million left. He went to Texas and dealt for a trainload of little Texas tarbacks. (Meaning sheep that had accumulated dirt on their wool mixed with the oily lanolin in their wool, making for a tar-like texture.) Those were little ewes, weighing 80 to 90 pounds, and they were not used to being herded.

After loading his huge band of sheep on the train, Mr. Marks went to Omaha, Nebraska to his lender to borrow the money to pay for the sheep. The main man at the bank cornered Mr. Marks in his office and asked him the pertinent question, "What do you have for security?"

Mr. Marks said, "Well, that's easy. I've got a train load of sheep headed for South Dakota."

Another good lesson for me. Several years later I went to Billings, Montana and bought seven loads of steers, using the copy-cat method of dealing.

Slim decided that he'd better bring his tractors and farmhands up to help stack hay. He ran one and Ab ran the other. Bert brought an old man down to help. I think that this man named George was down on his luck. He had had a post peeling business in Whitewood that had gone "bust."

In those days it was customary for a couple of men to be in the stack while the loader operator piled hay helter skelter up on to the stack. It was up to the pitchfork, guys to build the sides into a respectable-looking stack. George kept telling Slim that the hay was too wet. He said, "Slim, you need to go to town and buy some salt to salt down each layer so that it don't spoil. Slim would take a handful, feel it, and say, "Oh, it's all right."

Well, George was sure enough right on that one. Hundreds of tons of hay turned brown, and smelled like tobacco. This entanglement was so very hard to tear loose from the stack and throw into the hayrack for feeding.

I put up the second cutting myself, and allowed for much more drying time. This was the hay I fed to the sheep. I fed the tobacco-colored hay to the cows, and they were crazy for it.

I never made many pony tracks that summer, but was too busy to even notice.

Then, came the mules. Mr. Marks took my good team away from me and brought me a little team of 800 pound mules. I get mad just thinking about those dang long-eared freaks. He tied them in the manger one alongside the other and left. The next morning I'm sort of anxious to see what I got. I go in the barn to water the little buggers, and they gave me the business from both ends—braying and kicking at me. I don't know what to do, and I can't get to them from the front. About 9:00 o'clock here comes ole Bert to see how I'm getting along with the beasts. I tell him I can't even water them things, let along harness them.

He says, "Oh, well now. The first thing you gotta do is get their attention. He goes back to his Packard car and retrieves a chunk of tug with the chain still attached. He goes in the stall and just don't give them no chance to sass him. He just goes to wailing the crap out of them two mules. Now they are behaving like old maids at Bible study.

After that, I never had to lay a hand on them. All I had to do was go into the barn and rattle the tug chains. They were nice little boys until I would hook them up. Of course, when the boss was there, I think that they remembered the bald-headed guy, and behaved just fine. They would back up, side step, step

325

up, hitch good and unhook without a problem. Boy, by spring, after six months of feeding with them, I really had a grudge. And I still got one.

I once hooked them to the wagon to haul wood. I had the lines wrapped around the line pole in front of the wagon, I no more than put the last tug chain in the hook on the double tree, and away they went. I took a dive for the wagon, crawling and kicking my way in to the box to grab the lines. The mules were smoking up the road just as hard as they could go. I had their heads bent hard right, but, they just kept going straight. There was an auto gate coming up fast, and I think, "Oh, Boy." There is a wreck coming. They turned so sharp that they nearly tipped the wagon over and me out.

They never broke stride. Back up on the road we went hell bent for election. Me with my feet braced in the front of the box, pulling on the lines for all I was worth, sawing away at their mouths with the snaffle bits by pulling one line, then the other. No results. They finally decided that they had had all the fun they needed that day, and turned in to the yard on their own accord, stopping by the corral expecting to be unhitched.

I still had wood to haul. I backed the unpredictable little rats up, expecting another good ride, but I couldn't have asked for a better team than that after they blew off their little head of steam.

They had the habit of turning short and breaking out the tongue on the wagon. When you are feeding alone, the procedure is to wrap the lines on the line pole at the center of the wagon, then allow your team to walk forward in a straight line while the task of unloading is in progress. Once in a while, you may have to adjust the team's direction by a "Gee" or a "Haw."

I'd be busy concentrating on this unloading business, and those two little mules would, somehow, communicate with each other, and both, at the same time, would turn sharp until there was no more "give," and the tongue would be broken out. This sure never helped my disposition. All progress would stop until I went home to get tools and a new pole to replace the broken one. This usually took at least 2 hours if the job was done right.

I had 500 black heifer calves and 300 coming-two-year-old ewes to feed. I liked to be done by 10:30. This involved pitching on and off three good-sized loads of alfalfa hay. Those mules were throwing me off schedule something terrible. The third tongue I put in, try as they may, they could not break, but they would pull the ring off the end of the neck yoke in trying. Tongue no. 3 was an ash pole, six inches thick and green. It weighed about 180 pounds. They had asked for it. I did name those mules, but won't tell you what I named them.

I'll give them one thing, they could pull. I would come out of the creek bottom with a big load of hay on my rack, and they would get down on their bellies and claw like cats.

More lessons learned. Every time I see a mule, I think of those two nasty little buggers. Maybe it's like my dad explained to me about my dogs. You have to be smarter than a mule to teach him anything.

Early one morning, Willard Haines showed up with a load of sheep in his truck. Bert had bought them at the Faith Sale Barn. We no more than got them unloaded, and Bert showed up to instruct me on where to trail them and leave them to graze. This was a small flock of about 120. I saddled up and headed south up the creek with those little wooled peltors. I didn't have any better luck with those little ewe lambs than I did with his mules. Boy, they can be stubborn. There just wasn't no trailing them things. I just had to keep them pointed in the right direction and let them graze at their own designated pace.

It took me about 5 hours to move the flock about 2 miles. I heard Bert mention that he was going to his ranch north of Maurine to visit Arnold Bell. So, I cranked up the old blue International and drove over to see if I could talk him in to getting me a dog to make this sheep handling a little more tolerable. He agreed that I needed a dog, and he asked Arnold if he would loan me one of his. He had two really well-trained border collies. Speaking to Bert, Arnold said, "He can use Spike, but just as soon as he gets his own dog, I want him back."

Arnold grazed a huge band of sheep for Bert, and he rotated his dogs when he worked them hard, like at shearing time. One would have to be tethered and watered while the other worked, lest they got too hot. Those border collies would literally work themselves to death.

Oh, my. How I loved that Spike dog. Where the cactus was too thick, he would jump up in the saddle with me when I asked. He'd be so attentive about his balance. He was a wonderful companion and a great stock dog. Eileen and I took him with us wherever we went for fear of something happening to him. No more problems, moving sheep. He would move them as fast or slow as you wished, on command. A good, border collie never barks. They are stalkers. This seems to have psychological affect on sheep, resulting in their having great respect for the dog.

Mr. Marks came rolling in one afternoon with a female mix-breed pup about 4 months old. He told me to take her to Faith to Dr. Sletten to have her spayed. This was a nice, furry, lovable pup like most are. I took the dog and left her in Dr. Wayne's care. I went back the next day to fetch her. She seemed to be frightened of the whole situation, and she rode home with her head in my lap. In the night that little dog pulled all the stitches out, and her insides were hanging out, making for a gory sight. Two trips to town in two days for that dog's sake, and the good Dr. Sletten sewed her up again. This time it was more successful, and rapid healing occurred. This dog was a loveable family dog, but just no stock dog. She just never had the heart for it. Too timid. I told Bert that she was never going to make a working sheepdog. His instructions were to "Give her a black pill. I have no use for freeloaders, man or beast." In a gesture of departure, he threw up his right hand, turned and left.

I didn't have the slightest idea what the devil he meant.

Alvin Anderson and I were building a stout set of pens on the river place where Slim resided. Noontime came and I was sitting in his very clean shop eating a sandwich and sipping ice water. Slim came walking in and I asked him if he had any black pills. He gave me a quizzical look and said, "Why, yes. How many do you want?"

I said, "Just one." Mr. Marks said to give the little bitch dog a black pill."

"Don't you know what he meant?" Slim asked.

I said, "I don't have no idea. I've never heard of giving dogs a black pill."

Slim says, "A black pill is the end of a 22 shell. Bert wants that dog graveyard dead."

I was most bothered by my stupidity. I gave much thought about shooting that lovable dog that had showed us affection and companionship.

I counseled with Alvin, and he said, "You are riding for the brand. You got to carry out the boss's orders." That was not the counsel that I wanted to hear.

I shaved off the face of a huge pitch pine post that Alvin and I had painstakingly set to hang a gate on, and Slim entered the pen with a bucket for the purpose of picking up the wood chips. Also in his possession was a plumb bob used to line up the holes for the hinges. I'm just not feeling good about shooting the little dog, and I've decided to plead my case to Slim. I handed his 22 shells back to him and said,

"Would you just please come up to my place and shoot the dog? I could do it, but it would make me heavy-hearted."

Slim hands the shells to Alvin. Alvin is a noted hunter. He said, "Alvin, go shoot the dog."

In desperation I asked, "Mr. Robbins do you suppose Mr. Marks would care if I gave the dog to one of the neighbors?"

"You keep her around there until Bert comes around again, and you ask him," Slim says. "I'll tell him that I gave you permission. Remember, he has the final word, and it's up to you to buy dog food for her."

I had pleaded my case and was granted a reprieve.

The next time that Mr. Marks came around I asked him if I could give the dog up for adoption. I made sure that Eileen was present with her female influence.

"Well," he said, "if she means that much to you."

I was very careful not to ask how much time we had to find her a new home. We kept her for about a year, at which time we gave her up to a fine family with a boy name John Paul, and a girl named Jeanie. Me thinking all the time about what my dad had said to me about having to be smarter than the dog to teach one anything.

Chapter XXIX
Good Neighbors

Sundays and Sabbath means a day of rest for the A.J. Marx ranch hands. This made time for church and the meeting of many a fine and lasting friend.

There was Dale Haines, the stiff-legged cowboy with generous appetite for adventure. And, of course, Arnold Bell who lived to work and could handle a 16-pound mall like he was Paul Bunyan with an ax.

There were the Jim McGinnis's who had the very first big round baler. Those people abided by the Golden Rule as though they had written it!

Emmet Peters, from up the creek, who always was ready and willing to lend a hand in his quiet, but efficient manner.

There were the Wilson Boys and their wives—Jr. and Nita, Larry and Bobbi. Jr was a bit portly and of good humor. Nita, with a hint of "Texas" in her accent, baked a great cherry pie. Larry and Bobbi were friendly and the handsomest couple in 5 states!

Merle & Dorothy Heidler with their son, John and daughter, Jeannie, bring back such fond memories. I have no idea of how to start the description of the kindness shown by this family. They lived on the Moreau River – on the wrong side, if the water was up and they needed to go somewhere. That's just the way they liked it!

The Heidlers just sort of took us under their wing. They treated us like family. Many evenings were spent at their ranch, dining on the fine setting that

Dorothy had laid out. Playing dominoes with Merle while listening to his fascinating tales of adventure was a favorite pastime. Merle's father was a German immigrant who had learned the harness-making trade, and Merle, himself, was always cutting strings of rawhide or braiding his bosals and quirts.

Occasionally we would cut firewood together. He has a heavy old chainsaw that was run by hydraulics from the tractor. If a guy was man enough to handle that heavy contraption and drag the long hoses over the fallen logs and slag, he could be very productive with it. On one occasion, we were falling tall ash trees that had succumbed to drought. All of the sudden, Merle walked over to the tractor, killed the engine, and proceeded to load his saw in his pickup, without saying a word.

I'm sort of puzzled by his short run at the logs, thinking that maybe I'd made him mad about something. We had barely cut enough for two loads-one for him and one for me. He walked over his old rig and grabbed his water bag for a pull of water, and made me an offer to join him in quenching my thirst. I made mention that, maybe, because things were going so good that we should have stockpiled a load or two for future use. With a twinkle in his eye Merle said, "That's enough. You never want to cut too much wood ahead. If something happens and a fella should die, I sure as shootin' don't want somebody else burning my dang wood!"

The Heidler Ranch was nestled in a little bend on the west side of the river. Like any river, The Moreau would occasionally take enough drainage to flow bank full, or, even flow out of its banks. On the occasions when they needed to venture across the river, whether it be for business or activities for John and Jeannie, their school age children, they would, by necessity, have to cross back and forth across the river.

Merle made a tramway across the river by hanging a cable to big cottonwood trees on each side of the stream. To this he connected a box-like vehicle with pulleys. This gave mobile access back and forth across the river. One simply had to climb the ladder fastened to the tree, get the box, release the security system, grab hold of the cable and pull hand over hand until you reached the other side. That is, if you had nerve enough to climb into the thing and chance the ride! I'm sure their holdings would have been much bigger if they would have advertised for rides across the river on their tramway! It was far more daring than riding on any roller coaster, no matter what speed or height!

The rocking back and forth on the cable with muddy water swirling beneath was only for the heartiest of souls. Merle would climb aboard and sail across without a second thought. The kids made little mention of it, but Dorothy affectionately refers to the machinery as "Oh, that darn thing!!"

No one in the 1930's had much livestock because nature had taken care of all available grass and water in all of western South Dakota. A water hole was most prized possession, worthy of making a stand for when threatened to be consumed by outside cattle or horses.

Merle lived up in the Ottumwa country in the 30's during the height of the drought. He cleaned out a spring in order to water his small herd of horses and cattle. One day Merle rode down to water his stock and found his neighbor, Jack, watering his stock at the water stash. There was a limited supply of that precious resource, and it was vital to the survival of Merle's own stock.

Merle Heidler
A good old cowboy and his horse Chester.

Merle indicated that, maybe, he should kick somebody's butt for stealing his water. Jack pulled out a revolver and made the statement, "I'm just a little guy, but I've got the difference right here!"

"Jack," Merle said, "I think that your horses are thirstier than mine, by golly. You just go right ahead and water them horses right here in my water hole!"

It was customary for owners of large bands of sheep to only let a ewe raise one lamb. They were of the opinion that they would rather a ewe raise a good lamb as two poor ones. A pair of sheep tents would be set up in the night pen, which was usually moved daily by the camp tender. The smaller of the two lambs would be put inside one of them.

These extra lambs would be picked up daily, by people who had milk cows and could raise the bum (bottle fed) lambs.

If no one picked up the bums by the next afternoon, the practice was to destroy them. This only happened when no one could find the teepees that were set up the night before, or, if it became too wet for travel on the prairie.

Mr. Marks made it clear that he didn't want his help diverting any of their time raising bums! It was the general consensus that big sheep men wouldn't tolerate their help raising bum lambs because they would eventually have a brand of sheep of their own.

This would then create competition for their grass and water.

Dorothy Heidler always had a good milk cow and she had a knack for starting bums. That dear, sweet lady brought Eileen 17 started bums one spring, that she might have raised and sold herself. She was always one to help her neighbors.

Merle loved to visit, and his daughter, Jeannie, inherited this trait from her dad!

Then there is little J.P., the son. A cuter little boy you will never find. He was born with a shyness and attentive smile.

The culture off the reservation was much unlike what I was used to. This came about mostly because there were no axes to grind and no land disputes like on the rez. On the reservation, every five years your livelihood depended upon whether or not you were going top get your lease renewed, or if some neighbor was going to try to outbid you on it. This caused much suspicion and unrest amongst neighbors in this dog-eat-dog environment.

Over in the Maurine Country there was no tribal land, and people had deed to their property. They could sink root in satisfaction that their neighbor would not be a threat to their livelihood. The ranchers there, although separated by miles, were a tight-knit group that were more liken to family.

Another family that we spent a lot of our evenings with was the Junior Wilson Family. What wonderful people, as were Larry and Bobbi! They were your Southern gentlemen! One time Jr. and Nita invited us to motor to Sturgis, some 80 miles to the west, to see a movie. The movie, Lassie, had just been released in motion picture theaters. This was when they still made movies without all vulgar language and nudity. The movie and the trip with Wilsons to the old cavalry town adjacent to Fort Meade was much enjoyed, and never forgotten.

Arden Palmer is a soft-spoken man with a reputation for honesty and hard work. He also rode for the brand, managing one of A.J. Mark's ranches. Arden was a tried and true stockman who had the ability to handle cattle and sheep in an efficient manner to reap maximum production. This man, over the years, has brought much honor to the Palmer Family name. I had the honor of working with him several times, and he was an inspiration. I never ever heard one bad word said about this man.

When I first met Arden in 1957, his face and hands were marked from a terrible accident. He had been mowing a huge field of hay with a small tractor. This must have been a big land, because he started in the center of the field and mowed outward for many days, making the rounds longer and longer. He knew not the number of acres he had covered.

He was filling his tractor with gas, and the fumes ignited, causing an explosion. He never made light of this incident, but I'm sure that he suffered immense pain and agony. One must look very closely today, to see the evidence of his injuries. His endurance and God's goodness have healed his scars, but have not yet taken away his challenges.

Arden was my jack rabbit hunting companion. Rabbits were in abundance on the little creek bottoms where they would come out to feast on the tender alfalfa. In the late fall and winter, the rabbits would be adorned in beautiful fur, some even being snow white. These rabbits were in great demand by fur buyers, and could be sold in the carcass.

Arden had a 222 caliber rifle. He loaded his own ammo, using steel-jacket bullets that would penetrate, but not tear up rabbits. I had just bought my very first new gun-a Marlin lever-action 22 with micro-groove fillings. It was a dandy. Arden would plunk the ones that were just out of range for my little gun, and I'd get the close ones.

There were times when we harvested jackrabbits in abundance. This was a great sport for us. It also filled our pockets with spending money. However, the most rewarding thing for me was to be able to spend time with this great stockman.

Alvin was the workhorse down at Slim's place. If Alvin needed help, Slim would come up to our place and ask me if I would help with certain jobs. On one particular day, Slim came to get me to help replace water gaps that had washed out during a recent rain storm. When we were done dragging the wire out of the muddy banks across the creek in several places, Slim asked if we would, maybe, be interested in seeing John Nashe's cave.

After many questions by two inquisitive boys, he told us that John Nashe was a bootlegger who had a large still in a tunnel near where we were working. We were working in stifling heat and humidity, with mud and water up to our knees all morning. We'd been fighting mosquitoes and barbed wire, so both Alvin and I were ready for a break! We welcomed the chance to investigate the old still site.

Slim pulled up to a sharp bend in the creek and said, "There it is!" We neither one could spot a tunnel or cave like he had described, but noticed the grass around one particular site was taller and greener than the surrounding area, like, maybe, it was a feed ground, or a bed ground for sheep.

"There it is, right there." Slim was pointing at a high shale-sloped bank off the creek bank near a thick grove of trees. Alvin and I decided to investigate!

Sure, enough! When we got close to the spring-fed stream along the creek, we could see an opening in the bank that had been shored up with timbers like a mine. It very much resembled the placer mines in the hill surrounding Deadwood. The tunnel was shored up with timbers, but they appeared to be in a state of deterioration. Slim warned us that we shouldn't enter the cave because it might cave in.

The story goes that this little piece of real estate, with the live spring water, was the site of much activity. The Haley brothers freighted in barley and sugar on a regular basis for the still. There were hogs in large numbers that had become addicted to the mash they were fed. This was a by-product from the still that was being put to good use to fatten hogs. The hogs would then be loaded on to the freight wagons headed to town for the end result.

These hogs were also addicted to meat—horse meat!! Horses were brought down there and shot for the hogs to feed on. The range was so barren of grass that both horses and cows were being bought by the government by the thousands to be destroyed. The government paid $5 for a mature horse and $20 for a cow. The procedure was to dig huge holes to run animals into where they would then be shot by riflemen on the banks, and covered with dirt.

Some of the big, fat cows were branded E.R.A. on their left ribs. They were turned loose to escape the death pits. There was a government-indoctrinated program for these E.R.A. cows. To the hungry, drought-stricken homesteaders and ranchers, the interpretation of those letters meant "Eat Right Away!" The government-branded beef put much fresh beef on the menu for white man and Indian alike.

The horses were to be destroyed under contract by John Nashe. These horses were shot and skinned for hog feed. The horse hides sold for from 50 to 75 cents each. Considering the amount of traffic on the creek and around the still, there is a very good probability that the secret of its existence was never revealed, or, at least the revenuers never ever descended upon this location to destroy it.

This activity was the lifeblood of the economy in that area, employing many that needed income for their families. The Haley Brothers' freight wagons had false floors in them that contained stainless-steel cylinders that lay flat, and held the finished product from the still. After placing the beverage on the floor and replacing the top deck, hogs would then be loaded on the wagon for the 25-mile trip to town. Where there's a will, there's a way!

John was the manufacturer and retailer, and Milt was the wholesaler. Everybody knew if they had the price for a strong snifter of grog, Milt could fix you up!

Milt was a very distinguished-looking gentleman, in good standing with all who made his acquaintance. Milt wore a long topcoat, even in seemingly warm weather. This made him stand out in the crowd. Being the proper businessman that he was, he had several pockets sewn on the inside of his trench coat—just the right size to hold a pint of his fine depression medicine! This put money in Milt's coffer, but it did much more than that. It created an economy in the little homesteaders' town that allowed people to work and feed their families.

Prohibition was repealed Dec. 5, 1933, so all bootleg operations ceased when alcohol became available to the public.

Milt sent a stream of cars to Canada for the purpose of hauling legal whiskey back to the States. This made him one of the first sources of legal whiskey before United States manufacturers had time to set up their processing plants.

Always the business man, and always with partners, Milt went into partnership with Harry Krouse. Together, in 1938, they built the first auction barn in the area. This was called the Tri-County Commission Company. At this time there were not yet scales, so thousand of cattle, horses and sheep were sold through their commission company by the head — so much apiece!

Harry and Anna Krause worked for Milt, spending much time breaking and trading horses for him. They received $30 a month with no board or room furnished.

Milt's good friend, and partner, Billy Richardson, purchased the Chevrolet Garage in 1936, which they ran in partnership for many years. They further expanded their partnership and bonding their friendship by also purchasing and running the Mobridge Commission Company.

Milt made large charitable contributions and was instrumental in financing the Faith Memorial Hospital. Much to learn and know about his good neighbor.

Trips to the Mayo Clinic, accompanied by Billy, for treatment of a progressive terminal illness resulted in no relief or cure for Milt.

The Milwaukee Railroad had a pasture north of town where people could hold their livestock for their turn to load on to railroad cars for shipment. This was necessary because as high as two or three thousand cattle and sheep would descend on the stock yards at one time. There was not much room therein for the huge shipments to be held while awaiting their turn to be loaded. Because of this, the ranchers would await

344

their turn in the railroad pasture, grazing and watering their livestock until they got the word to bring them in.

Milt could stand the pain of his illness no more. He went to the railroad dam, stripped off his coat, folded it neatly, and laid it on the ground, stacking his billfold and diamond ring on top of his coat. He then walked into the dam and drowned himself.

Merle Heidler was one of the men that helped retrieve Milt's body. A hay rake, which was drug back and forth across the pond, was used for the search. Finally it passed over his body, retrieving it in the teeth of the rake.

The unbearable pain was gone. The legend lives forever.

Chapter XXX
Unforgettable Characters

The real trick to life is not to get bored! When you spend time around Dale Haines, this was just going to happen!

Mr. Marks had sold 710 steers to his old friend, Leif Hanson, who ran the commission yards at Fort Pierre. We gathered and trailed them to Dale's Ranch. Dale had put in a fair-sized scale where 12 to 15 steers could be weighed at a time, and several area ranchers took advantage of Dale's facilities for weighing and marketing livestock. This facility was also used by Dale, and was installed for that purpose. This was my first meeting with Dale and his kids.

Dale was all business, but seemed to be favoring his leg a lot while running the gate. However, he managed in an efficient manner.

The weighing was going hot and heavy. Every now and then, Leif would enter the herd and jump up and down flapping his hands with orders to "Hurry up! Get to work! These cattle are shrinking!" Leif knew full well that he was getting those old wild range steers worked up so that they would, indeed, lose a little of that belly full of grass and water before they went over the scale! This was to Leif's full advantage, him thinking that he might not have to pay for so much of that stuff that passed out the back end of a steer before he walked over the scale with it.

Now, at this time, we had not yet entered into the world of technology, and the method of adding the recorded weights of all those little scale pens of steers was with a tablet and a sharpened lead pencil. This was normally done by at least three people — the buyer, the seller and a third scholarly-type person. Then they would compare their figures to see if all came up with the same number to determine the total pounds. Once they agreed upon the pounds, they would begin the process all over again, by multiplying the decided-upon price per pound times the total pounds to determine the total dollar amount.

On this particular day, it was around 11:00 a.m. with the sun being nearly straight up, bearing down with much heat. "Now I'm going over to my car," says Leif, "and I'm going to do my figuring. I don't want any interruptions!"

Leif retreats to his car and rolls up his windows due to many flies that had come to the pens to visit the steers, making pests of themselves for both man and beast. The closed windows were to form a barrier between Leif and the flies, lest he should lose his train of thought in going over his long line of figures.

The drawback to this plan was that it was hotter than Dutch love in that car, and that big old Norwegian sweat so profusely that he had to keep wiping the perspiration from his eyes and forehead. However, Leif was not long in doing his share of figuring. He was a whiz at math, and Mr. Marks told me later that he very seldom ever come out with the wrong figure.

We finally got done with that hot, dusty job, and went to the pump to quench our thirst. All hands were relaxing along the edge of Dale's old red barn, visiting and joking, having a good ole time like cowboys do, about old Leif never tying his shoes or zipping his fly on his trousers.

I'm the youngest hand there, and soon to be the "huckleberry" of Dale's young son, Squeak. Squeak was probably 3 or 4 years old, but had developed his own unwritten lingo. I'm sitting flat on my butt and he walks right up to me and says, "Hello, you big old piss ant!" My face had never been redder before or since! Of course, much laughter and knee slapping followed, at my expense! This little male child of Dale's showed to be a chip off the old block!

Dale had married one of the Schulke girls, and that should have helped to sort of put a little better disposition into his offspring, but it didn't appear like the mating resulted in much improvement!

Dale had a partner, Jack Walker, and when they teamed up, something was sure going to happen! Jack was a big, soft-spoken bruiser, and he always tipped his hat to ladies, greeting them with his deep-down South accent. Jack made a very big thing out of having respect for the fairer sex, but, as far as I could see, that was where he drew the line on gentleness! He and Dale were a pair! When they would get to "playing", they could do about as much damage as a unit from the National Guard.

For instance, they could totally destroy a nearly-new Lincoln Continental while chasing coyotes or hunting antelope up on those hard-pan, sage-brush flats. One thing about that is that it was sure a lot more level to lope a horse over after they had made a few passes over the landscape with that Lincoln!

Every now and then Dale and I would trade work. He contacted me about helping him butcher a big 3-yr-old steer. I was sure longing for a little excitement, so I volunteered to help. I was on the butchering crew with Shorty Holloway at Parade, so I had sure take lessons on range butchering. I thought I may be able to take a meat saw and knife in hand and probably impress ole Dale with my splitting and skinning skills. Well, I guess maybe I didn't know anything about butchering! Dale instructed me to take his pickup over to where the steer was in a package of cows east of his house. He told me to shoot the steer and cut his jugular. "I'll follow you with my tractor and loader," he said.

We skinned out the legs and cut the tail off, split the hide down the belly and front legs, went down the brisket with the knife to where the jugular is, and the lesson began!

"You fasten these chains onto the loose hind legs on that old M Farmall with the loader extending it skyward a good 10 feet, don't you know!"

He backed his pickup up to the steer and fastened his chains to the hitch on the pickup's bumper. He made sure that everything was nice and even, with the length calculated to be the same coming off both hind legs. He hobbled over to his pickup and sticks 'er in low and says, "Here goes!" He puts tension on the chains and the tractor sort of rocked in resentment. The pickup just spun out! Three times!!

All of the sudden, he throws down into reverse, cussing a blue streak, and slams the beef up against the front of the tractor. He threw the pickup into the low and shoved the gas pedal to the floor. The steer flew up into the air about 25 feet, somersaulted, and came down hard! Hideless!

Dale slides out of the pickup and says, "Yuppers! That's how she's done—a little grass on the meat can't hurt!"

I was invited to help Dale and big Jack brand colts. Head and Heal, just like they were little cattle.

Branding was a wild event with many volunteers to help with the disposal of about a three-day supply of beer. Dale had about 700 cows—Herefords with little buckskin calved following them. They had white faces like their mamas. Dale said that they were Charolais. That was the first I had ever heard of them. He said that they were a breed that originated in France. Their large frame was necessary for the use as draft animals.

They were snaky little critters. Those calves would charge the wrestlers, making for much excitement. Many a rope settled beneath the tail of the saddle horses used to drag the calves to the branding fire. That caused more than a little excitement, too! No hard and fast on the horn allowed—daily only and every man for himself!

I'd mentioned to Dale that I was short on meat. The country was just overrun with big, fat mule deer, and Dale asked me if my wife would tolerate venison. I said, "Sure enough! That's what she was raised on."

Her father, Ray Bayless, was quite a successful hunter and he had raised his kids on antelope and venison.

"Well," he said, "why don't you go shoot a fat doe?"

I said, "All I have is a 22 rifle and a Savage bolt-action 30-30. I just can't even hit the big end of the barn with it!"

Dale says, "I'll come over and shoot your deer for you. Might even help you field dress and hang it in the shed!"

Next morning, early, here comes Dale, driving in the yard in his big, fancy Lincoln. I offered coffee, but he says, "Nope. After. Let's get 'er done!"

The morning was foggy and damp—cool enough to be comfortable with a light jacket. We took Dale's gun and slammed the doors on the old blue International and headed to the creek bottoms. All these bottoms were in alfalfa, and there were deer everywhere. It's just a matter of which one do we want! Now Dale is all the time telling me how good eating those fat dry does are. Well, they are all fat. I'm trying to decide how the heck one is supposed to tell if she's dry!

All of the sudden Dale says, "There's one!" He ordered me to "Turn left—turn left! Stop! Stop!"

All I could see was a big ole five-point buck on the edge of the timber, looking straight at us and not twitching an eyebrow. Dale says, "There is your Daisey!" He pulls his 30-06 out the window and CA-PLOOEY, he shoots right out the window! The noise was so loud in the cab of that pickup that it about broke my ear drums!!

Dale says' "Hot dam, he's down, he's down! Gimme your butcher knife and drive up close. I'll cut his throat!" He jumped out of old Blue and hobbled over the biggest old mule deer buck you ever saw, and proceeded to get on with it!

The big old buck jumped up and charged Dale with his head lowered and his front feet hitting the ground hard! Dale is so close—so close, in fact, that the buck couldn't get a run at him, but he didn't need one! Dale has shot an antler off right at the base of the head which must have just rendered the buck unconscious! He didn't stay that way for long! That big buck got up on his hind feet, slapping the crap out of ole Dale. This deer is inflicting pain! Dale's jacket is ripped to shreds. His nose is bleeding, and his pant leg is just about gone! Me—I'm a coward. I dived under the pickup in an effort to save myself! Not Dale! He makes a stand! He's got a death grip on one antler that's left and has his arm around the big boy's neck. They are going around in circles like they are on a runaway merry-go-round! Dale is just plumb mad and won't let go. He's hollering profanities—"Bring me the...........knife! I'll cut this.......throat!"

There's no way that I'm going to jump into that meat grinder, and I'm encouraging Dale to let go and run for cover.

Now Dale is hollering at the top of his lungs. "Get the gun!! Shoot this.........!

Finally Dale is totally exhausted. The deer slings him out there about 10 feet, and heads for cover.

I'm trying to give Dale my handkerchief to stop his nose bleed. I looked down at his torn pant leg and discover why he is so gimpy. The leg appears to be artificial!! No questions were asked by me — no words said by him — no deer hanging on the meat hook in the shed. When you are young, there's always another day!

A.J. Marks never owned a lot of cows, but he would, every spring, drive around and purchase steers. Mr. Marks had figured out that the cattle would eat a big, tall grass, and the sheep preferred the little grass (short buffalo grass). A large majority of the steers would come to us as bulls, with horns. There would be brockel faces, roans, dairy crosses, or anything that could be bought at a discount. The hands would clean them up and brand them. They would then be trailed to various pastures to graze with the sheep. Mr. Marks would run the steers from May though September, shooting for gain of 250 pounds. This method made him much money.

Slim Robbins had 600 steers on the north side of the river that he needed to move to the bottom southwest of the headquarters. He needed help, so he called on his son-in-law, Jim Reed, to help. Now this Jim Reed is a wirey little cowboy that is all cowboy times two!

There at the crossing where the river was to be forded, was a big washout, which splits into two big gullies. If things don't go just right, with a good man on the point, the steers would just break around the two gullies and split up to escape back into their summer range. Slim asked Jim Reed if he could prevent a wreck by handling the job of turning those big steers into the water so that they would ford the river.

"I can do that!" said Jim.

Jim Reed riding Scottie. He loved to ride his favorite color — Palomino. Good horse — good track, and a cowboy that knew how to get the most out of both.

Jim was mounted on a real good horse named Red Cloud. This horse came from Calgary, Canada where he had been used as a hitch horse to pull a wagon in the Chuck Wagon Races. The previous owner said that he wasn't fast enough for that, so he was sold to Mr. Marks, along with two other horses. Red Cloud was a registered Jockey Club horse, but due to his being born and raised "up north" he was big, and possessed more bone than the southern-born thoroughbreds.

The steers came running and bucking toward the river, thinking that they were going to make the bend in the gullies and return helter-skelter back into the rough river breaks. Jim Reed and Red Cloud were "Johnny-on-the-spot"! They came off the river full speed and Red Cloud jumped from one gully to the next, settling in front of the lead steers for a successful crossing.

Slim, who was a good carpenter, always had a tape measure clipped to his belt. He stopped to measure the distance that Red Cloud had jumped from gully to gully, and recorded that the first jump was 25 feet, and although the horse had had very little space to gather himself, the next jump was 15 feet to the second ledge!

This was my first acquaintance with Jim Reed and Red Cloud!

I later tried to buy Red Cloud from Mr. Marks. His reply was, "You'd just as well try to buy the ranch! The horse and the ranch are the same price!"

Jim came from a long line of pioneers who resided in the Faith area. His granddad, who was a freighter, moved in the area in 1911. He moved out of the area and went into freight business at Miles City, MT for a few years, but then moved back to the Faith area.

Jim's dad was a great cowboy who made his mark, also.

Fritz Judson was raised in the same country as Reeds. His dad died of pneumonia the same year that Chauncy Johnson's wife died of it. Fritz was raised by a rancher named Blake Crowser and his wife. Fritz married Jim Reed's sister. They ran a band of sheep, trailing them all the way to Whitehorse to summer pasture. This was a range of some 65 miles. When the lambs got big enough to sell, they would be sorted and trailed to Ridgeview and put on the train for shipment.

The ewes would then be grazed back to the winter quarters southwest of Faith in the Opal country. Fritz, rode horseback, with his wife following along in a pickup, pulling the sheep wagon. Every once in a while Fritz would go on a binge. Once when he was in Ridgeview country, he was headed across the street and met Fight Mac. Fritz asked Fight where he was going. Fight said, "The same place you are!" They both headed for Geisingers' the local bootlegger.

Fritz reports that during that time, he was a "mess". As he was telling me this, he opened up his mouth and said, "See. In there are two bands of sheep and a ranch!" Indicating that he had drunk up the sheep and the ranch.

Fritz tells that his father-in-law was a fair man, and not a troublemaker. But, he also was not one to be messed with! One time a much larger man kept sticking his finger in Mr. Reed's chest, looking for trouble. Mr. Reed soon got tired of that and "one punched him"! He dropped the big man like a beef! One always has to be wary of the quiet ones!

At one point his gentleman ran into trouble with the law. Horses were of no value in South Dakota, so Mr. Reed and two of his companions gathered a large herd. This took a period of much time and preparation. Their intention was to trail them to Indiana where there was a demand for horses. Or course, their hopes were to make a profit for their efforts.

On the morning of departure with the herd, they were crossing the Huddleson Bridge across the Belle Fourche River. Mr. Reed was riding "point". He got nearly across the bridge, and law officers descended on either end of the bridge. This entrapped a portion of the herd as well as the point rider on the bridge, with no way to escape.

The sheriff approached Mr. Reed and asked him where he was going. Mr. Reed replied, "Well, I WAS going to Indiana!"

Horses were being bought by the government for $5 each and destroyed because there was no grazing due to drought. But, here they have this man "dead to rights" with a bay mare that carried no brand, and was identified by the owner only by a white rear foot.

The balance of the horses, which had not entered the confinement of the bridge, scattered to the wind, along with the helpers!

Mr. Reed spent time in confinement. This was serious business, and left a mess of problems for young Jim and the family at home.

The better, I got to know this tough little cowboy, Jim Reed, the better I liked him. I only wish that he could have been one of my range buddies during the open-range days in Dewey County.

I had 300 bushels of oats down at my dad's place that Merle Heidler wanted. So, Merle, Jim, Jack Walker and myself motored to my parents' ranch on Green Grass Creek in Jack's old Studebaker truck for the purpose of transporting the oats back to Merle's. Also, Jim was interested in buying a buckskin saddle horse that I had traded Dean Reeves out of. He was not of the make up of the Reeves' horses. He reminded me more of a mustang. Dean has done some swapping with peg-leg Tom Maupin for him.

Dad had the horse, Tom, stabled in the barn when we got there. Jim threw his saddle on him and rode to the creek a time or two. He said, "Gosh, he's got a long reach at the trot. I believe I'll take him. I can't go wrong at $85. Do you want me to pay you now, or when I get home?"

Jack had a question, too. "How we gonna haul him? You all gonna stand him in them oats?"

Jim said, "Heck no! I'm going to ride him home. It's only 80 miles and it will be good for him!"

Jim dismounted and wrote me a check for $85. He pulled his latigo up a hole and said, "Well, I'd better get going. It's quite a ways." He asked, further, "What's the best way?"

Dad said, "This whole country is ruined with fences and gates everywhere. You'd best take the road, or you will be riding back and forth on the fences looking for gates."

Jim said, "I'm off!" and up the road he went.

The rest of us took turns scooping the oats onto the truck, leaving about 50 bushels for my dad because he was still taking care of my stud and six mares.

My sister, Linda, had 3 of her pretty piebald red roans around the buildings, and we gave them a bait of oats, discussing their merits.

Upon my mother's request, we went to the house for a cold drink of lemonade. She made an offer to fry us up some venison steak from the deer we brought along for her. It was yet 10:00 a.m., so everyone declined her offer. Speaking for myself, I was about full of venison as that's about all the meat I had had on my menu for a good long spell!

On our return trip we caught up with Jim Reed making pony tracks on a long trot. He has a grin on his face like a coon eating cactus! He was just east of Dupree and heading west — only 50 mile to go!

Our next encounter, Jim said, "Shoot! That old Tom horse made the trip plumb easy. It was only about 4:30 when I got home!"

I thought to myself, "That Jim Reed would have probably done all right carrying the mail for Wells Fargo!"

Mr. Marks purchased 203 Hereford cows and 5 bulls from Williams and Chalmers, who had lost their tribal lease on the Cheyenne River east of Carl Samuelson's outfit. He needed help trailing them to his holdings on the Moreau. Slim drove down to Jim's place to see if he might lend a hand. Jim said that he sure would, but that he was kind of busy right then. He was building a hay rack on a rubber-tired wagon, and he'd sure like to get that job out of the way first.

Slim said, "I'll make you a deal. If you help me trail those cows, I'll pull your wagon down to my place, and put it in the shop where I can build you a nice rack for your wagon."

Jim answered, "It's a deal! I'm not a very good carpenter, but I sure can trail cows!"

Slim Robbins showing Jim Reed how to fix it in his always Tidy Shop.

This was in October, and we were supposed to take to the trail with the cows the day after the calves were taken off.

Bed rolls, tents, horses and all possibles were made ready, along with a sheep wagon pulled behind a pickup, which was to be used for cooking and for the "old codgers". Bert and a few of his old buddies had decided that it would be great fun to relive the past by getting in on one last trail drive, sitting around the camp fires, sipping strong coffee, and maybe swapping a few yarns about "Do you remember when------?? Or, Do you remember this---or Do you remember who--?"

Of course their coming along involved four extra horses. Gentle ones!!!

Chapter XXXI
From Cheyenne to the Moreau

Chilly nights necessitated building a fire in the wood stove in our old house in order to be comfortable. We had an old wood burner that proved to be very efficient in making the house warm and cozy.

In order for the stove to be efficient, one had to control the damper on the chimney. The more open the damper, the hotter the fire, and, of course the faster the logs burn. If you wanted your house to stay warm all night, it was customary to pick out a "night log," which was a good, solid logwhich would just fit nicely through the door on the wood burner. Then you would close the damper to allow just enough draft for the fire to burn slowly and, hopefully, still have at least hot coals when the rooster crowed in the morning.

The damper on our old stove was tricky because the tension spring was gone. On the night before my anticipated departure to help trail Mr. Mark's newly acquired herd of Herefords, I banked the stove with a good-sized ash log. It was still a little green. I went to bed and woke up about 4:00 a.m. the next morning very dizzy and disoriented.

I tried to awaken Eileen, but hard as I tried, she did not respond. I did not know what was wrong, but the house was slightly smoke filled. I could not walk, so I crawled to the doors and opened them. I then crawled back to bed to try to revive Eileen. I could not wake her. I could tell that she was breathing, however.

I got my arms around her and drug her out of bed and on outside, dragging her by the heels. She was lifeless. Her head and arms just flopped like those of a rag doll.

I sat on the step with her head on my lap, stroking her forehead, asking her to please wake up. I was beginning to come to my senses in the fresh air. I decided to use my resources. Prayer! I asked God to please help me and not let her die! I stroked her forehead and she opened her eyes. Praise God!

We had both been exposed to carbon monoxide poisoning. The damper was pulled shut by gravity. This completely shut off the draft. The partially-green log just smoldered, filling the entire house with fumes. We were both a couple of sick kids for a while. In this crisis, that probably lasted only 5 or 6 minutes from the time I woke up, I never once panicked or shed a tear. I know that God had control of our lives, and his will would be done. No doubt, another 30 minutes and we have both been history.

Arnold Bell came over from Maurine with a truck to haul the saddle horses down to the cattle. The bed rolls and the like were loaded in the back of Slim's pickup. I had flu-like symptoms from the gas. Eileen kept saying that I should go ahead and join the others. She said that she was all right. By now I'd had time to think, and was very worried about her. I sure didn't know if I wanted to be gone for a week.

Slim was aware of the incident, and, in fact, was the person who figured out what had happened to us. He assured me that Eileen would be alright, and that he'd have someone check on her if I'd go on the drive.

Jim Reed and I were the only two that had enough staying power to trail the cows those 90 miles.

The weather looked rotten! The sky exhibited those tell-tale fish-rib clouds that meant moisture.

Arnold had the horses all loaded. Slim had the sheep wagon in tow with a load of bed rolls loaded in the back for his pickup. It was 1:30 in the afternoon. We were getting a late start. Although he never mentioned it, I know Slim stalled around to be sure that Eileen was going to be alright.

Arnold, Jim and I rode in the truck, which transported us, with Slim following behind. It started to rain! No one ever suggested that maybe they should postpone the drive due to inclement weather. They had their "huckleberries". Their names were Mel and Jim!

We drove like what seemed forever, and were barely on the reservation road when Arnold just stopped the truck. He said, "I don't like the looks of this. I'll get down there with this truck and I won't be able to get out. I don't want to be stranded in the middle of nowhere! This is as far as I go. You can ride the rest of the way!"

Arnold backed in to the ditch to make it easier for the horses to jump down, out of the truck.

Mr. Marks had informed me earlier that he was sending a grey horse down for me to ride. He flexed his hands (I was used to that by now!) It usually meant, "get ready for something!" He said, "He's a little green, but he'll be all right. He's a good looker, and you'll like him. Make a horse out of him!"

367

Bert assigned a real good buckskin horse called Chamus and a red roan. These two horses, the iron grey, and the red roan were loaded with our gear already on them, so, it was no problem to catch them coming off the truck."

"Do you suppose that them old guys are gonna ride?" Arnold asks.

We don't know!

Arnold says, "You'd better trail their horses down to the corral just in case."

I stepped on Grey and he goes to bucking! He's jumping high, but lighting light as a feather when he hits the ground. The mud goes Splat! Splat! Splat! My adrenalin is pumping and I'm ready to ride!

Jim swings on to Roany and he goes to bucking, also, kicking and squealing like a pig with a prickly pear stuck to his nose!

The rest of the remuda just stands there with their backs to the rain-turned-to-sleet, glancing around ever so often as it to say, "Are we supposed to be acting up like that, too?"

Jim gave me "that look" and says, "This could be interesting!"

Five extra horses, Jim and I headed south. It was now starting to snow. It was about 8 miles to the pens where the cows were milling around. The calves had just been taken off the day before! Those ole cows were bawling around there like they were auditioning for opera at Carnegie Hall!

Now we needed to be thinking, "Why are we going on this drive in this miserable weather?" The snow was wet and accumulating to about 2 inches of slush on the ground now! Here's the reasoning—If we don't pull out with those already-paid-for cows tomorrow, those cows are going to pull stakes and scatter big time, all over the reservation. It was going to take at least a week, and with more riders than we had, to gather them. By that time, at least three of those fat cows would be hanging on a meat pole, being cured for jerkey!

By the time we got to the pens, I was getting along pretty good with Grey. He's responding to leg pressure and has an understanding of the reins to establish direction of travel. I had to punch him in the belly pretty good with my Kelleys to get any sudden moves out of him. I've got his number—I'm doing what I do best. I'm making pony tracks! In an blizzard!

Slim had his chains on his pickup and he made it to camp plumb fine. He stroked up the fire in the little stove and I was pushing cattle to Jim for the final count before we took possession. The tally book recorded 203 cows and 5 bulls, 208 head, total. All were accounted for.

At last, only Slim, Mel and Jim were in camp. Slim said that the old cowboys decided, maybe, this wasn't going to be as much fun as they thought, and maybe Neil Crowley had a warmer place in town where they could swap lies! Neil would see to it that they would be warm both inside and out. Besides that, they hadn't seen his spur collection in a while!

When Jim walked by Slim's pickup he just stopped and looked at the beds. We squeezed into the sheep wagon for a cup of hot coffee and a bit to eat. Jim said, "Slim, you weren't very careful about the way you placed our bed rolls in the pickup were you?!

Slim said, "Why? I never paid a mind!"

"You sure didn't," says Jim. "You laid them in there with flaps up so they could catch the rain like a funnel!"

Slim countered with, "Oh, shoot! I never thought of that. Are they wet?"

"Well, they got them tarps on, but the water had to go somewhere!"

I got to spend the next 6 nights in a pup tent snuggled in a bedroll that had the first 12 inches of the foot end froze solid. The first night at the pens, Jim just sat in the sheep wagon by the fire. Slim was in the bed and would, one in a while, ask Jim if he wasn't maybe going to go to bed.

Jim said, "When you want to leave in the morning, just give the word. I'll be ready! I'm gonna sit right here by the stove!"

Visitors at the Wagon.
Jim Reed and Mel Anderson left to right on horseback. Jarvis, Carmel and Doris Risdall---
Just before the freak October storm.
Trailing cattle from the Cheyenne to The Moreau River.

Next morning I peeked out of the tent for a look-see. About 8 inches of slush—cold! Smoke is coming out of the chimney on the wagon. The top half of the Dutch door is open. I'm freezing, and I'm thinking, "It's so hot in that little shelter that they have to spill some heat by opening the door!! What a waste! Maybe

I'd have been better off if the gas had got me at the house!!!"

What a miserable night! I kicked my legs back and forth to stay warm. I think if I'd been standing I'd have made about 15 miles, figuring 3 ft. to the kick! I had slept about a total of 15 minutes all night!

I crawled out of the tent to retrieve my brand new yellow slicker. I was so glad that Eileen had insisted that I take my overshoes! I walked over to the wagon and greeted my compadres with fake, but cheerful, "Good morning!" I thought that Jim was gonna stick one on me!

Slim was pretty cautious and selective with his commands. This morning we decided that we weren't getting any closer to home just sitting there, so we went for our horses. It's good thing that Grey was confined to a small pen. He took one look at me in that yellow slicker! He snorted the loudest snort I ever heard before or since! He stomped the ground hard with his foot, sending slush in every direction. I remembered Bert saying, "He's a little green." Yup, he was! I caught him up and slapped my gear on him. He was really cold and shivering. Jim was saddling his roan, kinda of keeping an eye on my corner of the pen. My latigo was wet and slick, I knew it was gonna pull easy. I made two wraps and gave her all I had. Old Grey blows the plug!! My stirrups were popping up on top of the cantle! I ain't about to let go of the reins of fear that I'll teach him bad habits! He quit bucking, and walked right up to me, blowing out air out of his nostrils. I was kind of cautious for fear he would introduce me to his front feet. Nope. The horse was plump good. He was in remission, and ready to repent!

I stepped up, and he just kind of walked around with a hump in his back, like he's walking on eggs, don'tcha know!

"Now it's my turn," says Jim. He swings up and just buried his Crocketts in Roany's belly. The horse was bucking and squealing, hitting the wet show with a splat, splat, splat. Jim says, after he takes the snot out of his horse, "Okay, I'm warm. Let's get this show on the road!"

The cows were still reluctant to leave. They were still yearning for their babies, and they were carrying tight bags. It was not much trouble getting them started. They were cold and hungry. That helps. I only wish that Bert and his old fogey buddies could have seen Jim and Roany. That would have made their day. Oh, well, they were probably riding ranker horses in the municipal bar!

We whittled off a bunch of miles the first day. The only problem we had was those extra saddle horses! They were wanting to go home. Sometimes they would get way out ahead of us. Then one of us would have to leave the drive to capture the horses and bring them back to the cows. This was getting old fast!

Slim abandoned the sheep wagon because of poor roads. He packed lunch to us along with our frozen beds, stopping at certain agree-upon locations.

Jim had some authority and in no uncertain terms told Slim that we were going to leave the extra saddle horses some place where they could be loaded.

He would have to send someone to get them. We were on gravel quite a bit of the time, and the cows were getting sore footed. This was making them hard to move, and it was about impossible for one man to keep the herd lined out while the other of us went chasing after horses.

The second night was not so bad as the first. I had Jim for company in the little tent, and our body heat seemed to keep it warm, although the bottom part of our beds was still froze stiff!

We visited, and I was very interested in Jim talking about his army days. He was drafted right out of high school. He did his Basics at Fort Livingston. The war winding down by the time he was sent to Germany in WWII.

He talked about the evidence of destruction after a battle as he walked back to Paris, France. I asked him if it was true that the French girls were really interested in the American soldiers. He may have answered. I don't know. I was tired. I slept.

The next day began with the same routine. The only difference was that Jim caught the good horse, Chamus for the day's ride. Grey was fagged and looked like a greyhound!

I was thinking that, maybe, I should, probably, catch one of those extra horses we'd been chasing for two days. Then again, maybe not! Bert had said to ride this one. I don't think that the deal with the dog had set very good with him. I didn't want to make any more mistakes!

There is nothing that will make you more tired than, riding a tired horse. You have to make him do everything. He is not willing.

Slim met up with us on day three, and told us to leave our horses at the Chicago Outfit's Camp. Arnold was to come and pick them up. What a relief! Bert accompanied Slim on this trip to report to me that Eileen had fully recovered from the house fumes. He also wanted to check on the overall operation of trailing the cows. It's now or never if I'm going to ask for a change of horses!

I said, "Mr. Marks, this horse is getting pretty hollow gutted. Do you suppose I should ride something else?"

Bert looked him over and said, "Oh, he'll live. I'd sooner have his hide as his tracks!" And that was that!

After we got rid of the burden of the extra horses, we had been at it long enough so that the cows were trail broke. They just ambled along at a steady pace. We trailed from Cheyenne to Moreau in 6 days, averaging 15 miles a day.

Jim Reed brought his six up to the faith stock show parade pulling two freight wagons. Jim riding the left hand wheel horse handling all six horses with one line. Called a jerk line.

Chapter XXXII
Disappointed

The winter was pretty much routine, with the feeding of cows and sheep. The exciting thing in our lives was that we were expecting our first born. Audey Ray was born June 8, 1958 on his Grandmother Rose's, birthday. Audey was named after Audie Murphy, World War II's most decorated soldier, who later became a movie star. More importantly, however, he was a great horseman. If you've ever seen him in a western movie, it is important to know that the fine horses he rode were registered quarter horses that he raised and trained himself.

Eileen had planted a garden down on the bed grounds where there was a windmill and a large underground jug to store excess water. This served well for irrigating the ground which had been made fertile by hundreds of sheep.

We were watching our son grow and very much enjoyed taking time to go to church and visit neighbors. Occasionally we would motor to Eagle Butte to visit our families. Eileen was expecting another baby and we were living like normal civilized people. I still had my stud and mares at my folks' place, but I had lost my lease, so needed to do something with my little covey of cows. I was out of time on the horses, also, because Dad said that one year was as long as he would keep them. It was going on two years.

I was mowing hay northeast of the house on a creek bottom when Mr. Marks showed up where I was. He waited for me to cut around to where he was parked. The days are long in June and although it was nearing 9:00 p.m. it was not yet dark. I stopped the tractor and dismounted to go see what my boss wanted. He met me about half way and preceded the conversation with small talk about weather and the prospects of a good hay crop. He also questioned me about why I was still out in the field, as it was normal on his ranches to quit at 6:00 p.m. on the dot. I told him that I thought it wise to get the rest of the hay cut on the north side of the creek because I would need help moving and if I could finish cutting on this side first, I would only have to ask for help once. My boss is now getting the idea that I don't take orders well!

Mr. Marks finally got around to telling me that he was going to build a feedlot in Arizona, and needed $25,000 right away. He asked me if I was interested in buying this little ranch I was on. He laid out the terms: $25.00 an acre and he would finance all but the $25,000. He would also build a big new shed on the east side of the road for that price.

I was very happy about this offer. I remembered my dad had told me that he would help me get started, and although I always thought he was going to take me in as a partner on the home place at Green Grass Creek, I had grown to understand it was too small for Dad to take his 3 sons in as partners.

This would be an excellent opportunity for him to help me get started if he would just lend me the money to make a down payment on the Marks Ranch.

I know Dad had the money. I just had to figure out a way to get him to go along with this deal. I was only 21 years old, but by now I really liked this little ranch and the surrounding neighbors. It was only 22 miles to town, which was just about right for me.

I went to the house to tell Eileen of this exciting news, and we made plans to immediately travel to Eagle Butte and on down to my parents' place to get the $25,000. There was no time to waste! Mr. Marks needed his answer in a week.

It was a 75-mile trip to my parents' house and of course with no telephone in those days, no way to notify them of our intentions of coming. It was well after midnight when we got there, and of course, everybody was in bed. Mother was somewhat startled at our arrival because of the late hour. She was sure there was something terribly wrong.

I explained the intention of our mission to my parents, and Mother was very excited about helping us with a loan. I offered my pitch in the purchase of the ranch to Dad, pleading my case for about 2 hours!.

He never got out of bed, but you could tell he was doing a lot of heavy thinking. He finally reared up, resting his head in his hand and said, "I told you I was going to help you, and I am. I'm not going to give you a damned thing!" It took me 30 years to figure out how, by not giving me anything, was going to help me.

I left their house that night so very anger. I had no intentions of ever coming back to see my father again. All I could think of was how I was going to show him how I could sure as the devil make it on my own without his help, and maybe, for sure, have more money than he ever had.

It was a long trip home for this young couple with down-trodden hearts, and very little conversation.

Art Anderson had planted his seed! I sure hated to tell Mr. Marks that I couldn't come up with the money. But, to this day I think he was banking on me not getting the money and would have been very surprised if I had.

The place was sold to Arden Palmer. I don't think Mr. Marks did Arden a favor. The little ranch was just too small to make a good living and raise a family on.

I now had a burning desire to show my dad how I could make it on my own, and this beautiful little ranch definitely did not match my ambitions.

I never did shoot that little dog that Mr. Marks told me to shoot with the "black pill," and in my mind, because I went against orders on that one seemingly small thing, I was not on his short list for permanent employment.

The disappointment of not getting the funds to purchase that little ranch and the setup to get me off the place without having to fire me, was by far and away better than any college-earned diploma ever. I came to realize that if we were going to make our mark in the world we could count only two things – God's blessings and ourselves------unless---

I'd better go talk to my Uncle Jim.

Chapter XXXIII
Back to the Reservation!

Always needing a little extra spending money, I had worked for my Uncle Jim on and off at his lumber yard in Eagle Butte when I was a freshman in high school. I got along with him and my Aunt Esther very well, and held them in high regard.

The Cheyenne Agency had to be moved off the river because of the building of the Oahe Reservoir. Jane Warnock (who moved to Eagle Butte in 1920 with her husband, William, to manage the Diamond A Cattle Company for Cap Mossman) had much influence in Washington, DC, as she was the National Republican Committeewoman for many years. She was definitely instrumental in having the Cheyenne Indian Agency moved to Eagle Butte.

My Uncle Jim and my cousin, Leonard, played a big part in supplying contractors with material from their lumber business. They also farmed several hundred acres and had a ranch 25 miles south of Eagle Butte where they ran cattle on the old Eli place. This, combined with a flourishing feed business, kept them on the run.

I asked Uncle Jim if, possible, he needed help running his ranch. He was very much in favor of this, but his daughter, Beverly, and her husband, Bob Durpis, were on the ranch at that time. They were waiting for a house to be built so they could move to their newly-acquired lease and herd of cattle that was located in the vicinity of the Sid and Rose Nordvold

Ranch. So, we had to wait for Bob and Beverly to move out before we could move in.

In the interim, I was to move my little family into a trailer house, temporarily, so that I could help out in town. Eileen had not accumulated much in the line of furniture or household goods, so it was not a huge job to move. The biggest regret I think was to leave that beautiful garden behind.

The first order of business at the lumberyard after we got moved was to build fifteen outhouses for construction workers at the Oahe Dam project! Very humiliating for a cowboy!

Our good friend, Merle Heidler, helped us move back to Eagle Butte by volunteering his pickup truck for hauling household items. Merle said that he sure hated to see any more people move into the country, but he'd sure as heck help them move out! The country was just getting too crowded for him!

I offered my last paycheck to Bert Marks for his good horse, Red Cloud, but to no avail!

I did purchase 300 of his 4-year-old-ewes for $12 per head to be picked up after the lambs were taken off in the fall. I had no idea where I was going to graze them! No money borrowed up to this point, and no money owed.

We are back on the reservation with no idea of what a rocky road we are about to embark on.

Comments

Ride along with Mel in Volume II:

What happens when he finds his blue roan saddle horse?
When he negotiates the purchase of his first little ranch.
His experience managing the Tribal Sale Barn
The killer storm of 1966
The price you pay when you go against God's written word
The tornado
Chance meeting with Indian girl he saw at the river
Marriage and successful ranching with a school teacher
Trailing cattle through the Badlands
Floating down the river on a big slab of ice
Muskrat hole in dam
And much more---------

385

**Big Grass and wildflowers Cheyenne River Indian Reservation
Dewey County –South Dakota**

**Mel and El Diablo
He gave this Paint Gelding to his friend Chuck Smith**

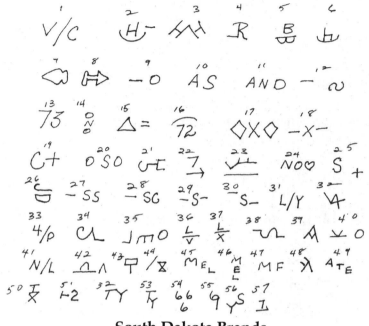

South Dakota Brands

Hog tied and ready for branding.

To order this book or contact the author:

Send payment plus $2.00 shipping and handling fee to:

Mel Anderson
The 73 Ranch
22144 Elm Springs Road
Wasta, South Dakota 57791

Price of book $24.95

For Publishing Information contact:

Art in the Heartland
408 Washington Street
Columbus, Indiana 47201
812-376-3465

sbreeding@artintheheartland.com